performing jane

performing jane

A CULTURAL HISTORY OF **JANE AUSTEN** FANDOM

SARAH GLOSSON

Louisiana State University Press   Baton Rouge

Published by Louisiana State University Press

Manufactured in the United States of America
First printing

Designer: Barbara Neely Bourgoyne
Typeface: Whitman
Printer and binder: Sheridan Books

Library of Congress Cataloging-in-Publication Data

Names: Glosson, Sarah, author.
Title: Performing Jane : a cultural history of Jane Austen fandom / Sarah Glosson.
Description: Baton Rouge : Louisiana State University Press, [2020] | Includes bibliographical references and index.
Identifiers: LCCN 2019044176 (print) | LCCN 2019044177 (ebook) | ISBN 978-0-8071-7195-0 (cloth) | ISBN 978-0-8071-7335-0 (pdf) | ISBN 978-0-8071-7334-3 (epub)
Subjects: LCSH: Austen, Jane, 1775–1817—Influence. | Austen, Jane, 1775–1817—Appreciation. | Fans (Persons)
Classification: LCC PR4038.I52 G58 2020 (print) | LCC PR4038.I52 (ebook) | DDC 823/.7—dc23
LC record available at https://lccn.loc.gov/2019044176
LC ebook record available at https://lccn.loc.gov/2019044177

The paper in this book meets the guidelines for permanence and durability of the Committee on Production Guidelines for Book Longevity of the Council on Library Resources. ♾

For Lee, bringer of coffee and instigator of dance parties.

I'm your biggest fan.

Contents

Acknowledgments

This project was born in the American Studies Program at the College of William & Mary, where it was nurtured and raised by a village. Foremost I thank Arthur Knight, Charles McGovern, and Karin Wulf. I have the utmost regard and respect for these exemplary scholars. They have mentored me in more ways than they can possibly know. Special thanks to Daniel Cavicchi at Rhode Island School of Design for asking great questions.

I am deeply grateful to Virginia Torczon, first for her role in establishing the Michael R. Halleran Dissertation Fellowship and second as my most excellent boss and fellow advocate for graduate students. She has cheered me on to complete this project twice now; I couldn't be luckier to have her support.

Jenny Keegan at Louisiana State University Press is a rock star with deep reserves of patience. Her incisive reading has been a godsend. I'm so happy we found each other. Everyone at Louisiana State University Press has been superb, start to finish. Copyeditor extraordinaire Elizabeth Gratch offered an expert eye and elegant suggestions. As Jane Austen wrote, "Where so many hours have been spent in convincing myself that I am right, is there not some reason to fear I may be wrong?" Any deficiencies in this project are mine alone.

I am constantly inspired and challenged by my extraordinary colleagues and students, past and present. I simply cannot imagine these years of reading, research, and writing without Sarah Adams. Diana Floegel, with whom I can always share a good squee, makes sure I'm up-to-date with pop culture. Special shout out to the smart women of freshman seminar Jane Austen in America.

Members of my local Jane Austen Society of North America (JASNA) chapter were welcoming and kind. Amy Stallings and Virginia Lee offered encouragement and help. I am grateful to all the JASNA members near and far who have ever taken time to talk to me about their passions, especially Gracia Ellwood, Lorraine Hanaway, Jim Nagle, and Joan Ray. Many Austen fans on Tumblr and FanFiction.net offered me their time, sharing their love of Austen through friendly and lively correspondence. I can't imagine a kinder, lovelier community of fans. Juliette Wells and Nancy Magnuson of Goucher College have been gracious allies. Tara Olivero and her staff at the Special Collections and Archives at Goucher College always made it a true pleasure to conduct research there. Likewise, my dear friends and former colleagues at W&M Libraries' Special Collections Research Center made George Tucker's quirky notebooks accessible to me. I have become very fond of the Austen enthusiasts of past generations whom I have gotten to know through the legacies they left in the archive. I am grateful to Barbara Winn Adams, Henry and Alberta Burke, David Gilson, Jack Grey, and George Tucker for sharing their obsessions with the world.

If I'm a fan of anything, it's my family. I can't express here just how much I owe to them. My husband, Lee, is my most stalwart supporter and more marvelous than even Captain Wentworth. Calum and Aidan were busy becoming young men as I worked on this project. When Calum was only seven or eight, he made up the phrase *Pride and Polyjuice*—he gets full credit for that. My parents, Joe and Eunice, paved the way for me and now help do the same for our boys. I love you all.

performing jane

Introduction

PERFORMING JANE

One half of the world cannot understand the pleasures of the other.

—JANE AUSTEN, *Emma*

In the 2008 British TV miniseries *Lost in Austen,* the protagonist, Amanda Price, rereads *Pride and Prejudice* so often that she becomes drawn into the world of Mr. Darcy, literally. When a portal opens from her bathroom into Elizabeth Bennet's attic, Amanda and Lizzie switch places and become trapped in each other's worlds. Amanda quickly discovers that to survive in Lizzie's world, she must put to use her extensive knowledge of the plot and narrative of *Pride and Prejudice* as well as her understanding of Regency era manners and customs. Yet her presence confounds the plot; she disrupts all of the romantic entanglements and finds herself having to choose between remaining faithful to Austen's text and becoming the heroine herself. Should she leave her beloved Mr. Darcy to his intended true love and salvage the purity of the novel? Or should she choose love and Darcy, overturning the sacred text? In the end, she remains with Darcy, while Lizzie Bennet takes up a new life, enjoying the comforts and freedoms afforded to women in the twenty-first century.

The miniseries opens with a voiceover from Amanda that reads as if it were taken from one of the hundreds of blogs and websites maintained today by Austen fans: "It is a truth generally acknowledged that we are all longing to escape. I escape always to my favorite book, *Pride and Prejudice.*

I've read it so many times now the words just say themselves in my head and it's like a window opening. It's like I'm actually there. It's become a place I know so intimately, I can see that world; I can touch it. I can see Darcy."[1] Amanda is recognizably a fan. She repeatedly immerses herself in the alternate world of her beloved text, and she knows that text inside and out.

Seeking immersion into a favored text and garnering knowledge about its world are central to fannish life. Fans also engage in elaborate social rituals through which they perform their insider knowledge and loving admiration, such as through fanfiction, attending conventions, or dressing in costume or regalia. Once Amanda is trapped inside the world of *Pride and Prejudice,* she must survive by performing what might be deemed the definitive version of these social rituals of fandom. Whereas the fictional Amanda escapes into the past through a magic portal, actual Austen fans rely on metaphorical means of time traveling. These imaginative acts of time travel form the crux of this book.

While Jane Austen fandom provides my primary case study, this is not particularly a book about Austen. Nor does this study attempt to address, as others have done, the question of why Jane Austen has remained perennially popular and what it is about her, her characters, and her world that continues to captivate readers.[2] Instead, I trace the pursuits of Austen's most enthusiastic readers, individuals who—past and present—read and reread Austen's novels, watch and re-watch Austen screen adaptations, collect and curate "Austenalia," and who thrill to discuss "Jane" and anything related to her novels, personal life, or the times in which she lived. Previous scholarship on Austen's devotees has grown out of literary studies and emphasizes what it is about Austen and her novels that inspires such devotion among her readers.[3] I instead emphasize the activities of these enthusiasts, seeking to theorize and contextualize them and recognizing individuals as fans even in contexts in which that term might not at first glance appear well suited.

American fans of Austen have been particularly active and so receive the lion's share of attention throughout this work. I recognize that Austen's appeal is global, evidenced in recent years by the founding in 2013 of an active and scholarly Jane Austen Society in Italy (JASIT);[4] the appearance of several Bollywood film adaptations, including *Kandukondain Kandukondain* (2000), based on *Sense and Sensibility*, and *Aisha* (2010), adapted from *Emma;* the development of a Brazilian television series *Orgulho & Paixão* (2018), inspired by *Pride and Prejudice;* and the emergence since the 1980s of Chinese fans of Austen introduced to her works though English language curriculum and subtitled film adaptations.[5] However, I have chosen to delimit my scope to Austen's American fans as a means of tracing continuity across nearly two hundred years of vibrant engagement. Austen's emergence in America was immediate even if modest, whereas the rest of the world developed a love for her works gradually and at different moments, particularly as availability of adaptations and translations of the novels brought Austen global visibility. Many characteristics of the Austen fandom, including nostalgia for the Regency era and a complicated relationship to notions of cultural hierarchy, while not uniquely American, are particularly visible in American contexts.

This book recounts the history and characteristics of the Jane Austen fandom as far back as the 1830s, pushing against the boundary of fandom history. Throughout I explore three distinct modes of fan practices: collecting memorabilia, texts, and objects; writing fanfiction, or what Abigail De Kosnik more capaciously refers to as "archontic literature";[6] and the practice of literary pilgrimage to sites both real and fictional. I introduce these modes of practice within the context of the nineteenth century in part I. Each of the remaining three sections, parts II–IV, returns to one of these three modes in greater detail and with more specific theoretical consideration as I trace Austen fandom into the twenty-first century.

Fan practices today have precedents in the past, despite major changes in discourse made possible recently by the internet and digital technologies. In part I, I detail the origins of the Austen fandom in America and situate it in the context of nineteenth-century transatlantic literary fandom. Austen's readers have long sought additional means of entry into a world they love to inhabit. Nineteenth-century readers engaged with early forms of fanfiction, made pilgrimage to literary sites, and collected personal treasures related to a favorite author. Long before 1889, when the term *fan* first appeared, these traditions of fandom were part of readers' lives. Jane Austen fandom did not, after all, spring fully formed from the head of Colin Firth in 1995. In fact, evidence of nineteenth-century Austen fandom reveals characteristics still visible today, suggesting remarkable continuity within the fandom over time. Part I reveals the place of Austen in the American public imagination, tracing the earliest forms of Austen proto-fandom in the mid-nineteenth century through the moment before the first major Hollywood adaptation of an Austen novel appeared on the big screen.

Part II picks up the history of Austen devotees in America in 1940, the moment when MGM released its much-anticipated adaptation of *Pride and Prejudice,* starring Greer Garson and Lawrence Olivier. Austen collector Alberta Burke of Baltimore, Maryland, documented this moment in detail in her Austen-related scrapbooks with magazine clippings about the cast and production. The chapters in this section detail the devotion of Burke and three other contemporary "Janeites" who enacted their enthusiasm for Austen by collecting Austenalia and creating scrapbooks over several decades. Scrapbooking is a form of leisure intended to be productive, representing a labor of love. These were collectors and bibliographers whose scrapbooks were emblems of their devotion to Austen. Highly capable amateur scholars, their protracted search for knowledge of Austen and her world was conducted against the backdrop of the developing professionalization of novel studies in the mid-twentieth century that attempted to codify legitimate forms of reading. They document years of seeking and attaining objects and knowledge, with each scrapbook allowing the creator to relive and keep alive otherwise ephemeral experiences along the way.

Like part II, part III begins with a galvanizing moment in the history of Janeites: the 1995 release of the BBC television adaptation of *Pride and Prejudice.* At the very moment the internet was becoming an indispensable part of daily life, this adaptation burst into the collective imagination, driving the greatest-ever resurgence in Austen's popularity. I explore the ways the visual culture of screen adaptations and the internet have influenced both the reception and creation of archontic works, including fanfiction and spin-offs. In Austen fanfiction, for example, the visual influence of screen adaptations is evident in the ways writers reference familiar settings and actors in their reworkings of Austen's narratives. These stories also reveal a manipulation of the female gaze influenced by the visual pleasure that period dramas offer to women in particular. Analogous to the material creations and collections covered in part II, the archontic works discussed in part III provide opportunities for fans to re-access Austen's world and keep alive the affective experiences of fandom.[7]

Austen has had admirers in America since she was first published here in 1816, and since 1979, the Jane Austen Society of North America (JASNA) has institutionalized this fandom into a highly organized and lively group of enthusiasts who celebrate the life and novels of Jane Austen with a large annual conference and smaller, regional events including literary teas, historic house tours, lectures, and dances. Part IV focuses on literary pilgrimage as a mode of engagement. There are two types of pilgrimage associated with Austen fandom: attending conventions and special events such as those sponsored by JASNA and traveling to Austen-related sites in England. Separate from quotidian demands, these events and journeys offer fans a chance to share in more social experiences of fandom and to imagine themselves getting closer to Austen and her world. There is a consistent rhetoric evident within representations of literary pilgrimage on screen and in the popular press, which helps to inform the practices of fans and their expectations of what pilgrimage can offer. Pilgrimage of this sort requires resources of leisure time and money not available to all, but for those with the means, it offers the pleasure of temporal displacement in ways that fannish activities within everyday life do not.

Ultimately, this study demonstrates how Jane Austen fans connect to literature, to each other, and to an imagined past. The modes of engagement I describe offer fans a means of time travel. Specifically, I argue that through their activities, both solitary and communal, fans continually forge new meaningful experiences by reviving and reliving their favored texts and the pleasurable experiences they have enjoyed through those texts. This is made possible by performance. The practices of fandom can be understood as performative acts, which open up "creative retrospection," a term anthropologist Victor Turner coined in other cultural contexts.[8] Performative acts, including rituals, make accessible to a community the social modes and meanings it usually keeps hidden from itself. Performance allows communities to be self-reflexive and to navigate social distinction. These performances can take place within the everyday routines of fans as well as within ritual spaces apart from the quotidian. In other words, through performativity, fans create space to be creatively reflective and to find and express meaning within everyday life (e.g., writing or reading fanfiction), as well as within special circumstances detached from the everyday world (e.g., attending a Jane Austen festival).

Performativity is a theoretical concept with multiple meanings. It can connote "performance-ness," or the quality of being similar to a theatrical performance, and it can signify the notion that performance is key to constituting subjectivity. Performativity is a lens for understanding the way words, gestures, actions, and behaviors can constitute a lived reality.[9] It is this connotation that helps account for characteristics of fandom. In fandom, performativity imbues the liminality of pilgrimage; the playfulness of fanfiction, dress-up, adaptation, and reenactment; the everyday devotion of a collector, curating an assemblage of material objects; and the social performances that offer participants social distinction and help form or negotiate subjectivity. The concept of performativity—in all these related forms—is fairly portable and therefore applicable to the interrogation of cultural activities such as fandom.

In this study, I highlight the performativity of fan activities that take place in both the day-to-day lives of fans as well as in special occasions outside of the quotidian.[10] I suggest that in fans' everyday lives, performativity is visible in practices that rely on a process of what historian Joseph Roach has called "surrogation." Apart from everyday life, fans engage in performative activities that take place in liminal, or in-between, spaces that allow them to build community, share knowledge, and experience the affective experiences of imaginative time travel. By applying the ideas of surrogation and liminality to the study of fandom, I propose a useful framework for approaching common activities of fandom.

The chapters ahead offer a long view on the history of fandom by studying an enduring literary phenomenon rather than a media fandom such as those surrounding *Star Trek, Doctor Who,* the vast Marvel franchise, or countless others. Cultural historian Daniel Cavicchi has demonstrated continuity in the history of music fans, connecting the habits of today's music fans with those of the nineteenth century. I likewise interrogate the connection between today's fans and those of earlier periods of the American past. In particular, I explore three factors that have influenced the fandom from the beginning: nostalgia, Austen's complicated position within cultural hierarchy, and an air of respectability that pervades her world. I sketch a portrait of the Austen fandom that demonstrates continuity over time and across media environments. The earliest Jane Austen enthusiasts may predate the use of the term *fan*, but their predilections would not seem unfamiliar to today's Janeites or to participants in other fandoms.

CHANGE AND CONTINUITY

In 1892, the *Boston Journal* expressed that a "recognized Austen cult" could be attributed to a nostalgic yearning for a simpler time: "The telegraph, the telephone, the steam cars and the newspapers were not the factors in rural life that they are today. The dates of Jane Austen's life embrace some of the most momentous events in European history. But she seems to have taken no particular interest in them." The article declared Austen's novels "dateless," suggesting, "nobody in his senses would speak of them as 'old novels.'"[11] Even earlier in the nineteenth century, in the 1830s and 1840s, when her novels began to circulate more widely, her works evoked nostalgia for an unspoiled past, in contrast to looming modernization and industrialization. This was particularly true for white American fans for whom Austen's world represented a nostalgic connection to an Anglo heritage. Barely a generation had elapsed since the novels first appeared (first editions were published from 1811 to 1818), yet already they represented a bygone era. This historical yet timeless aspect of Austen's work continues to shape how her fans engage in meaningful ways with her world.

Many Austen fans today cherish the Regency era as much as the novels. The ways they relate to this historical past are an important part of how they experience their fandom. As historians David Thelen and Roy Rosenzweig have suggested, individuals tend to relate to the past—not specifically to history but, rather, to a more generalizable past—in deeply personal ways, even when they view History (with a capital *H*) as dull or uninteresting. When people engage with the past, it is as a source for understanding their own experiences and identities.[12] For Jane Austen fans, this relatable past is viewed as a simpler time, replete with extensive social structures and manners that magnify niceties and obscure less pleasant aspects of life. The nostalgia found in Austen fandom is a longing for both a particular vision of the historical past as well as for the fictional world represented within the novels and in adaptations.

Cultural theorist Svetlana Boym has explained that although nostalgia appears to be a longing for a place, it is more accurately a "yearning for a different time." However, this yearning is a romance with our own fantasies, not with an actual historical past as it really was.[13] Nostalgia, therefore, is utopian. Boym's descriptions of nostalgia resoundingly resemble the drives that fuel fandom: individual desire for affective experiences, the building of community through collective memory, and the constructed continuity of a narrative world. For fans, nostalgia is a means of selectively playing with and imagining the past.

In *Lost in Austen,* Amanda tries to convince her roommate Pirhana to join her briefly through the portal to the world of *Pride and Prejudice.* Pirhana responds: "Amanda, I'm Black. What's more, I can't live without chocolate, electricity, and bog paper [toilet paper]."[14] Pirhana is not such a Jane Austen fan that she is willing to endure the risks associated with time traveling to that world. She is not nostalgic for Austen's world, thank you very much. Nostalgic time travel to Regency England more readily welcomes those who are white, cisgender, and privileged, much like Amanda. This is not to say, for instance, that nonwhite, queer fans are not welcome in Austen's world or do not also yearn for it but, rather, to point out that the nostalgic impulse to seek refuge in Austen's world may either be less enticing or require more selective imagining for some. Time travel to Jane's England does not easily make space for fans of color, disabled fans, and LGBTQ fans, so they must make space for themselves. Fortunately, fandom allows for this.

Nostalgia is often treated as a problematic form of expression. The term *nostalgia* is used dismissively with regards to certain types of sentiments or traditions. Boym says that *nostalgia* is often considered a "bad word" or at best an "affectionate insult."[15] Some scholars have suggested ways that nostalgia problematizes contemporary views of Austen's historical world with a tendency to erase England's exclusionary class system and destructive imperial tendencies in favor of a rosier view of the past.[16] Austen's version of Regency England (and representations of it on screen) may indeed understate actual historical problems of class and imperialism, but by claiming that fans are nostalgic for Austen's world, I do not denigrate their desires or pass judgment on ways they prefer selective erasures of historical actualities. Instead, I contextualize the pleasures that Austen fans seek. Fandom is a playground in which to explore a world alternative to one's own. In that world, certain problems, fears, and desires are worked out, underscored, or ruptured, while others are set aside or ignored. These tactics—visible throughout the history of Austen fandom—make fan practices useful and pleasurable to those who employ them.

The place of Austen's novels and related spin-offs, adaptations, and comic books in cultural hierarchy is wonderfully complex. Jane Austen has become popular culture with a highbrow affect and aesthetic. Like Shakespeare's plays, Austen's novels have at different moments moved unstably between highbrow and popular realms, according to the shifting desires and needs of audiences. Historian Lawrence Levine has said that Shakespeare was domesticated and humanized by nineteenth-century America before being turned into a "classic." Americans "digested" his plays, making them part of a shared public culture;[17] the same could be said of Austen.

Roberta Pearson has called for more scholars to consider highbrow fandoms (such as "Bachies" and "Bardies"), and to a certain extent, this book does that.[18] But Austen cannot be considered fully highbrow, even if champion of the literary canon F. R. Leavis did, in 1948, dub her the "inaugurator" of the great English novel.[19] Her position is more complicated than that. Compared to other popular novelists whose works inspire fannish devotion, Austen enjoys a unique bimodal position. Works such as J. K. Rowling's *Harry Potter* series are indeed studied in academic settings, but they are generally presented as popular culture worthy of study for their artistic merits as well as in acknowledgment of the deep impact such works have on culture through their vast reach. *Pride and Prejudice* and *Emma* are studied as literature in high schools and universities across the world, and regardless of one's views on the concept of a canon, it would be difficult to find someone today to argue that Austen's novels should not be part of the Western canon of great literature. Yet unlike many other canonical works, Austen's novels also circulate easily within the realm of popular culture through numerous adaptations, spin-offs, YouTube videos, fanfiction, and Austen-related merchandise.

In her lifetime, Jane Austen sought to have her novels published alongside other popular reading material. Her works entered the market modestly in the early nineteenth century and gained only a narrow readership at first.[20] However, by the late nineteenth century, as novels by her contemporaries fell out of favor, her works gained both wider, popular readership and simultaneously began to be viewed as "classic literature," a trend that continued into the twentieth century. From the 1870s, Austen was marketed as a "popular" author to a wider audience in more affordable editions. This moment coincided with—or precipitated—an increased demand for classic literature as highbrow readers sought to distinguish their tastes from lowbrow readers.[21] In the early twentieth century, even as adaptations proliferated for stage, radio, and eventually film, Austen was being added to college curricula. St. John's College in Annapolis, Maryland, known as the Great Books school, added *Pride and Prejudice* to its senior year reading list in 1950, alongside Aristotle, Hegel, Melville, Proust, and Tolstoy.[22] Although Jane Austen has shifted easily between the realms of popular and high culture, this bimodality has caused conflict: as popular audiences claimed her as their own, scholarly readers decried her misuse and sought ways to distinguish their mode of loving Austen from those less lofty.[23]

In the first half of the nineteenth century, when Austen's novels were gradually becoming available to more readers, contemporary fiction was considered the domain of popular entertainment, and like most popular entertainments, novels attracted both proponents and detractors. Detractors of the novel included evangelical critics who feared the literary genre would corrupt female virtue. Jane Austen playfully contradicts this notion throughout *Northanger Abbey*, and in *Pride and Prejudice*, she alludes to James Fordyce, whose published sermons included an indictment of novels. Fordyce feared novels were "in their nature so shameful, in their tendency so pestiferous, and contain such rank treason against the royalty of Virtue, . . . that she who can bear to peruse them must in her soul be a prostitute."[24] An extreme position, to be sure, but the sentiment is reminiscent of critics of fandom today who derisively express discomfort with what they view as excessive and obsessive behaviors. Although Fordyce and others were concerned over the effect of novels on young women's morality, it appears that Austen's earliest fans—like her fans today—were in fact mostly shielded from negative criticism.

Austen's bimodality as both literature and popular culture, her respectable and realistic narratives, and her reputation as a highly regarded daughter of a clergyman have protected her fans from the kind of derision sometimes aimed at other fandoms, especially compared to those that predominantly attract women.[25] Picture the familiar negative stereotype of the geeky Trekkie obsessed with *Star Trek* minutiae; recall the scorn hurled at women and girls who found themselves enamored with Stephenie Meyer's *Twilight* series. Although mainstream society will sometimes raise an eyebrow at a group of grown women and men in Regency attire dancing and drinking tea at an Austen event, these fans are viewed as quaint and quirky, rather than dismissed as obsessive losers. Society views the fandom's trappings of fancy attire and the refined manners of a historical age as more acceptable than pointy ears and homemade communicator badges or "Team Edward" T-shirts. Moreover, the whiteness associated with Austen serves as an additional protective factor. American nostalgia for Austen's era is protected from scorn and legitimized because at its heart Austen's world represents the white patriarchal hegemony that society itself strives to uphold. Although fandom has in recent years come out of the shadows and is more accepted by the mainstream, there remains a sense that some fandoms and their idiosyncrasies are more acceptable than others.

The negative stereotype of fans as losers who just need to grow up and deal with the real world is partly dependent upon a notion of escapism understood pathologically and implying a lack of self-control.[26] However, fans often use the term *escape* in positive terms. One Austen fan I spoke to used the word *escapism* in a positive sense three times in a conversation of half an hour.[27] She described falling in love with Austen's novels at age thirteen, as a refuge from real-world troubles during the Vietnam War era. As Ken Gelder has suggested, students of literature in the classroom are taught a serious, slow, careful style of reading, but reading popular fiction sometimes encourages the opposite: "reading fast, reading at leisure, reading to 'escape.'"[28] Mainstream society differentiates reading that is serious (work) from reading that is for pleasure (play). A classist hierarchy normally underscores this distinction, placing serious reading of so-called classics above lower forms of entertainment. When readers escape into Austen, it problematizes this distinction, creating tensions for those invested in upholding such hierarchies. It is well worth recuperating the idea of escape within fandom from the grips of elitism since it offers a form of play that is often quite meaningful.[29]

Sociologist Jock Young suggests that leisure cannot exist without work and that the two things inevitably inflect each other. He argues an "ethos of productivity" attempts to "legitimize and encompass" the world of leisure.[30] When adults engage in a true form of play without inhibition (as opposed to simple leisure), it is frequently viewed by mainstream society as problematic. Often aspects of fandom that most resemble play, such as dressing up and enacting roles through cosplay, are those most derided by normative society. Young's suggestion that leisure is inflected by an "ethos of productivity" may help explain why many fans often engage in expressive forms and activities that resemble productive labor, such as writing fanfiction or creating scrapbooks. Such practices align more closely with leisure activities deemed suitable for adults than the more playful modes of fandom. Many of the Austen fans discussed in this study participated in forms that resemble professional or scholarly work and exemplify the labor of love common to fandom, and, moreover, highlight the Austen fandom's relative respectability.

The air of respectability that surrounds the Austen fandom has distinguished it from the beginning and continues to shape fans' modes of engagement. Within the fandom, many Austen enthusiasts play out their sense of Austen's bimodality and its relation to notions of respectability when they either self-identify as scholars or as non-scholars and in the ways they describe their love for and devotion to Austen. When is a person not a fan but an "enthusiast" or "connoisseur"? How do we draw such distinctions and why? Attempting to answer these questions reveals anxieties over cultural hierarchy and distinctions among literary enthusiasts over "proper" ways of reading. Many of the performative aspects of fandom are concerned with mitigating these anxieties and social distinctions. Anecdotally, a colleague casually mentioned to me that while she loves attending Jane Austen conventions, she would never dream of attending a similar event for her other great obsession: *Doctor Who.* For her, there is a line to be drawn between fan activities that are acceptable or suitable and those that are not. Among fans and fandoms, a cultural hierarchy exists yet is not a simple matter of high and low but, rather, is something subtler and more complex.

TERMS AND TERMINOLOGY

In his landmark work on *Star Trek* fans, *Textual Poachers: Television Fans and Participatory Culture,* Henry Jenkins emphasizes the notion that fan activities, especially the writing of fanfiction, turn the consumption of a commodity (the text) into a form of production. He argues that fans are "cultural scavengers," or "textual poachers," who pose a challenge to official culture producers by writing fanfiction, making videos, and otherwise remaking source material.[31] Like other early scholars of fandom, Jenkins was attempting to recuperate the reputation of fans by arguing for an understanding of fan practices as active and productive, not as passive or even deviant, consumption. Foregrounding the productivity inherent in fandom distances fans from the criticism that they are engaged in nothing more than a form of infantile commodity fetishism or "repetition compulsion" driving a desire to relive and keep alive an experience with a text.[32] However, Jenkins's early writings on fans rest upon a false dichotomy. Rita Felski has critiqued the emergence and subsequent naturalization of a production/consumption dichotomy in which production is understood as good and consumption as bad.[33] This dichotomy is furthermore understood—and coded within social discourse—as gendered: production is masculine (good), and consumption is feminine (bad). By championing the idea that fan productivity should be viewed as constructive, early fan studies scholars unintentionally underscored the dichotomy described by Felski.

Jenkins's assertion that fans are not simply engaged in a form of commodity fetishism remains valid today. Fans engage in mindful—not mindless—consumption. The argument that fans are not driven by infantile repetition compulsion remains equally valid.[34] While I agree that the desire to reread, re-watch, and remake texts should not be viewed as a regressive impulse, I recognize the important role repetition plays within fan practices. The impulse to revisit a text can better be understood through the notion of surrogation. I propose that by focusing on the acts of surrogation that occur through fan engagement, we make both a tactical maneuver in favor of feminism that corrects Jenkins's false and gendered dichotomy of production and consumption, and we recuperate the idea that repetition in fandom is not simply an infantile compulsion.

Joseph Roach has explained surrogation as a performative process of memory and forgetting. He describes the "three-sided relationship of memory, performance, and substitution." I suggest that fans create things—scrapbooks or fanfiction, for example—to act as what Roach calls "effigies." The effigy is a mnemonic object, "a contrivance that enables the processes regulating performance . . . to produce memory through surrogation." Fans create these effigies to stand in for something lost, such as a past affective experience related to their beloved text. However, it is a substitute that can never produce an exact fit and is destined to disappoint. Therefore, one must continuously audition new stand-ins in the hopes of finding a better match.[35] Repetition and memory are at the heart of this process. First, the fan seeks to repeat a past act or experience, such as reading the text for the first time or attaining a prized book for a collection, by creating an effigy. Second, the fan revisits the effigy (a scrapbook, e.g.) seeking a way of remembering the past experience. And finally, the fan must continue to make new effigies, repeatedly attempting to attain a better substitute.

Performativity is visible within fan practices both in the performances in everyday life that happen through acts of surrogation and in the performing of subjectivity that takes place within liminal spaces—apart from the quotidian—provided by forms of literary pilgrimage. In these liminal spaces, fans perform in much more explicit ways, such as through dressing up and playing roles. Acts of surrogation allow fans to keep alive in their everyday lives the special liminal experiences attained through pilgrimage. Through collecting, scrapbooking, and reading and writing fanfiction, fans revisit the world of the text in ways that are always familiar but also always new. The mnemonic objects fans create are performative: they make manifest, transmit, and reinvent each individual's affective experiences.[36]

Fan activities and creations have recently been described as taking two predominant forms: "transformational" and "affirmational." Both involve the same types of activities and are not mutually exclusive, but at their core, each uses a different set of tactics in order to celebrate the beloved text. Transformational fandom subverts intended meanings. "Obsession_inc" (a pseudonym of the fan who coined these terms) describes transformative acts as "laying hands upon the source and twisting it to the fans' own purposes, whether that is to fix a disappointing issue (a distinct lack of sex-having between two characters, of course, is a favorite issue to fix) in the source material, or using the source material to illustrate a point." Affirmational fandom, on the other hand, restates the source material and operates according to certain canonical rules and norms regarding characters, details, and the central concepts of the text.[37] Fan practices that are transformational have received greater attention from fan studies than affirmational ones. However, I have found that Jane Austen fandom employs a rich and lively set of affirmational practices. The Austen fandom is mostly conservative compared to other fandoms in that it affirms rather than resists the messages within the original texts, often restating core narratives, rarely challenging them, even when creatively adapting and modernizing Austen in new forms.

Transformational practices are viewed as predominantly carried out by female fans, and affirmational ones as mostly male. Matt Hills has critiqued the use of these terms precisely because they suggest a false binary, particularly regarding the gendering of fan activities.[38] The predominantly female Jane Austen fandom, and its mostly affirmational modes, complicates critiques of this gendered distinction. Moreover, the modes of Austen fandom resemble those of other more transformational fandoms. Austen fans play with irony and incongruous representations of Regency manners as a way to pry open the text but without overtly resisting the social mores and norms found within Austen's texts or in contemporary adaptations of her texts. Fan studies scholars tend to favor those aspects of fandom that are transformational and seem to demonstrate resistance to hegemony.

However, the creations of fans such as those in the Austen fandom that tend toward the affirmational are just as important (even if less sexy).

Jane Austen fandom may not exemplify the kinds of resistance to hegemony that many media fandoms do, but the alternative community it offers fans—mostly women—plays an important role in the lives of the individuals who seek it out. Jenkins describes the "alternative social communities" in which fans celebrate and constitute alternative social networks apart from the mainstream. He says, "Fandom offers . . . an alternative reality whose values may be more humane and democratic than those held by mundane society."[39] Fandom is not so much a removal from reality as it is a strategic move toward an alternative. For the (mostly) women who love Jane Austen, her world allows for that strategic move toward a different way of living in the world and relating to others than that offered by twenty-first-century life.

I want to be clear that by describing the fandom as nostalgic and by pointing out the non-subversive nature of the practices of Austen fans, I am by no means making a value judgment. Fandom scholars tend to champion fans who demonstrate creative resistance and the disruption of hegemony in popular culture. I myself favor fan creations that disrupt white, patriarchal power structures, but I suggest that it is well worth recognizing the importance of affirmational fandom. Whether overtly subversive or conservative and nostalgic, fandom serves individual needs and desires. I am wary of privileging resistance above affirmation or valuing one fan's pleasures over another. Moreover, as fan studies scholar Rukmini Pande has recently pointed out, transformational fandom is perhaps not as inherently disruptive of hegemonic norms as often thought, particularly as regards race; rather, Pande shows that so-called transformational fandom shares the same biases that plague the very media that fans are attempting to transform.[40]

WHO ARE AUSTEN'S FANS?

Although the term *fan* did not come into regular use until after 1889, when it became fashionable in the United States to describe baseball fanatics as such, several instances of what we now recognize as fandom come to light much earlier, particularly surrounding literature and literary figures. I acknowledge it is problematic to apply the terms *fan* and *fandom* anachronistically, but they accurately describe the devotion of Austen's earliest enthusiasts whether they had a word for it or not. I use *fan* to encompass a broad historical phenomenon, even where applying it is, admittedly, anachronistic. Moreover, I suggest that to call an enthusiast a fan regardless of historical or social context should be viewed as a compliment redolent of devotion and depth of knowledge.

Some of today's Austen lovers will balk at being referred to as "fans," preferring other terms they feel are more appropriate for devotees of great literature. Normally, when *fan* is applied to a lover of a cultural text, the text itself is automatically viewed as popular culture. By contrast, it might seem unsuitable to apply *fan* to avid devotees of opera, today viewed by some as one of the highest forms of culture. Concerns over hierarchy persuade society to view some obsessions as belonging to fandom and others as belonging to something else. Even among devotees of popular culture, there are factions, such as a subset of Sherlockians, that abhor the term *fan*, a preference that perhaps reveals a hierarchical preference for certain forms of media or genre over others.[41] But I suggest such distinctions, built on the basis of cultural hierarchy, are in many ways irrelevant; it is the behavior, tendencies, and social modes of interaction of the audience that distinguishes fans from enthusiasts, not the genre of the text or its place within cultural hierarchy. And yet the social modes of fans and connoisseurs are not entirely distinct. Some Austen lovers eschew *fan* for what they view as its frivolous connotation that does not capture a sophisticated and enduring affection. Yet *fan* is a useful term that connotes a wide range of serious as well as frivolous pursuits. Whether one is comfortable calling an Austen enthusiast a fan or not says more about perceptions of highbrow versus popular culture and social distinction than it does about the actual characteristics of a fandom. As this study of the Jane Austen fandom demonstrates, in different settings these distinctions play out or are mitigated through performance.

As in most fandoms, among Austen enthusiasts, there exists simultaneously a shared nomenclature as well as communal disagreement over its use. Even the term *Janeite* has come under fire as a derogatory term among some devotees of Austen who view *Janeite* as connoting a shallow devotion. I have found feelings on this subject to be as varied as they are subjective, but I acknowledge a schism exists between those who call themselves Janeites, and those who find such an appellation beneath their dignity. Yet others seem to feel the term connotes the highest devotion to Austen. Whatever these Austen lovers—past and present—choose to call themselves, I suggest they share common attributes and experiences as fans, whether their approach tends toward scholarly or escapist.

In 2008, Jeanne Kiefer, an Austen lover and research consultant who designs online surveys for corporations, sought to determine whether there is such a thing as a typical Janeite. She shared her findings, a "fully-rounded portrait of Jane Austen's current readership," in *Persuasions,* the journal of the Jane Austen Society of North America. The survey was self-limited to participants who had read all six of Austen's novels and "considered themselves to be 'sincere admirers.'"[42] Over forty-five hundred people responded to the survey. Respondents were overwhelmingly women (96%). They represented a wide age range, with roughly one-third of respondents under age twenty-nine, one-third between ages thirty to forty-nine, and one-third over fifty. Among respondents over the age of twenty, 81 percent were college educated and 45 percent held a graduate degree. A large proportion have held positions in fields related to education or library sciences. Nearly half claimed to listen "frequently" to National Public Radio. Respondents were much more likely to view themselves as liberal (55%) than conservative (25%), and their households tended to be more affluent than the U.S. median. Questions on race or ethnicity are conspicuously absent from the survey. This oversight reveals an assumption that respondents would predominantly be white. Taken together, the results of Kiefer's survey suggest that a typical Janeite is essentially a white, educated, affluent woman—just what one might anecdotally assume.

As for me, I have loved Jane Austen since I first watched—in a single five-hour sitting—the 1995 BBC adaptation of *Pride and Prejudice.* I was in my first year of college at the time. After seeing that production for the first of many times, I began reading Austen, but it was not until after college, when I had more time for pleasure reading, that I really began to appreciate Austen's prose. By that time, the post–Colin Firth frenzy was in full swing, and adaptations of *Emma, Sense and Sensibility,* and *Persuasion* were becoming available. And as it happened, I was working in eighteenth-century costume in Colonial Williamsburg as a historical interpreter by day and musician by candlelit night. I was, in a sense, living and breathing (and earning my livelihood) in a romanticized American version of the era of Jane Austen's youth. My roommate at the time was also a Janeite, and together we watched and re-watched adaptations and compiled lists of actors with whom we would recast our own adaptations. I believe I was a fan by anyone's standards. For a number of years after that period, I reread the novels, read a few of the "sequels" and spin-offs, but eventually, Austen and I grew apart. As my lifestyle changed, so did my interests. I still love Jane Austen, and I never grow tired of her prose, but I no longer deserve the designation "fan." As a scholar I enjoy an interesting vantage point; I am not an outsider, but nor am I entirely an insider. I am like many of the fans I study: I am a white woman from a privileged background that includes an advanced education. I am admittedly not as committed to the texts nor as engaged in the activities of the fandom as the fans I have encountered, but I certainly pass for a fan thanks to my gender, class, education, and knowledge of Austen, even if not consciously trying to. Having once wholeheartedly been a Janeite, however, I am well positioned to fully appreciate those who are and to time travel beside them. And I can nearly keep pace with their knowledge and enthusiasm.

I

JANE AUSTEN AND TRANSATLANTIC LITERARY FANDOM 1816–1940

Prologue

In Louisa May Alcott's *Little Women* (1868), the March sisters enjoy an entertainment derived from an activity rather like the writing of a fanzine, inspired by their admiration for Charles Dickens.

> As spring came on, a new set of amusements became the fashion, and the lengthening days gave long afternoons for work and play of all sorts. . . . One of these was the "P.C."; for, as secret societies were the fashion, it was thought proper to have one; and, as all of the girls admired Dickens, they called themselves the Pickwick Club. With a few interruptions, they had kept this up for a year, and met every Saturday evening. . . . Three chairs were arranged in a row before a table, on which was a lamp, also four white badges, with a big "P.C." in different colors on each, and the weekly newspaper, called "The Pickwick Portfolio," to which all contributed something; while Jo, who reveled in pens and ink, was the editor.[1]

Alcott followed this description with a comical and charming example of the "Pickwick Portfolio," the sisters' weekly newspaper complete with poems, jokes, sensational stories, and even advertisements. The real-life Alcott sisters, on whom the March girls were based, themselves formed a Pickwick Club, and examples of their actual "Pickwick Portfolio" survive today.[2] It is from among these original newspaper entries, written between 1849 and 1853, that Alcott excerpted the selections found in *Little Women*.[3] The fannish admiration of Dickens documented by the Alcott sisters and represented by the fictional March sisters was surely meant to be a familiar scene to readers in the mid-nineteenth century, not an outlandish one; these were young women engaging in good clean fun. Yet fans, their obsessions, and their behaviors have always been viewed by some as eccentric at best and deviant at worst. It is no accident, then, that Alcott characterizes the girls' secret society as industrious—and therefore virtuous—amusement.

The chapters in part I provide examples, like that from *Little Women*, that demonstrate that literary fan practices analogous to those today were commonplace in mid-nineteenth-century America, when Austen's novels began to take root there in the cultural imagination. Today's Jane Austen fandom has origins traceable to the 1830s, long before the appearance of adaptations and spin-offs that would later help make the fandom much more prevalent. By 1940, when MGM's film adaptation of *Pride and Prejudice* captivated audiences, the stage had already been set for expanding participatory interaction with Austen's texts. In addition to tracing Austen fandom from the earliest reception of the novels through a moment of burgeoning spin-offs and adaptations at the turn of the twentieth century, the following three chapters reveal several characteristics of the fandom that were as notable in the nineteenth century as today, demonstrating remarkable continuity.

Early Austen fans used ideas about the novelist's morality and the decency of her work to support their claims of respectability in the face of criticism leveled at them by a society ambivalent about novels and uncomfortable with unfettered fascination with them. For every fan of literature who emerged in the eighteenth and nineteenth centuries, a detractor found their enthusiasm and habits problematic or even immoral. To overcome this disapproval, literature lovers learned to perform virtue through their reading habits, rendering an obsession with literature safe and blameless by casting both their own activities and the object of their fascination as moral. By performing an affinity to Jane Austen, readers performed virtue. Whereas some fandoms today receive criticism for their obsessive behaviors, fans of literature benefit from an aura of respectability. Society might look askance at Trekkies (or Trekkers, as many prefer) or censure the exuberance of teen girls over K-Pop stars, but Janeites are spared for the most part or are at least tolerated thanks to the way Austen aligns with certain ideas about class, race, and gender. I suggest that the air of respectability Janeites enjoy today relative to other fandoms is visible in the nineteenth century through Austen fans' performances of virtue.

Austen, like other literary figures of the time, inspired fans to feel a personal connection to "Jane," a sensibility that the fandom retains today. The modes of literary fandom I describe here are not unlike those seen today, in which fans—through performative means—seek personal connections to texts and authors, pursue affective experiences related to their reading through play, and seek out a physical link through material objects and pilgrimage. Today fans can easily connect to a greater community online through social media and can readily travel great distances to come together in person. Although such connectivity and community were harder to achieve in the nineteenth century, personal correspondence and circulating print media provided a vibrant means for fans to participate in like-minded communities. The activities of fans described in part I are antecedents of those detailed later in the book.

In the first chapter, I offer brief context for eighteenth- and nineteenth-century transatlantic literary fandom, particularly highlighting the tendency, well documented by literary scholars and historians, of nineteenth-century fans to seek a personal connection with a beloved author or fictional world. In the second and third chapters, I detail evidence of a Jane Austen fandom that was in full swing by the time her first biography became available, in 1870, a moment that sparked even greater and more widespread admiration of Austen. In the 1830s through 1850s, Austen's fame and fandom existed on a more modest scale than in later decades, but I suggest that allusions to Austen and discussions of her novels in early-nineteenth-century print media help shed light on the emergence of the fandom. Periodicals, so influential on the American cultural imagination, reveal views on Austen that influenced the characteristics of the fandom. Chapter 3 offers examples of three main modes of fan engagement—fanfiction, collecting memorabilia, and pilgrimage—from the early nineteenth through early twentieth centuries, bringing the history of Austen fandom up to another pivotal moment: MGM's release of *Pride and Prejudice* on the silver screen in 1940. By this time, Austen's appeal was ineluctable, and she had taken hold in the cultural imagination, particularly in America. I propose that the modes of fandom visible in the nineteenth century enabled and shaped the Austen fandom that would become so recognizable in the twentieth century and beyond.

1

A "Sense of Kindred" in Nineteenth-Century Transatlantic Literary Fandom

In the mid-twentieth century, American literary critic Lionel Trilling lamented a trend whereby Jane Austen was frequently removed from "the proper confines of literature" and instead was read and loved in a manner that Trilling felt might be considered "objectionable" or even "illicit" and which stemmed from a self-congratulatory and "extravagantly personal" form of admiration.[1] Yet Austen was never solely within the "proper confines of literature" to begin with and has long inspired very personal forms of veneration among her fans. Precedents for loving Austen and her works in all sorts of ways have a long history in the nineteenth century. And Jane Austen was not alone: nineteenth-century readers loved literature and adored writers. This chapter provides brief historical context for the milieu into which early Jane Austen fandom emerged and highlights a feature prevalent in nineteenth-century fandom generally: a personal sense of connection fans felt—and sought—to their favorite authors and other celebrities.

There persists a notion that what we recognize as fandom today is a much more recent phenomenon driven by the advent of film and especially of television, with its appealingly serialized, often open-ended narrative format. While it may be true that the characteristics of fandom, as defined by fans as well as fan studies scholars, are more pronounced today and amplified by social media, they are certainly legible in fandom's past. Fan studies scholar Matt Hills defines fans with regards to several key traits: fans are obsessed with a particular text; they retain detailed information about that text and can quote favored segments; they are highly articulate about their fandom; and they tend to interpret texts in "a variety of interesting and perhaps unexpected ways."[2] Perhaps most important, fans participate in communal activities and are not isolated or atomized readers/viewers. This communal aspect of fandom is further explained and indeed emphasized in the definition offered by Henry Jenkins, who characterizes fans as acting within an interpretive community through distinct yet interconnected dimensions of fan culture. According to Jenkins, fans engage in particular modes of reception and traditions of cultural production, and they form alternative social and cultural communities within which they are active participants working to shape the very texts they consume.[3] This foregrounding of community in contemporary media fandoms makes sense given the great capacity for connection between fans made possible by the infrastructures of modern society. Yet even in the more atomized world of the nineteenth century, the role of personal correspondence and circulating print media, which I will return to in the next chapter, can be understood as providing social modes of participation for fan communities analogous to those today.

Just as rapid technological advancements and cultural changes made possible an expansion of fandom in the twentieth century, so too did the mid-nineteenth century witness changes that amplified celebrity worship and certain forms of fandom. Advances in technology and communications enabled the rise of mass media, such as the penny press. Improved media infrastructures and the proliferation of photographic images in print media fueled fascination with human interest stories, which in turn engendered more active than passive audience responses, a hallmark of fandom.[4] In the nineteenth-century transatlantic world, broader audiences gained access to ever-increasing varieties of performances and print materials, which in turn encouraged new, more inclusive forms of social discourse and engagement, including fandom.

When Jane Austen's novels first began to capture fans' admiration and imagination, a culture of literary fandom already existed, rooted in modes of engagement that included pilgrimage, collecting objects, and writing fanfiction. An intense attachment to or identification with beloved authors and the characters they created often characterized this early literary fandom. To understand the modes of fandom familiar to nineteenth-century lovers of Jane Austen, it is worth momentarily considering literary fandom in eighteenth-century Europe around the rise of the novel and the growing fame of novelists.

Cultural historian Leo Braudy suggests the inclination of audiences to be obsessively curious about famous individuals began with men of widespread fame such as Jean-Jacques Rousseau. Early enthusiasts sent letters and made pilgrimages in search of an intense identification with famous writers and, in some cases, with the literary worlds they created. The fame that surrounded Rousseau rendered him into an object of fascination—a mere aura—molded by his audience to their own desires. Never before had an audience taken to so actively shaping and defining its idols; this is, for Braudy, the marker that distinguishes a passive audience from a fannish one.[5]

Literary theorist Mikhail Bakhtin also historicizes the rise of fans in the second half of the eighteenth century, referring to the unique "local cults" that emerged around literary works as fans began to seek out pilgrimage as a means of personal connection to beloved authors, characters, and stories. Readers began to feel impelled to visit factual sites where fictional events had taken place. For instance, in Goethe's fairy tale for children "The New Paris," fantastical events are linked by evocative description to an actual segment of Frankfurt's city wall, leading young readers to make pilgrimages to the spot. Bakhtin suggests it was the mixing of "real spatial markers with fantastic ones" that encouraged the development of a cult around the literary work.[6]

Readers of early novels also sought a personal connection to beloved authors through spin-offs and continuations. Samuel Richardson's novels *Clarissa; or, The History of a Young Lady* (1748) and *Pamela; or, Virtue Rewarded* (1740) inspired avid fandoms with readers rewriting Clarissa's tragic end and recuperating the dastardly Lovelace who ruins her.[7] As Elizabeth Judge has pointed out, fans were so personally invested in Richardson's characters that they felt they were better equipped than the novelist to rescue them from what they viewed as shortcomings in the novels.[8] *Pamela* inspired numerous spin-offs, both admiring and satirical. While the parodies were meant to be just that, readers turned to the continuations (unsanctioned by Richardson) to assuage their hunger for more time with characters with whom they had developed an intense relationship.

Evidence of readers' desire to possess commodities that sentimentally correlated to beloved books appears almost as early as the impulse of fans to visit pilgrimage sites and read and write fanfiction. By the mid-eighteenth century, sentimental literature began to stimulate the creation of spin-offs in the form of commodities. Fans of Richardson's *Pamela* could purchase items including straw bonnets, teacups, engravings, and paintings related to the novel.[9] This trend continued into the nineteenth century and encompassed not only literature but also music and performances of sentimentality. Daniel Cavicchi has shown that nineteenth-century music lovers demonstrated starstruck personal attachment to performers such as singer Jenny Lind and other traveling virtuosos.[10] Lind was beloved as much as an icon of virtuous, Christian womanhood as she was for her singing. Her name and likeness were found on a wide range of commodities, including paper dolls, brandy, teakettles, and sleds, meant to evoke the sentimentality of her performances. The spin-off commodities audiences purchased made possible a material means to both represent and experience fandom in daily life, bringing themselves closer to the idealized and idolized characteristics associated with Lind or Richardson's Pamela. Such objects help collapse for consumers the distance between cultural habits such as reading and attending performances and buying and using things that represent taste and affinities.[11]

Nineteenth-century music fans engaged in a range of practices that resemble those of fans today. They kept diaries to document the performances they attended, recording the emotions they felt at different moments; they made pilgrimages to sites associated with great composers; they collected memorabilia and sheet music; they reproduced the experience of concert going at home with amateur performance; and they formed idealized connections with star performers such as Jenny Lind.[12] Shrewd P. T. Barnum promoted Lind to the public as simple, innocent, and good, appealing to audiences' sensibilities regarding womanhood.[13] Audiences identified with Lind yet also sought to fill in Barnum's cultivated public image of her with more personal details. As with Austen, a sense of kinship with the woman herself motivated Lind's eager fans to pursue greater familiarity and intimacy with her through any means available.

Austen scholar Deidre Lynch claims, "Jane Austen fosters in her readers, as most other literary giants do not, the devotion and fantasies of personal access that are the hallmarks of the *fan*."[14] Lynch is only half-correct: Austen has indeed inspired devotion and fantasies of personal access, but so too have many other literary figures. Literary fandom was prominent enough by 1839 that social theorist and essayist Harriet Martineau felt compelled to bemoan the sentimental, personal identification readers expressed toward the likes of Chaucer and Shakespeare. The sentiments, especially, but also the practices of fandom were already familiar enough by the mid-nineteenth century to warrant commentary.[15]

Unsurprisingly, Martineau did not observe fan devotion with equanimity. Writing in the *London and Westminster Review*, she described the rise of what she termed "literary lionism," which we might today recognize as proto-fandom.[16] The "lion," as she called the proverbial literary genius, represented "the 'interesting creature' round whom young ladies flutter, with bashful praises of his 'divine poem.'" And the "lionizers" represented fans, young ladies specifically, driven to utter "urgent requests for 'one line' for each of their albums." Martineau teased that lion and lionizer were locked in a symbiotic relationship, whereby the author soaked in much needed praise and adoration and was obligated to perform his greatness in public, so that the lionizers—the fans—might collect treasured objects associated with the lion to be "locked up in lavender, cherished like a gem" (139). Martineau's censure of these literary fans resembles the response prompted many decades later by movie-struck girls of the early cinema days.

Books, complained Martineau, had become commonplace and were no longer the "scarce fruit of solemn and protracted thought" but instead had been made available for anyone. In her view, this led to the development of a broad class of lions as well as lionizers, each dependent on the other. The rise of adoring literature fans furthermore fueled the rise of popular literature. Martineau ostensibly blamed "the deterioration of literature" and the mediocrity of the public intellect on the emergence of fan culture (141).

However, Martineau allowed that the fandom surrounding literary figures originated in commendable sentiments, such as those "in veneration for intellectual superiority, and gratitude for intellectual gifts" (139). After all, in her autobiography, Martineau referred to Jane Austen as the "queen of novelists" and claimed to read "with more pleasure than ever" her "old favourites," Miss Austen and Scott.[17] Her greatest complaint was not that fans adored their lions or that literature had become available to a wider segment of the populace; she actually celebrated that literature had "interested a different order of people from any who formerly shared its advantages." Rather, much like Lionel Trilling more than one hundred years later, she complained that the flattery of genius, formerly a "noble" pursuit, had been degraded by lower forms of selfishly based admiration. She lamented, "As the blessings of literature spread, strong *personal* gratitude mingled with the homage" (140).[18] With a sneer, she imagined readers who, "on the heath, or in the shadow of the wood, whispered to themselves, with beating hearts, while communing with some mastermind, 'I also am a poet.'" These readers, she opined, "could not hear the very names of Chaucer or Shakespeare without a glow of personal interest, arising out of a sense of kindred" (147).

This "sense of kindred"—a personal attachment to literature—recollects the experience of fans yearning for a connection with the likes of Walt Whitman and Elizabeth Barrett Browning, both of whom were well aware of readers' strong reactions to their work and avid curiosity about their lives. While Martineau disparaged readers' devotion to literary celebrities, writers such as Whitman and Barrett Browning basked in the attention and even encouraged it.

Whitman inspired messianic devotion and admiration on both sides of the Atlantic; his admirers included Bram Stoker, Oscar Wilde, and others recognized by their contemporaries as great men of letters. These admirers formed societies and made pilgrimages, and some of his disciples even came to believe that Whitmanism might become a form of religion to rival Christianity.[19] After reading and falling in love with Whitman's *Leaves of Grass*, Bram Stoker felt the urge to connect as directly with Whitman the man as he had with his words. Stoker, besotted with Whitman's ideals and persona, wrote to the poet in the guise of friendship: "If I were before your face I would like to shake hands with you, for I feel that I would like you. I would like to call you Comrade and to talk to you as men who are not poets do not often talk." The sentiment is much like the letters young fans write to favorite celebrities today. In a fervently personal manner, the twenty-five-year-old Stoker continued, "I have been more candid with you—have said more about myself to you than I have ever said to any one before."[20] He did not send this letter, written in 1872, until four years later, when he found himself moved to express his admiration yet again to Whitman and mustered the courage to mail multiple letters at once to his idol. Three weeks later, Stoker received a warm, if brief, response.

An activist, working to shape his beloved texts, Stoker's fandom resembles examples of today's television fan activism.[21] He sought to edit lines from Whitman's works that mainstream Americans found objectionable so that the poet would forever be found on the bookshelves of every home in America, rather than be censored and then forgotten. Stoker felt the sacrifice of a few lines of poetry was worth ensuring his idol's lasting renown.[22]

Elizabeth Barrett Browning was keenly aware of reader's tendencies toward obsessive adoration and actively cultivated her own fans; moreover, she was herself a fan of other writers.[23] Browning described herself as "capable of all sorts of foolishnesses," admitting that upon receiving a letter of praise from William Wordsworth, her response was to kiss it. Reminiscent of Martineau's lionizers, a droll Browning admits, "I might, if I were tempted, be caught in the overt act of gathering a thistle because Wordsworth had trodden it down."[24]

Following the 1856 publication of her blank verse novel *Aurora Leigh*, about, as it happens, the life of a young woman writer who achieves literary success and inspires fans, Browning received fan mail that she found extravagant. She described the "mania" the poem caused among "quite decent women" reacting with "a sort of effervescence" that astonished her.[25] The letters to Browning from her fans describe the performative ways they experienced their love of her work. Some fans memorized long passages of Browning's writing, and others wrote their own poetry in response. In one instance, a fan had a portrait painted of herself in the garb of Aurora, imitating (in very meta fashion) an act of fandom that takes place within the work.[26]

In 1887, when Sherlock Holmes burst onto the literary scene, the public was primed for a fanatical and deeply personal response to the detective and his adventures. Sherlockians appeared immediately, signaling a shift at the end of the nineteenth century toward a type of devotion that gave more attention to characters or fictional worlds than to the literary genius responsible for creating them. When Conan Doyle killed off his eponymous detective in "The Final Problem" in 1893, fans took the death personally and channeled their grief into activism. Holmes devotees were so shocked and hurt by the detective's death that they wore black armbands in public and wrote scathing letters to Conan Doyle and his publisher in protest. Thanks to the fans, Sherlock Holmes returned from the dead ten years later in a new set of stories. In 1902, the first example of "Holmesian speculation" appeared. In this main facet of the Holmes fandom, the fan writes as if the characters of Conan Doyle's stories are real people and speculates, as Holmes himself might, explanations for the discrepancies that riddle Conan Doyle's plots. Notably, this has always been a fandom devoted to the creation rather than the creator; Conan Doyle has always played second fiddle to Sherlock.[27]

Austen, by contrast, has inspired as much intense personal devotion as even her most beloved characters. When Martineau referred to Austen as the queen of novelists, she supported the honorific by adding, "the immortal creator of Anne Elliott, Mr. Knightley, and a score or two more of unrivalled intimate friends of the whole public," pointing in equal measure to both Austen's genius as a writer and the deep connection felt by her readers to the "intimate friends" they met within the novels.[28] Austen was indeed an "immortal creator"; in contrast with other literary figures of the nineteenth century who inspired a sense of kindred in readers, by the time Austen had fans to adore her, she was long gone from this earth. An affective sensibility of attachment to Austen has remained a hallmark of the fandom.

Most Austen scholars agree that the 1870 publication of J. A. Austen-Leigh's *Memoir of Jane Austen and Other Family Recollections* was a watershed moment in Austen's reception history. Written by her nephew, the intimate look into Austen's life drawn from personal recollection and family lore inspired greater interest in Austen and her works than ever before. The *Memoir* did indeed animate readers, leading to a significant boost in her popularity; however, I suggest that the fandom predates this moment, as the next two chapters will show. Print media of the 1820s through 1840s demonstrates how Jane Austen—her persona, her novels and her characters—began to take up residence in the cultural imagination, setting the stage for an emerging Austen fandom and a deeply rooted sense of kindred for Austen and her characters long before the *Memoir* helped readers gain more intimate footing with their dear Jane.

2

Performing Virtue

JANE AUSTEN IN THE PRESS AND IN AMERICAN CULTURAL IMAGINATION, 1830–1850

Nineteenth-century depictions of Jane Austen and her novels in the press reveal the place of Austen within the cultural imagination and bring to light the ideas and sensibilities that helped shape her early fandom. Throughout the nineteenth century, tastemakers and fans fostered a mythos surrounding Jane Austen of moral and agreeable womanhood, similar to that which surrounded the "Swedish Nightingale," Jenny Lind. This mythos helped promote Austen's novels and aligned her readers with good taste and virtue. A notion of Austen as a quiet, young Christian woman of good education and pedigree but little experience in the world provided evidence that her novels were of good quality and worth reading, even for impressionable minds. Legitimate society, including taste-making literary periodicals, argued in favor of certain novels, such as those by Jane Austen, because of the good morals and suitable didactic aims to be found within them. Before exploring the evidence found in print media, I begin with some context: a brief publishing history and discussion of how the novels themselves began to circulate.

Emma was the first Austen novel made available by an American publisher. In 1816, Carey & Lea of Philadelphia produced a small printing of probably 500 copies.[1] It was not until 1832 that the other novels began to appear in American editions, so it seems that *Emma* did not initially create much demand for additional works from the author. By 1832, however, Carey & Lea seemed certain that more Austen would be welcome by American readers. They sold the first American edition of *Pride and Prejudice* in August 1832 and followed with the rest of the novels in quick succession: *Persuasion* in September; *Mansfield Park* in December; *Northanger Abbey* in January 1833; and *Sense and Sensibility* in February. The second American edition of *Emma* appeared in June 1833. The 1832 edition of *Pride and Prejudice* was produced in an edition of a cautious 750 copies, but subsequent publications of the other novels were increased to 1,250 copies. This success is modest but clear. Just six years later, in 1838, the same firm (now Lea, Carey, & Blanchard) published the first American collected edition of the six novels and then, in 1845, produced separate editions of the individual novels once again.[2]

Between 1816 and 1832, editions of the novels available in America were so costly that only wealthier readers could afford to purchase the books. Other readers may have encountered the books in circulating or subscription libraries or in the private collections of acquaintances. One of only six copies extant today of the 1816 Philadelphia edition of *Emma* was once owned by a circulating library in Rhode Island.[3] Eventually, between 1832 and 1869, cheaper editions of the novels began to appear.[4] In competition with Carey & Lea, the Bentley Standard Novels editions were advertised to middle-class readers in 1833, and Godey's Uniform Editions became available in 1839.[5] But at three dollars each (roughly seventy-eight dollars in 2018, according to consumer price indexing) for the Godey's editions, Austen's books would remain out of reach for the working classes until the 1880s, when they were published by George Munro's Seaside Library in America, in cheap editions.[6]

Throughout the century, certain editions of the novels were presented in a manner that would appeal to contemporary readers. Inclusion in a series such as the Bentley Standard Novels and later the Seaside Library signaled to readers that Austen's works had been vetted as acceptable, commendable books. The illustrations added to some nineteenth-century editions were meant to convey the readability of these books. Many included illustrations that reflected contemporary styles of dress, as opposed to the older Regency look, thus encouraging readers to view the novels as current and relevant. It was not until the 1890s that the illustrations were retrofitted to represent the era in which Austen set the novels. These later editions also began to include editorial, scholarly material, placing the novels back into original historical context and lending them an air of venerability as literature from a past era, rather than as contemporary entertainment.[7]

Some scholars have claimed that Austen-Leigh's *Memoir of Jane Austen* both generated increased interest in Austen and her novels and was responsible for initiating the type of intimate personal interest in Austen that remains a prominent feature of the fandom.[8] Claire Harman has said that between Austen's death in 1817 and the publication of the *Memoir* in 1870, Austen "was hardly mentioned in the public sphere."[9] Referring specifically to British readers, Deidre Lynch argues it was following the publication of the first biography that "readers began thinking of Austen as an author with whom they might be on an intimate, first-name footing."[10] However, as Tamara Wagner has proposed, fervent love of Austen began "decades earlier than analyses of her canonization and the publication of biographies at first suggest." Similar to my own findings in American periodicals, Wagner's examination of early Austen sequels and spin-offs proves a longer history of the personal uses of Jane Austen than many scholars recognize.[11] Not only was Austen's name circulating in the public sphere; it was resonating in homes and parlors. American readers and admirers of Austen, especially, exhibited a sense of something deeply personal about their involvement with the author of the beloved novels. Lynch and others are correct that the years from 1870 to 1900 saw an increase in Austen readership and fans, but the first-name-basis devotion to Austen—Martineau's "sense of kindred"—arose much earlier.

Austen's name appears in newspapers from Portland, Maine, to New Orleans and San Francisco, as booksellers announced newly available titles and the literati espoused her virtues in editorials and reviews. Austen's presence in the American cultural imagination is brought to light through these periodicals, a body of evidence mostly overlooked. Recently, Juliette Wells has explored the earliest advertisements for Austen's novels and biographical information about Austen to circulate in the United States through periodicals. Whereas Wells focuses on the earliest readers, I focus on allusions to Austen and reviews of her works to trace the earliest features of the fandom, features that are still apparent today.

Nearly all the reviews and mentions of Austen's novels found in nineteenth-century periodicals emphasize the goodness, morality, and sensibleness of the novels, not just their quality. That they could educate as well as amuse and lacked objectionable material, coarse satire, or sensationalism made the novels suitable for the widest possible readership—for both men and women. The traces of Austen in American periodicals reveal the role of the novels in readers' lives, suggesting that reading Austen in Victorian America was a performance of virtue. Moreover, discussions of Austen's novels in taste-making periodicals enacted a performance of the praising of virtue by applauding Austen's character and the quality of her writing. This anticipates a feature of today's fandom: that aligning oneself with Austen is a means of signifying attributes society associates with Austen's works.

Reliant upon complex relationships among writers, readers, and editors, periodicals were central to culture formation in American life.[12] Circulating socially, they connected swaths of American society, cultivating ideas, taste, and worldview. Their reach and influence was vast. By the 1870s, nearly forty-three hundred inexpensive weekly magazines enjoyed a combined circulation of 10.5 million, roughly one-third of the U.S. population.[13] As part of a growing concern within the upper class over stewardship of American culture, magazine publishers attempted to guide and improve the tastes and manners of the middle classes across all the regions of the growing nation.[14] Periodicals were an important part of a burgeoning worldview that encouraged American readers to "revere culture, to actively pursue mental cultivation and good manners, to heed Christian ethics, and to view America as eternally progressing and rightfully propelled by the upper classes."[15]

The first allusion to Austen in an American periodical that was neither an advertisement of books for sale nor an early biographical notice based on her obituary was in an 1820 edition of the Boston-printed *Atheneum; or, Spirit of the English Magazines*. In a piece called "Female Literature of the Present Age" that describes worthy women writers, Jane Austen receives a paragraph of attention and praise. The fact that this praise for Austen was extracted from an English magazine, *New Monthly Magazine*, does not inspire much confidence that Austen's work had become well-known in the United States by that time. However, Anglophile readers of the *Atheneum* would have been alerted to Austen's value by this glowing review: "We turn from the dazzling brilliancy of Lady Morgan's works to repose on the soft green of Miss Austen's sweet and unambitious creations." The article then listed the four Austen novels available at that time, which, the writer claimed, "have a simple elegance, which is manifestly the natural and unlaboured result of a singularly harmonious mind." Furthermore the books were recommended because readers would find themselves disposed "to pensive musing," as Austen "tranquillizes every discordant emotion."[16] Following the appearance of this piece in 1820, the American press fell mostly silent on Austen for seven years.

In April 1827, a piece from the English magazine *Blackwood's*, offering a "beautiful eulogium upon female authors," appeared in the *Casket*, from Philadelphia, and again in September in the *Philadelphia Album and Ladies' Literary Gazette* and the *New York Mirror*. It exclaimed: "Oh, Sirs! What a glorious galaxy of female genius and virtue have we to gaze on with admiration, pure and unreproved in our native hemisphere." Among the stars in this galaxy, the editors named Jane Austen, Joanna Bailie, Maria Edgeworth, Elizabeth Hamilton, Mary Russell Mitford, and Mary Tighe, all of whom bring together "genius and virtue, and religion, and morality, and gentleness, and purity."[17] This style of describing an author's virtue and morality, typical of attitudes toward sentimental fiction and its writers, appears in most descriptions of Austen's writing found in periodicals throughout the century.

Following the 1832 and 1833 publication of American editions of the novels in Philadelphia, Austen's name became more widely recognized among novel readers. In 1834, the *Literary Inquirer* stated, "The works of Jane Austen have quietly won their way to the public heart, as all works of genius will." Already Austen was being viewed as superior to other novelists: "Miss Austen's works may safely be recommended, not only as among the most unexceptionable of their class, but as combining, in an eminent degree, instruction and amusement."[18]

In 1837, the "esteemed authoress" was highly recommended by the editors of *Lady's Book* (later *Godey's Lady's Book*), who claimed, "A good novel is a picture of life which a young lady may study to advantage."

Yet this endorsement came with a caveat: "In saying this, we would not be understood to commend all, or indeed, but very few of the works of fiction which inundate our circulating libraries; the overflowings of the 'Minerva press,' which the cupidity of some of the American publishers have poured over our own land, can hardly be too severely censured." The *Lady's Book* credited the genius of Austen's novels to the fact that the author was a good person "whose disposition and character was, as a woman, perfect." Austen's "works are a picture of . . . excellence. Read them, young lady—the novels of Miss Austen should have their place in your library, beside the moral essays of Miss Hannah More. One will convince the understanding of the beauty of virtue, the other will draw the heart to practice it."[19] Such strong recommendations seem to have had an impact on Austen's popularity because by the following year, in 1838, we learn that "it is needless to pronounce any eulogium upon works so well known and universally admired as Miss Austen's productions." The novels "are worthy a place in every library that contains the works of Scott, and other master minds."[20]

Yet with a certain level of acclaim comes some criticism. From the "Editor's Table" of the *Journal of Belles Lettres* in 1838, we learn that although many readers gave Austen "a very high rank" and that her novels "deserve commendation no one doubts," the editors were not convinced that "readers of the nicest discrimination will ever place them beside Miss Edgeworth's for talent, deep knowledge of human nature, pathos, sensibility, humour, or even nature." And two of Madame d'Arblay's (Frances Burney's) novels they found "superior." "Yet," they conceded, "Miss Austen maintains her station among the new race of novel readers that is springing up, notwithstanding numerous rivals."[21] An exception to prove the rule, this editor was dismissive of the quality of Austen's novels and therefore, by not praising her work, had no need to praise the virtues of her character, as did more favorable reviews. Contributors to periodicals who admired Austen's novels applauded her character as well as talents as a means of performing their own alignment with Victorian values.

As early as 1838, periodicals began to employ rhetoric that commended Austen's creative genius and revealed a personal attachment to the novelist like the sense of kindred Martineau decried a year later. The *Ladies'*

Companion offered a rapturous paean to Austen's creative genius in the midst of a review of literature discussing eighteen other works of fiction, biography, and history. The segment of this review on Austen's novels is forty-seven lines long (roughly 475 words), while the rest are mostly four to six lines long (about 50 words each).[22] Yet it is not simply the length of the piece that is remarkable; it is the tone of breathless devotion and attitude of defensive support for Austen that marks it as distinctive from the rest of the descriptions within the review. The article argued that Austen's novels "are as true to life as the master-pieces of Gainsborough, possessing all his exactness and literal fidelity." However, Austen deserves greater esteem than the master painter because she lacks his "coarse vigor." Austen's works are "among the most original that have appeared since the 'Amelia' of Fielding." Unlike the works of some authors, they offer "no traces of thoughts, or incidents, or characters, supplied by other writers; they are self-suggested throughout." Last, the editor stated, "wit without malice, humor without grossness, refinement of touch without apparent effort, and repose of manner without insipidity;—these are the main characteristics of Miss Austen's productions, who in her own circumscribed sphere has never yet been rivaled, and most likely never will be so."

"These novels of Jane Austen I have read thrice, each time with renewed pleasure," wrote a contributor to the *American Review: A Whig Journal*. "They are always charming. I take them up in happy moments, and they cheer me in unhappy ones,—for sorrow comes to all. Even in solitude they introduce you to the most agreeable company, for all Jane Austen's characters are either old friends, or persons that you are confident are living somewhere on the earth. . . . They seem to be in the very room with you." Like any good fan, this Austen lover rereads the novels and is especially drawn to them in emotional times, both happy and poignant, finding comfort in "old friends" who seem very real. The contributor speculated fondly about the creator of these characters: "Miss Austen could never have written this sweet story of love [*Mansfield Park*] without having experienced it herself, with all its rapturous enjoyments and torturing fears."[23]

By the 1840s, Austen's name was well enough known to avid readers of literature that the *North American Review* could drop her name by way of comparison to a brand-new work, such as Lady Georgiana Fullerton's

Grantley Manor, without needing to first explain who she was or to remind readers of what she had written.[24] She had simply become "Miss Austen,—dear Miss Austen,—who never says a brilliant thing, nor paints a perfect character,—who is neither witty, nor passionate, nor eloquent,—is still minute, homelike, and true; and by these qualities alone, she twines about the inmost fibres of her readers' hearts."[25] This is Austen viewed as an old friend, flawed but beloved for simple qualities rather than greatness or brilliance. This review depicts Austen not as a great genius on her pedestal but as deeply familiar and well-worn—as one of us.

Periodicals of the 1830s discussed Austen in a manner that set the stage for a fandom to emerge in the 1840s. Even though the public would know little about her until 1870, adoration of Austen was already strong by this time, and the language used to describe her works—particularly in the 1840s—reads like the rapturous outpourings of today's fans and enthusiasts. These lovers of Jane Austen, writing in the pages of widely circulated periodicals, performed their own good taste and virtue. By performing praise of Austen's novels as well as her character, they aligned themselves with the Victorian ideals she represented to the reading public.

3

Three Modes of Fandom

FANFICTION, PILGRIMAGE, AND COLLECTING

Before the publication of Austen-Leigh's *Memoir of Jane Austen* provided hungry fans with a way to become better acquainted with the woman herself, fans who wanted more had to seek other means to gain a personal insight into Austen's life and a greater intimacy with her beloved characters. By the 1840s, as the novels were becoming more widely available on both sides of the Atlantic, a recognizable fandom began to take shape, with fans writing fanfiction, going on literary pilgrimage, and collecting material objects—all recognizable features of fandom related to an obsessive and affective engagement with the beloved author and her works. This chapter introduces these fan practices, each to be explored in much greater detail in parts II–IV, and begins to suggest their performative features.

Eliza Leslie (1787–1858) was an early fan of Austen. An American author, Miss Leslie, as she was known, gained popularity for her numerous cookbooks, books on etiquette, and works of short fiction. She also edited an annual gift book in the 1830s, *The Gift*, which included works by Lydia Sigourney and Henry Wadsworth Longfellow, among others. One of her works of fiction, "The Beaux, A Sketch," was published in five serial installments in *Godey's Lady's Book* between January and May 1842. A frivolous yet didactic story about young women of courting age in Philadelphia, "The Beaux" brings to mind several obvious analogues to characters and plot devices found in Austen novels. I propose that this work relies on rhetorical strategies common in fanfiction today and can be understood as an example of derivative literature, or, better put, archontic literature.

"The Beaux" predates the first recognized Austen spin-off, Catherine Anne Hubback's novel *The Younger Sister* (1850), which turned Austen's incomplete work *The Watsons* into a lengthy Victorian romance.[1] While it is perhaps anachronistic to name this work fanfiction, I suggest it is the earliest example of Austen-related archontic fiction yet discovered.

Borrowing the term *archontic* from philosopher Jacques Derrida, Abigail De Kosnik has suggested a useful framework for approaching fanfiction as well as the sorts of sequels, spin-offs, and imitations that appear in professionally published spheres.[2] Rather than favor potentially derogatory terms such as *derivative* or *appropriative,* which imply that a work will necessarily be lesser or somehow stolen from the original, De Kosnik prefers *archontic* because it connotes the intertextuality at the core of fanfiction. The term foregrounds the idea that the world of the text is like an archive that is ever expanding and always open-ended. As new versions of a text appear, as spin-offs, adaptations, or fanfiction, they deliberately locate themselves within the world—or archive—of the original text and do so in creative and original ways. As De Kosnik explains, the archontic text adds to the text's archive, becoming a part of the archive and expanding it. Most important, the archontic text offers variations on the primary text and explicitly reveals them as such.[3] Since first suggesting the use of *archontic* to theorize fanfiction, De Kosnik has expanded on the term, using *archontic production* to more capaciously include all types of fan works, and she has begun to more explicitly suggest the ways archontic production is performative.[4]

Without the benefit of evidence of how nineteenth-century readers reacted to works like "The Beaux" and others discussed here, I focus on the creative ways early writers of Austen-related archontic literature would weave allusions to Austen's works into their narratives, creating performative texts. I suggest that certain writing practices found within the creation of archontic literature characterize it as performative; there exists playfulness at the heart of intertextuality and a double consciousness of both reader and writer that the work is not the original, yet is not *not* the original. Like theater, which draws its raw materials from an original source, recombining and referencing familiar elements of the "real" world to construct a fictional one, archontic literature references and recombines existing elements from the "real" text to form something new. Both the author and reader of an archontic work therefore experience an awareness, or double consciousness—like that experienced by performers and audiences in theater—that the archontic work is both real and not real.[5]

Writers create archontic literature when they are both fascinated and frustrated by their favorite texts and narratives; subordinate groups—especially women—have used archontic literature to work against dominant culture as a means to record, express, and publicize their opinions for over four hundred years.[6] Eliza Leslie seems to have become part of this long tradition when she wrote "The Beaux." The story is built upon allusions to characters and conceits lifted from Austen's corpus, yet Leslie revised aspects that frustrated or troubled her. As a writer, she performs her knowledge of Austen and her allegiance to the idea that a love of books and reading is a positive trait; Leslie's readers, in turn, get to experience the pleasure of recognizing what Leslie has done, themselves joining the performance and aligning themselves with the notion that reading and knowledge make a young lady desirable and good.

In "The Beaux," the story's heroine, Sabina, is an amalgam of wholesome traits found amid Austen's female characters: she is sweet and kind like Jane Bennet, timid like Fanny Price, and possessed of superior taste and accomplishments like Jane Fairfax (characters from *Pride and Prejudice, Mansfield Park,* and *Emma,* respectively). Fanfiction readers today might interpret Sabina as a "Mary Sue," an all-too-perfect heroine who is mostly an empty vessel to be filled by the reader's interpretations. The heroine's foils, three bubbly and foolish sisters, reveal their frivolousness time and again through their ignorance and outright disdain for literature, education, and the arts. They find it odd that Sabina would enjoy the company of her own brother rather than the exciting company of beaux, and they caution Sabina not to reveal too much of her bluestocking nature or risk losing the attentions of young men. One of the sisters complains that she had tried reading but could never stay awake, and since none of the gentlemen who come visiting are "at all literary," having books on hand could serve no practical purpose. The sisters begrudgingly offer Sabina access to the household books kept out of the way in a storeroom but warn her that "reading girls never take" with the beaux. When Sabina surveys the selection of books to choose from, she finds "none that were new to her," so she picks one that she has read before. "She carried to her room Miss Jane Austen's very entertaining novel of Pride and Prejudice; and, as is the case with all really excellent works, she found it improve on a second reading."[7]

The mother of the silly sisters, Mrs. Denning, is a busybody like Mrs. Jennings and is prone to ailments like Mrs. Bennet.[8] Even the name—Denning—seems to resonate with both Bennet and Jennings. When Anna, one of the three sisters, runs away with a dashing midshipman in the navy, the reader is reminded of Lydia Bennet's elopement with George Wickham.[9] The midshipman, the brother of a dressmaker, is of a lower class and, like Mr. Wickham, turns out to be a good-for-nothing, dishonorable man cut off by all his former acquaintances due to his debts and unseemly habits. Shortly after the elopement, he tires of Anna and never returns; much like Lydia in *Pride and Prejudice*, Anna is too foolish to fully comprehend her circumstances.

Mr. Jackaway Jempson, a pompous, mincing, stupid fellow reminiscent of Mr. Collins (the ridiculous clergyman of *Pride and Prejudice*), brings color to the story. He fancies himself a writer and rails heartily (and for many pages) about the derelict publishing industry, which, it seems, wants nothing to do with his driveling plays and poems. Although he disdains Sabina for her novel-reading habits, looks down on her good-natured demeanor, and willfully misunderstands her character, he fancies himself her suitor, much as Mr. Collins does with Elizabeth Bennet.

Sabina, like the accomplished Jane Fairfax, sings and plays with great style (and in languages other than English!), and her behavior never garners reproach. Much to everyone's surprise, like Miss Fairfax, Sabina is quietly engaged to a gentleman all along. In Austen's *Emma*, Jane Fairfax is a foil to the novel's meddlesome and self-centered titular heroine. Yet in an inversion of didactic conventions, Jane Fairfax, while admired as a perfect young lady, harbors the secret of a surreptitious engagement to rakish Frank Churchill. By contrast, Eliza Leslie's Sabina is too wise to fall for a capricious man like Frank Churchill; rather, she is promised to a man who values her accomplishments and intellect, and the fact that he is rich and very handsome is merely an incidental bonus. Like Emma and Mr.

Knightly, Sabina and her fiancé have known each other for a long time and are fond of each other, making the match romantic but also sensible, not the infatuation of a moment. This surprise outcome provides the moral of the story and serves to show the silly Denning sisters what it takes to win a husband who is truly worth having.

In several instances, the dialogue is reminiscent of Austen. When Sabina asks to borrow a book from the sisters to pass the time, one of the girls asks with surprise, "Is it possible that you are literary?" Sabina replies, "By no means, I am only very fond of reading."[10] A reader familiar with *Pride and Prejudice* would recognize this exchange as similar to that between Elizabeth Bennet and Caroline Bingley. "'Miss Eliza Bennet,' said Miss Bingley, 'despises cards. She is a great reader, and has no pleasure in anything else.' 'I deserve neither such praise nor such censure,' cried Elizabeth; 'I am not a great reader, and I have pleasure in many things.'"[11] In the first installment of "The Beaux," Mr. Denning, the Mr. Bennet–like father of the three sisters, teases his wife when she inquires whether he made a point of publicly spreading the news of his youngest daughter's engagement. Mr. Denning responds to the inquiries of his wife and daughters with evident cageyness: "I don't know . . . I believe I did not. The news from Europe must have put it out of my head." This response riles his wife and children, who press him, sure that he must have had the good sense to spread their gossip. But Mr. Denning is evasive, stating, "I do not perceive in what way the engagement of a daughter of mine can interest the whole community."[12] This scene echoes Mr. Bennet's teasing of his wife in the opening dialogue of *Pride and Prejudice.*

These details, so similar to Austen, are presented as though Leslie winks at the shrewd reader, hoping the barely veiled allusions will be understood. Writers of fanfiction and other archontic literature depend on their readers to recognize allusions, ironies, and clever conceits that reference the original text.[13] Leslie mentions *Pride and Prejudice* early in the story and gives the novel a hearty accolade for good measure, alerting the reader to the source of inspiration and performing an allegiance to all that Austen's novels stood for. Moreover, by drawing the reader's attention to the distinction between "reading girls" like Sabina and ignorant ones like the Denning sisters, Leslie performed through the narrative her own alignment with Victorian sensibilities; the reader—presumably herself a reading girl—was meant to identify with Sabina and, through gleaning Leslie's allusions to the virtues of being well read, also enacted a coherence to Victorian ideals.

The aspects of Austen's novels that may have troubled Leslie and which she sought to rectify in "The Beaux" stem from concerns over propriety. Austen's characters do not exhibit a singular unwavering set of traits, habits, or morals but, like real people, are fraught with contradictions and complexities. Jane Fairfax is in all ways well-mannered, accomplished, and mature—certainly compared to Emma and her meddling—yet she secretly engages herself to a man who, while charming, misuses people and behaves badly on several occasions. Leslie would not be the first or last reader to be frustrated by Frank Churchill as unworthy of Miss Fairfax or to question whether she deserves her sterling reputation. In "The Beaux," Leslie revised this scenario by giving Sabina a more suitable fiancé than Austen gave to Miss Fairfax. As a writer of conduct books, Leslie's concern for propriety is hardly surprising. She drew characters that were unambiguous and easily delineated as good or bad, kind or mean, wise or foolish, creating allegorical figures rather than realistic ones. She remedied the narrative difficulties posed by ambiguous characters by making obvious each individual's flaws or assets. This tactic supported her didactic aims by making clear that good characters get happy endings and foolish, ignorant, or catty characters do not. Like fanfiction and other forms of archontic responses to literature, "The Beaux," possibly the earliest example of Austen-related archontic fiction, offers both writer and readers a means to reenter a familiar and beloved text and perform affinities and sensibilities by recognizing the original source even as it is reinvented and made new.

Andrew Lang was a prolific author, collector of fairy stories, literary critic, historian, poet, and anthropologist whose works were popular on both sides of the Atlantic. He was also a Jane Austen enthusiast. In addition to twelve volumes of fairy stories, he published translations of Homer; essays on myth and religion; edited volumes of Scott, Dickens, and Coleridge; and more. Among his more than 150 published works is *Letters to Dead Authors* (1886), which includes a letter to Jane Austen that describes the kinds of readers who appreciate her works in his day. In 1890,

Lang published, simultaneously in London and New York, *Old Friends: Essays in Epistolary Parody,* in which he compiled imagined letters, or "parodies," between famous individuals, some fictional and others historical. In some cases, the characters corresponding with each other were taken from the same novel, but in others, he created examples of what in fanfiction today is called a "crossover," combining characters from different settings into a new alternative universe.

Letter 11, "From Catherine Morland to Miss Eleanor Tilney," is just such a crossover. Using the conceit of a letter from the heroine of Austen's *Northanger Abbey,* Catherine Morland, to her friend Miss Tilney, Lang imagined the impressionable Catherine visiting the home of Mr. Rochester, the brooding hero of Charlotte Brontë's *Jane Eyre.* Catherine writes to Miss Tilney to give an account of the opulence of the house, the strangeness of Mr. Rochester, and, just as her character might in *Northanger Abbey,* the observations her overactive imagination has turned into terrors. The reader of this parody is quick to realize that in Mr. Rochester's house, there really is a hidden secret; instead of the imagined murder of a wife that Catherine conjures in *Northanger Abbey,* in *Jane Eyre,* there truly is the horror of a concealed wife suffering from mental illness.

However, what Catherine uncovers in Mr. Rochester's home is not a dreadful reality but, rather, a laughable and ridiculous farce of terror. As soon as Catherine enters Mr. Rochester's home, she comments to Miss Tilney that she felt "a cold chill struck through me, as with a sense of some brooding terror."[14] She wonders what could make Mr. Rochester, a man surrounded by the elegance and splendor of "Turkey carpets and large mirrors" and "red Bohemian glass . . . [and] crimson couches," so morose, and why at dinner his conversation should be "confined to the governess (a Miss Eyre), whose position here your Catherine does not understand" (98–99). When Catherine is conducted to her bedroom by Miss Eyre, through a narrow, dim corridor, like that "in some Blue Beard's castle," she is told by Miss Eyre to be "silent as death," for she hears "the chains rattling." Catherine describes how Miss Eyre then placed "her finger on her lip and her meager body convulsed with some mysterious emotion." Thoroughly distraught, Catherine proceeds to test the walls of her bedchamber for secret panels and look for "assassins in the usual place," but she is haunted by "an unnatural sound of laughter." She tries to go to bed but is troubled: "The laughter seemed to redouble. I heard a footstep at my door. I hurried on my frock and shawl and crept into the gallery. A strange dark figure was gliding in front of me, stooping at each door; and every time it stooped came *a low gurgling noise!* Inspired by I know not what desperation of courage, I rushed on the figure and seized it by the neck. It was Miss Eyre, the governess, filling the boots of all the guests with water, which she carried in a can" (100–101). Catherine Morland, who, in *Northanger Abbey,* reads so much gothic fiction that her mind races with imagined terrors at all hours, finds herself in a house that truly holds a secret, yet she discovers only a silly (albeit strange) encounter with Jane Eyre.

Lang expected his reader would ascertain that Catherine's account is very much in character yet find humor in how out of character Jane Eyre's behavior is. The playful intertextuality of this work of archontic fiction depends on the reader's knowledge of the habits of the characters in the original texts. Lang forged obvious linkages and fissures between his work and the originals. Catherine, who always sees what is not there, in this case does not see what is actually there.

Several scholars have recently questioned whether or not such literary responses should be considered equivalent to the genre of writing we recognize as contemporary fanfiction. Balaka Basu convincingly argues for continuity in the rhetorical strategies of fanfiction, examining Sir Philip Sidney's *Arcadia* (late sixteenth century) as a queer fanfiction response to Virgil's *Eclogues.*[15] By contrast, Anne Jamison proposes that continuity is found only in the age-old habit of borrowing from existing sources, suggesting that not all writing that resembles fanfiction actually is and preferring to reserve the term *fanfiction* for the kind of community-driven writing found on the internet today.[16] I suggest that the examples presented here are best understood as archontic literary responses to Austen's novels; they draw from the original texts in obvious ways, relating the new to the old and adding to the archive of Jane Austen. Although they predate the term *fanfiction,* I suggest they share features and conventions with fanfiction. Moreover, these nineteenth-century examples demonstrate what others have only assumed to be true: written responses to Austen that resemble today's fanfiction have precedent much earlier than previously supposed and are not limited to continuations of Austen's unfinished novels or direct spin-offs of her major works.

In 1856, the *North American Review* critiqued Henry T. Tuckerman's *Month in England* in an article titled "Recent Books on England." However, the Boston native's book about his literary pilgrimage is more about Americans seeking cultural roots abroad than it is about England per se. The review claimed that England, more than the Continent, was attractive to Americans because of its literary riches: "It is only as the land of literary pilgrimage that England presents to the American traveler attractions which must needs outrival those of all the Old World besides. . . . No where else [but in England] has literature so multiplied its shrines, and lavished its oil of consecration, and become so truly the *genius loci* of almost every rood of soil, as in England." The reasons, the reviewer claimed, were obvious: "Strong and enduring associations between persons and places can spring up only where domestic life is stable and cherished."[17] By midcentury, the notion of literary pilgrimage hardly needed explaining to readers, as it was already a familiar practice, driven by a nostalgia for a preindustrial lifestyle.[18]

A Month in England was published in New York in 1853. Tuckerman viewed literary pilgrimage and enthusiasm for great writers and artists as transcendent, an experience apart from the quotidian. He observed, "A true enthusiasm for letters, art, and humanity, lifts the memory of their disciple, like a star, far above the oblivious monotony of trade, into the serene firmament of posthumous renown."[19] Throughout the meandering tale of his travels to literary sites, he used the terms *literary pilgrim* and *literary enthusiast* to describe those engaged in such pursuits. His descriptions greatly resemble today's fan practices, even when couched in overwrought language.

Tuckerman's account of this journey is steeped in nostalgia. He described how one might lose oneself in England's past, summoning to mind ghosts of the nation's history in a "spell of retrospective fancy" (7–8). The "transatlantic pilgrim" craves something different from what is "familiar at home," and to slake his craving, he must travel a few hours from the modern cities, taking himself "from new to old, and from the commonplace to the romantic" (8–9). Thus, he described the movement of the pilgrim from the quotidian to the liminal, just as anthropologist Victor Turner proposes.[20] In the noisy complications of modern life, Tuckerman asked, "What room is there for retrospection, when steam and electricity thus concentrate the significance of every passing hour?" As with entering the liminal zone of pilgrimage to make room for what Turner has called "creative retrospection," Tuckerman chose to "flit from the new to the old, from modern . . . everyday England," to the realm of Shakespeare (12).

Upon visiting Shakespeare's grave, he found evidence that many had come before: "The evidence of universal sympathy, so apparent in the pilgrimage of multitudes to a common shrine" (211). His visit was not, therefore, an anomaly but part of a common occurrence. Furthermore, being a literary pilgrim in England, he claimed, was a uniquely American practice:

> With a foreigner for his companion, when travelling in England, an American soon becomes aware of the greater intimacy of relation which he enjoys with the past and present of the country. No infantile reminiscence, musical with nursery-rhymes, startles the Frenchman beside you, when the guard bawls at the car-window, "Banbury Cross"; the German friend, on whose arm you lean, walking through Holborn, does not pause instinctively, as if his boot-nails were glued to the pavement by a magnet, at the sight of Day & Martin's sign . . . . An hour by "Shrewsbury clock" is no more significant to a continental than that noted by any other dial; he will scarcely think at Bath of Frances Burney, Jane Austen, or Smollett; or of Coleridge, Southey, and Wordsworth, at Bristol. The cliff at Dover to his eyes is only an abrupt elevation of jagged chalk; no blind Gloster [Gloucester] stands on the ledge, nor samphire gleaner, midway down, follows his "dreadful trade." It is from our sympathy with the mind of the country that her landscape often wears an occult charm. We have an a priori attachment to London because the soul of Shakspere [*sic*] encamped so long in its midst. (240–41)

I do not attempt to argue that Tuckerman is right, that literary pilgrimage to England is uniquely appealing to Americans; I do, however, wish to point out that he felt very strongly that this was true. His claim that

American sympathy for the English mind adorns the landscape with "an occult charm" rings not only of an Anglophile nostalgia but also of fandom.

Anna Cabot Lowell Quincy (1812–99) was another American who described a pilgrimage to a site of literary importance in England. The youngest child of Josiah Quincy (1772–1864), president of Harvard University, and Eliza Susan Morton Quincy (1773–1850), she was born into an Austen-loving family. Beverly Wilson Palmer, editor of Anna's diaries, has suggested that Anna was deeply influenced by Jane Austen, crafting the journal entries of her youth to resemble Austen's novels and turning to writing as a serious avocation later in life.[21] Published in the *Atlantic Monthly* under her married name, A. C. Waterston, Anna wrote reverently of her visit to Jane Austen's tomb: "In the old Cathedral of Winchester stand the tombs of kings, . . . of queens and noble ladies, of crusaders and warriors, of priests and bishops. But our pilgrimage led us to a slab of black marble set into the pavement of the north aisle, and there, under the grand old arches, we read the name of Jane Austen."[22] As this pilgrim gazed upon the slab, she experienced memories of "happy hours, gladdened by her genius, weary hours, soothed by her touch." These memories, "many-colored as the light which streams through painted windows," also included friends and loved ones: "the honored and the wise who first placed her volumes in our hand; the beloved ones who had lingered over her pages, the voices of our distant home, associated with every familiar story" (235).

Waterston's descriptions of Austen's world hold an evident nostalgia for the preindustrial world. Regarding the modes of travel and narrow range of movement available to a woman like Austen, she observed: "Steam, that genie of the vapor, was yet a little household elf, singing pleasant tunes by the evening fire, at quiet hearthstones; it has since expanded into a mighty giant, whose influences are no longer domestic" (235). Like Tuckerman, she yearned for a world in which steam and industry did not shape every moment of life. For both Waterston and Tuckerman, a pilgrimage to England offered means of stepping out of the modern world and into a liminal space in which communion with the past—and with literature of the past—became possible. Nostalgia drives their desire to seek out a liminal experience that will remove them from the constraints of everyday life and bring them closer to the literary world that stokes their nostalgia.

Near the end of the essay, Waterston outlined several anecdotes of great men who favored Austen's work, including the oft-quoted praise of Sir Walter Scott. One of these, "a pleasant anecdote told to us on good authority in England," illustrates Austen's "power over various minds." At a gathering of "distinguished literary men . . . of high reputation, . . . it was proposed that each should write down the name of that work of fiction which had given him the greatest pleasure. Much surprise and amusement followed; for, on opening the slips of paper, *seven* bore the name of 'Mansfield Park'—a coincidence of opinion most rare, and a tribute to an author unsurpassed" (236). She speculated that if she had been among that party of gentlemen, she would have claimed "the *last* novel by Miss Austen which we have read" as her favorite, but if pushed to make a selection, she "should have named 'Persuasion'" (237). This response is typical of many fans of Austen, who find choosing a favorite impossible, until pressed.

As a younger woman, Anna Quincy made several mentions in her diaries of the family reading Austen at home. In April 1833, she wrote, "Finished Persuasion,—& felt as if we could not bear to part with Anne Elliot & Capt. Wentworth." This affective engagement by a reader wishing a novel would go on and on is often what drives readers to become writers of archontic literature. In May 1833, she "staid at home—drew & Mama read loud in Mansfield Park [*sic*]."[23] One week later, on a rainy day, they read aloud from *Northanger Abbey*.[24] In addition to mentioning the family's reading of Austen, she also makes casual allusions to Austen, evoking the traits of certain characters to record events in her daily life. In one instance, she seems to compare some visitors to the annoying Mr. and Mrs. Elton of *Emma* by mentioning, within quotation marks, a "barouche landeau" as their means of conveyance.[25]

When preparing her piece on Jane Austen for the *Atlantic Monthly*, Waterston corresponded with the editor, James T. Fields, expressing her unpretentious intentions regarding the publication of the article. She stated that she was not in any hurry to see it printed or to see her name in print ("except of my visiting card"): "Were I entering the lists, as a magasine [*sic*] writer, then indeed should I have watched for the proof—but as I wrote at your request, & out of love for Miss Austen . . . the case is quite different."[26] Moreover, she left all decisions regarding the timeline of publication and the appearance of her byline to Mr. Fields. Writing for the *Atlantic Monthly* was something she did out of "love for Miss Austen," rather than for gain.

Anna Waterston was not the only Austen lover among her immediate family. In 1852, her eldest sister, Eliza Susan Quincy (1798–1884), wrote a letter to Sir Francis Austen, a surviving brother of Jane Austen, in which she depicted her family's admiration for the novelist. Describing the familiarity with Jane Austen that the Quincys enjoyed at home in Boston, Eliza wrote, "For many years her talents have brightened our daily path, and her name and those of her characters are familiar to us as 'household words.'"[27] Eliza, the eldest of Josiah Quincy's five daughters (collectively known as the "articulate sisters" for their erudition), was an artist and self-fashioned family archivist and historian.[28]

Thirty-five years after Jane Austen's death, Eliza's "voice of praise from across the Atlantic" reached Sir Francis. The letter, from a "family who delight in the companionship of Jane Austen," was written by Eliza and sent under the auspice of her father. Although she feared that "transatlantic admiration [would] appear superfluous," Eliza wished to assure Sir Francis that Jane Austen's "genius is extensively recognized in the American Republic, even by the highest judicial authorities" (114), and she gave credit to Chief Justice John Marshall and Justice Joseph Story for introducing Austen's novels to American society through their esteem and praise.

The purpose of her letter was not merely to express esteem; she requested more information about Austen's life and asked to be sent an artifact such as an autograph or "a few lines of her handwriting," which would be placed among the "chief treasures" of the Quincy family. She closed the letter by assuring Sir Francis that the name and reputation of her family were worthy of being entrusted with such a treasure, as a prominent family with many high-ranking "public stations of trust and responsibility" in the "colony and state of Massachusetts" since their emigration from England (115). What the Quincys received in response to their missive exceeded their expectations.

Upon hearing that her sister had received a reply from Sir Francis that included a lengthy letter written in Austen's hand to her dear friend Martha Lloyd, Anna Quincy Waterston exclaimed: "I am quite excited at the idea of the Austen letter . . . not exactly in the style of Miss Bates,—but still the fact, that you have received a letter from the Admiral & have actually in your possession one written by the very hand to which we own so much, quite carries me off my feet!" Anna emphasized her excitement by alluding first to chatty Miss Bates from *Emma* and then to *Sense and Sensibility* and *Persuasion:* "Mrs. Jennings's delight at the idea of Col. Brandon marrying Elinor is nothing to it! . . . Dear Admiral Austen I think he must have been like Capt. Wentworth, when he was young, and just like what Capt. Wentworth would be at this age.—He has replied with true naval promptness, and evidently deserves to be Miss Austen's brother. . . . I never expected we should get so near Miss Austen in this world, tho' I have always hoped to find some 'little coterie in Heaven' where I might catch a glimpse of her." She closed the letter, "With love to all and congratulations to all true lovers of Miss Austen," but added a postscript: "If the house catches on fire tonight,—please save the letter—I cannot die without the sight."[29]

The Quincy family is a model of early American Austen fandom. By writing to Sir Francis and then treasuring the gift of a letter in Austen's hand, the Quincys sought to bring themselves closer to Austen and her world. Members of the Quincy family read and reread Austen's work, they shared their knowledge of Austen through allusions within diaries and letters intended to be read within the family and through Anna's published magazine essay, they went on literary pilgrimage, and they sought to collect a prized piece of memorabilia from Austen's remaining relatives. Anna Quincy Waterston's relationship to Austen resembles the personal attachment to the novelist reminiscent of Martineau's "sense of kindred." Thanks to the family's elite status and role in Boston society, their papers, which detail much of this rich affective experience with Austen, have been preserved. It is reasonable to speculate that other families whose papers may not have landed in the archive shared a similar devotion to Austen and similar ways of expressing that devotion.

Other fans of Austen may not have been so fortunate—or so elite—as to have Austen's own kin bestow the gift of an autograph letter upon them to help satisfy their curiosity and hungry admiration. Others made do, as Henry Tuckerman did, with the experiences available to them, such as pilgrimage. But by the 1890s, an increasing number of biographies on Austen were available, which helped both spread Austen's fame and offered her devotees more of the personal connection they craved. In 1902, a piece in the widely circulated *Ladies' Home Journal* commented on this ability of Austen to continually attract readers who found great interest in her as an individual and held for her "a personal affection."[30]

By the end of the nineteenth century, even as Jane Austen was being raised to the highbrow pedestal reserved for classic authors, she remained the personal property of readers. Two reviews of Austen biographies published in the early 1890s perfectly illustrate this bimodal position; they highlight a contemporary awareness of the devoted sense of kindred to Austen that is visible throughout the century as well as the emerging perception of Austen as "classic." In 1891, the *Chicago Herald* reviewed a new biography of Austen by Oscar Fay Adams. The review stated that although several biographies of Austen had been recently published, "we do not think the present volume untimely or unwelcome." Evoking the personal attachment of her fans, it continued, "The world cannot know too much about the 'Divine Jane' or read her incomparable novels too often," and in the next breath, the review references her highbrow status, saying, "She is one of the few immortals in English literature." Particularly appealing about this biography, according to the review, was the personal touch Adams offered, having "spent a summer in visiting the places in England" associated with Austen, allowing the biographer to mix the popular genre of literary pilgrimage with biography. The reviewer strayed quickly from the task of discussing the biography and instead took the opportunity to praise Austen, reminding readers that men considered great thinkers had placed Austen in Shakespeare's rarified company and stating, "Certainly no works of fiction have ever met with higher praise."[31]

A year later, the *Boston Daily Advertiser* stated with optimism, "One of the interesting and cheerful signs of the times is the recent revival of interest in Jane Austen's life and works." This review compared the 1891 Adams biography with one by Goldwin Smith published in 1890. Further commenting on the Austen revival and its bimodal nature, the review states: "One or more of her works have long been a requirement of the course at Harvard. They have been in demand at the Public Library. And now Roberts Bros. announces the early publication of a sumptuous edition of her writings, in 11 elegant volumes. The love of the best in English literature is certainly increasing among the American people."[32] At the turn of the century, the novels were becoming more widely available in more editions and were beginning to circulate in new ways as well.

Adaptations and spin-offs to Austen's novels contributed greatly to her popularity. By the 1890s, Austen spin-offs and sequels had begun to emerge in greater numbers, and stage adaptations of the novels had become increasingly popular fare. These archontic works captivated American audiences and kept Austen circulating within the popular imagination well after her contemporaries had been forgotten. They also helped propel her relevance and popularity into the next century.

In May 1901, an adaptation of *Emma* was performed for "gentlemen's night" of the Worcester Woman's Club: "The story which will be well known to most of the audience, is laid in the first part of the last century, and will afford ample opportunity for the display of old fashioned costumes and manners. There is also a ballroom scene, with an old time minuet."[33] Whereas the producers felt the story would mostly be familiar to their audience, in many cases, as today, adaptations provided a way to introduce classic literature to new audiences, especially young women. The press of the 1890s and early 1900s was full of articles devoted to concerns over what girls were reading and, more to the point, what they ought to be reading. In 1900, the members of Wellesley's Zeta Alpha society "appeared in an original and most acceptable dramatization" of *Pride and Prejudice.* A full page of images shows the students of Wellesley College costumed for various productions. A caption reads, "At Wellesley College the drama is encouraged as an adjunct to literature, and the presentation of plays by the girl students has a definite purpose."[34] This purpose was perhaps to make the classics more palatable to young audiences. It seems to have been successful: once the popularity of adaptations caught on, it never abated.

Through the 1920s, many examples of archontic literature appeared from Britain and circulated in the United States. These include Constance Hill's *Jane Austen: Her Homes and Her Friends* (originally published in 1902 but reprinted many times through 1923) and works such as A. B. Walkley's collection of essays, *Pastiche and Prejudice,* which features an epistolary parody that places some of Austen's more ridiculous characters in new settings. An English drama critic, Walkley wrote as much about Austen in his essays as he did about Shakespeare; the title of his essay collection alone is testament to his affection for Austen. In 1914, Sybil Brinton published *Old Friends and New Fancies*, a sequel of sorts that throws most of Austen's heroes and heroines into one social context and lovingly imagines certain events beyond the scope of the original novels that Austen herself alluded to in family correspondence and conversations. These speculations were made public in the 1870 *Memoir* by Austen's nephew and include notions about the future lives and husbands of Kitty and Mary Bennet and insights about early married life for Emma and Mr. Knightley. In 1922, Lily Adams Beck, a British-born Canadian author, wrote "The Darcys of Rosings" under the pen name E. Barrington. This continuation of *Pride and Prejudice* appeared in *The Ladies! A Shining Constellation of Wit and Beauty*, published by the Atlantic Monthly Press. Works such as these fed readers' desire for more Austen, and moreover, the creation of this archontic literature served the desires of its writers. Writers of fanfiction frequently do not seek to establish their own individual voices as professional writers do but, instead, wish to reproduce the voice and style of the original text that inspires them; this is especially true of writers of Jane Austen fanfiction, who desire to re-create the voice they most long to hear more of: Austen's.[35]

Numerous adaptations for stage and later radio, most of which were written by women, began appearing in America and Britain in regular intervals by about 1895.[36] These adaptations brought Austen's novels to audiences in a new way, helped spread her popularity, and fostered a growing and visible fandom. In 1927, English playwright and columnist Arnold Bennett remarked that the "reputation of Jane Austen is surrounded by cohorts of defenders who are ready to do murder for their sacred cause. They are nearly all fanatics."[37]

In 1940, the first major motion picture adaptation of *Pride and Prejudice* helped propel Austen into the American collective imagination more widely and firmly than ever, and from that point on, she has never been dislodged from her throne. The film makes substantial changes to the original plot and characterization, highlighting the romance, the marriage plot, the spunk and charm of Lizzy Bennet (Greer Garson), and the handsome profile of Mr. Darcy (Lawrence Olivier) while downplaying Austen's social commentary on class and gender disparity. When the film was released, Austen's novels had been canonized as classics yet had continued to entice popular audiences. The next section begins at the moment of anticipation, as fans awaited the arrival of *Pride and Prejudice* to the big screen.

II

FANS IN THE ARCHIVE
1940–1995

There are some paths in life that we may follow only with our intellects; some we may follow only with our hearts. But only occasionally do we find paths like these that we may follow with both.

—PHILIP A. SHREFFLER, *Sherlock Holmes by Gas-lamp*

Prologue

In 1940, the year MGM released the first film adaptation of *Pride and Prejudice* starring Greer Garson and Lawrence Olivier—a watershed moment for Austen fans—an American collector of Jane Austen named Barbara Winn Adams, of Bethesda, Maryland, wrote to a bookseller in London with the hopes of purchasing a very rare 1816 American edition of *Emma* that had recently become available.[1] Also in 1940, another Austen collector, Alberta H. Burke, of Baltimore, Maryland, wrote an impassioned letter to the Columbia Broadcasting System hoping to purchase a copy of a script for a radio adaptation of *Pride and Prejudice* she had just heard.[2] Both Winn Adams and Burke were unsuccessful in these particular attempts to augment their respective Jane Austen collections. However, Winn Adams could console herself knowing she had already collected an 1816 London edition of *Emma,* and by 1940, Burke possessed several first editions and Austen autograph letters and had begun building up her collection with other types of unique items.[3] Attaining objects is paramount to a collector's experience of pleasure, yet the thrill of the chase and the moment of success in procuring objects are mere punctuations—although keenly felt—within the long years of a collector's painstaking research, reading, and other everyday activities.

Part II considers Austen fandom in the twentieth century through the scrapbooks of four serious Jane Austen enthusiasts—Alberta Burke, Barbara Winn Adams, George Holbert Tucker, and David J. Gilson—each of whom spent the better part of a lifetime collecting Austenalia. Their scrapbooks document their experience with collecting both objects and knowledge related to Austen, their collective obsession. Scrapbooks, as historian Ellen Gruber Garvey says, illustrate aspects of *how* readers read and thought about the scraps of print material they felt were worth saving.[4] The scrapbooks of these four collectors demonstrate in material form how each individual read, collected, studied, thought, and felt about Austen, her novels, and her world. More important, they are performative objects, material embodiments of meaningful experience that capture moments and stand in for them, allowing the scrapbook creator to revive and share momentous, affective experiences over time.

I suggest that the practices of scrapbooking correlate to practices of fandom familiar and common today. Scrapbooking resembles what Henry Jenkins names the "DIY" (do-it-yourself) practices of today's fans.[5] The digital tools that today facilitate fan creativity have antecedents in photocopiers and videocassette recorders and, even before that, scissors and paste. Today's readily available digital technologies offer fans creative control over the media they consume, allowing a wide range of means to reshape and recirculate content.[6] In the past, scrapbooking offered active engagement to audiences wishing or needing to manipulate the messages being presented to them. Scrapbooks allowed fans to insert themselves into the narrative and preserve, in tactile material form, evidence of their encounters with a text. The four collectors discussed in the following chapters used scrapbooking in this way as well as to resist the ephemerality of the print material they gathered and to make lasting the pleasures of collecting. Each scrapbook represents the collecting habits and subjectivity of each collector as a fan of Jane Austen.

Collectors and fans have much in common. Two notions in particular, central to collecting, resemble material aspects of fandom. First, as objects enter a collection, they are converted from profane to sacred, and second, the collector experiences the collection as an extension of the self.[7] The practices of both fans and collectors are imbued with an emotional investment. Both collectors and fans actively seek—and create—for themselves an alternative realm that helps them make sense of an imperfect world. Moreover, collectors derive great joy from sharing their obsession with like-minded others and will go out of their way to contrive opportunities to share. Fans do the same. I do not mean to suggest that collecting is a type of fandom—although certainly some collectors are fans and some fans are collectors—but merely that the two habits resemble each other and overlap.

Scholars generally understand collecting as a practice related to subjectivity.[8] I suggest that while collections and objects such as scrapbooks may indeed display or stand in for the subjectivity of the creator, they also serve as stand-ins for the affective *experiences* of the creator. The scrapbooks discussed in this chapter were created between about 1935 and 1987 to document the attaining of objects and knowledge related to Austen and to resist the ephemerality of particular moments that briefly punctuated the daily lives of the individual Austen collectors who made them. The moments captured by the scrapbooks are those of discovery and, most important, those in which a sought-after object is attained. Cultural theorist Walter Benjamin explains that collecting hinges on attainment: "The most profound enchantment for the collector is the locking of individual items within a magic circle in which they are fixed as the final thrill, the thrill of acquisition, passes over them."[9] As material objects that can be revisited, the scrapbooks keep alive for the collector the final thrill of acquisition, which can only be experienced once. As Susan Stewart theorizes, a scrapbook "lends authenticity to the past"; its function, as a souvenir, is to "envelop the present within the past."[10] Like a live performance, once the collector's moment of attainment is over, it is gone; the collector must create a mnemonic object if she wishes to relive, remember, and share the experience of that final thrill.

Relying on Joseph Roach's notion of surrogation, a performative process of memory and forgetting, I suggest that scrapbooks are akin to what Roach calls effigies; the effigy is a mnemonic object that attempts to stand in for something lost. The effigy is created through performance, and it enables performances when put to use. Yet as a substitute, it can never offer an exact fit, and so one must continuously seek new stand-ins in the hopes of finding a better match. Therefore, a metaphor of loss permeates acts of surrogation. This metaphor is applicable to the practices of literary fans and enthusiasts: a book can only be read for the first time once, and when the experience is over, a sharp sense of loss is often felt. In some cases, the author is dead; there will be no more novels. Literary fans seek a means of staving off the sense of loss—loss of an experience now past—through collecting, scrapbooking, and other practices. The scrapbooks discussed in part II serve as effigies for the original experiences of collecting and reading. To perform, according to Roach, is to make manifest, to transmit, and to reinvent something lost.[11] Mnemonic objects such as these scrapbooks are performative: they make manifest, transmit, and reinvent each individual's affective experiences and their collecting habits. In other words, the creation of a scrapbook is the making of an effigy; its creation is a performance and sharing it is a performance. The scrapbooks created by these four individuals perform more fluently than the rare first editions and other prized objects in the collections themselves.[12]

In the nineteenth century, a scrapbooker's goal was to sift through a glut of cheap and disposable print material, selecting that which was important or useful. Scrapbookers ensured that a selected clipping would endure by deeming it valuable, and by making it valuable, they made it last.[13] The act of transforming scraps into a treasured resource was viewed as a productive leisure activity. The material saved in the pages of a scrapbook was often meant to entertain and especially to edify. In the nineteenth-century American worldview shaped by the Protestant work ethic, leisure time was meant to have purpose and be productive, making scrapbooking a commendable activity that was didactic, utilitarian, fruitful, and moraı.[14] Moreover, scrapbooks were meant to exemplify and convey the values of the individual scrapbooker.

Historian Katherine Ott has studied nineteenth-century men's professional scrapbooks, created as an accessory to paid professional work rather than emerging from a private or domestic pursuit. Men's scrapbooks aligned with professional labor have been mostly overlooked by historians in favor of scrapbooks that represent everyday domestic history. Aesthetically, Ott finds that most men's professional scrapbooks, many of which were related to medical careers, were "subdued and stately." In some cases, however, they were packed admiringly with portraits of famous physicians, in addition to more serious texts documenting the history of medicinal practice. In these instances, the albums resembled celebrity scrapbooks kept by young fans to celebrate favorite actors and musicians.[15]

Like scrapbooking in the nineteenth century, and particularly like the professional albums studied by Ott, the twentieth-century scrapbooks discussed here display a curious blend of characteristics. They are subdued and academic yet show a deep fascination with Austen and an obsession with trivia. They illustrate the blurred line—and tensions—between professional and amateur, expert and fan, vocation and avocation. They are both public and private.

Folklorist Danielle Elise Christensen has argued that contemporary scrapbooks represent a performance-centered form of material culture in which the domestic and ephemeral moments of everyday life are made enduring and public. Scrapbookers today, predominantly women documenting domestic life and family milestones, value the acid-free, keepsake book format of scrapbooks precisely because they help resist the ephemerality of domestic labor and everyday life. The aesthetic work that women put into their scrapbooks renders domestic labor less ephemeral and therefore constitutes it as more lasting, public, and valuable. Today, as in the past, a scrapbook's permanence through its materiality is of crucial importance to its creator. Moreover, the materiality of the scrapbook allows for a public, performative demonstration of types of labor that may not otherwise be visible.[16]

This is certainly the case with the scrapbooks of the four individuals discussed in part II whose love of Austen manifested in labor-intensive, scholarly work that each individual wished to make visible and lasting through their scrapbooks. Scholars disagree about the extent to which these objects are intended for public sharing. Whereas Christensen suggests that scrapbooks today are often meant to be shared, Garvey asserts that in the nineteenth century, they were frequently viewed as too personal to be shown to others.[17] However, I would suggest that even if a scrapbook were created with the intention of being kept private, there is always the audience of one—the self—for whom the object will be evocative, allowing the object to be performative even if not public.

Today, as in the past, scrapbooks can offer fans—who love to share intimate knowledge about a beloved subject matter—a perfect expressive format to invite public display and evaluation. Jenkins has documented well how fans form "dynamic, collective, and reciprocal" knowledge communities, and Nancy Baym has demonstrated how sharing knowledge is central to the affective experiences of fans.[18] Fans are keen to show off their competencies to others who can appreciate the depth of their knowledge; Jenkins refers to this tendency as "epistemaphilia," which he suggests is not simply finding pleasure in knowing but, more to the point, is finding pleasure in the *exchange* of knowledge.[19] At times this knowledge production and exchange take the form of a type of labor for which fans are paid in satisfaction rather than in cash. This knowledge community, or perhaps knowledge economy, is central to fandom and is part of what blurs the line between fans and academics, as both depend on demonstrating depth of knowledge to determine who belongs and who is an outsider.

Fans generate all manner of material creations in different media, including artwork, clothing, accessories, and replica props. These forms routinely garner attention from scholars, while fan scrapbooking has rarely received mention. Yet scrapbooking appears to be prevalent today even if it is not as ubiquitous and visible as digital creations of fandom.[20] It is my hope to fill in some of the historical gaps in our understanding of fandom by considering the labor of love involved in the production of scrapbooks by extraordinary Austen enthusiasts. Alberta Burke's collection and scrapbooks have received some scholarly attention, but the scrapbooks of Barbara Winn Adams, George Holbert Tucker, and David Gilson have been overlooked or were inaccessible until very recently.[21]

The four Austen enthusiasts represented here collected Austenalia in the twentieth century and chose to document and curate their efforts through scrapbooks in unique ways. Revealingly, all four deemed these scrapbooks important and valuable enough to be given to an archive for the future use and enjoyment of scholars or anyone interested in Austen. These scrapbooks are neither purely academic nor purely fannish. For these individuals, scrapbooking offered a means to participate in literary culture through what Ellen Gruber Garvey describes as creative and thoughtful reuse and recirculation of print materia1. Moreover, the materiality of scrapbooks gives them a certain authority, being similar to published books.[22] Like academic research, these scrapbooks were made and maintained over long periods of time, requiring diligence and sustained interest. As the creations of individuals devoted to Austen and intellectually driven to document that devotion, the scrapbooks discussed in the following chapters share characteristics but are also distinctive.

More than the others, Burke's subjectivity as an obsessed and serious Austen enthusiast is on display. Her scrapbooks were intended for sharing with others as a supplement to her collection from almost the moment she began creating them. By contrast, Winn Adams's scrapbooks were the most private of the four, demonstrating a desire to easily access print material and keepsakes for her own uses. Tucker's scrapbooks most represent the notion of "epistemaphilia," the fan's enjoyment in sharing knowledge. Gilson's scrapbook reveals his desire to make a substantive contribution to the field of Austen studies as personally fulfilling. All four document the urges and practices of literary fans in the mid-twentieth century. These include a desire to possess objects and knowledge related to Austen and to contain and catalog them; a strong intellectual and emotional drive to connect in personal ways to Austen's world; and a long-term devotion through the investment of time and effort and, when possible, money.

I foreground an issue of terminology throughout part II. Many scholars agree that fandom involves an intense identification with a text, author, or character that drives a set of practices, yet the question remains (regarding past and current social modes of fandom), when is a fan not a fan? At what point does an intense identification or obsession transform into behavior other than fandom? I believe the difference in terminology between *fan* and *enthusiast* or *connoisseur* is a difference of class and privilege. The four individuals discussed here might have preferred to think of themselves as "enthusiasts" rather than "fans." Although their habits and practices fit today's generally accepted definitions of fandom, the term *fan* carries with it an association with popular entertainment that lovers of literature and other highbrow genres (e.g., opera) may find inadequate for describing the seriousness of their pursuit and the value of the celebrated text. These collectors were quite serious about collecting and researching Austen, and their habits were all-consuming. Privileged, white, and educated to varying degrees, these were obsessed literature enthusiasts who would not likely have embraced the appellation *fan,* and yet the record of their love of Austen embodied by scrapbooks preserved in the archive is testament to lives permeated by the practices of what is today called fandom.

4

"My Very Happy Pastime"

ALBERTA BURKE'S JANE AUSTEN COLLECTION AND SCRAPBOOKS

Anything which is in anyway related to Jane Austen is of intense interest to me.

—ALBERTA BURKE to the Columbia Broadcasting System, November 24, 1940

Alberta Hirshheimer Burke (1906–75) was a lifelong collector and formidable amateur scholar of Jane Austen. Her Austen collection remains one of the most significant in the world. Born in La Crosse, Wisconsin, in 1906, she graduated from Goucher College in 1928, then attended the University of Wisconsin, earning a master's degree in English literature. In 1930, Alberta married lawyer and accountant Henry G. Burke (1902–89), a native of Baltimore, who shared her love of Austen and other literature.

Alberta and Henry Burke began collecting Austen materials following their first trip to England in 1935. Henry later described the moment when they first arrived in London and "drifted" toward a book kiosk, where their "eyes naturally fell upon Lord David Cecil's attractive paperback edition of his *Jane Austen*." The acquisition of this volume "marked the dividing line between just owning Jane Austen books and embarking on some sort of collection."[1] For nearly fifty years, the Burkes built an extensive, fine private collection of Austen books and manuscripts, including first editions of all of Austen's novels and several autograph letters. They also amassed a notable collection of books related to late-eighteenth- and early-nineteenth-century costume, decorative arts, architecture, and landscape gardening. Beginning in the 1940s, they collected translations of Austen's novels, locating rare foreign-language editions that had been previously overlooked by bibliographers. Using Geoffrey Keynes's *Jane Austen: A Bibliography* (1929) as their model, the couple methodically sought out articles from historical periodicals on Jane Austen and her works. Henry described that "when an early *Dublin Review, Atlantic Monthly,* or *Nation* came our way, we felt as though we had discovered some medieval manuscript."[2] Any article, book, or dissertation about or related to Jane Austen's life, times, and novels was worthy of adding to their shelves. While Henry handled many of the actual purchase transactions, Alberta curated the collection, entering each item they attained into her card catalog and indexing them according to the numbering systems of the various bibliographies available to her. It was a pursuit the Burkes enjoyed together, but Alberta was clearly the primary architect of the collection; collecting Austen was her avocation, or what she called her "very happy pastime."[3]

In 1940, just five years after their collection began to take shape, Alberta Burke wrote a letter to the producers of the Helen Hayes Theatre program of the Columbia Broadcasting System (CBS), requesting a copy of the script of an adaptation of *Pride and Prejudice* she had just listened to on the radio. Burke described in her own words her collection and fascination with all things Austen:

> I have a collection of several hundred items of material by and related to Jane Austen, including several autograph letters, first editions of all her novels, biographical and critical works, magazine material, and the script which was used in a broadcast version of Jane Austen's life (her first appearance on the air). My collection is my own private diversion, and is not connected with any sort of institution, public or private. I can therefore promise that if you do permit me to purchase a copy of the *Pride and Prejudice*, no commercial or any other use will be made of it. It would be merely a private possession of which I should be extremely proud. Anything which is in anyway related to Jane Austen is of intense interest to me, and an item in which her name is associated with that of the actress for whom I have a most unbounded admiration, would be indeed a highly prized part of my collection.[4]

To lend weight to her request and increase the likelihood that CBS would comply, Burke offered to pay whatever the company might ask for it because, she explained, "to one who is a whole-hearted admirer of Jane Austen, her appearance in a new medium is a most thrilling and interesting event." This is remarkable considering she later wrote a note in one of her Austen scrapbooks that this Helen Jerome adaptation was "very poor," with "no continuity, no development," and would be impossible to follow for someone unfamiliar with the actual story.[5] Despite the fact she was unimpressed by the radio play, she felt she simply must attain a copy for her collection, and she scrapbooked about the experience of trying to acquire it by clipping the broadcast schedule, annotating her opinion, and saving the letter from CBS denying her request.

The Burkes began planning the bequest of the collection in the 1930s, in the early stages of acquisition. Alberta Burke's prescient awareness that her collection was to become valuable and important is reminiscent of American women connoisseurs in the Gilded Age, conscious of creating something important and lasting. By the time Alberta died, in 1975, at age sixty-eight, her collection had grown to over one thousand volumes, and her scrapbooks held more than twenty-eight hundred indexed clippings, articles, letters, and other Jane Austen–related ephemera. Henry survived Alberta, and the couple had no children. In accordance with Alberta's will, the collection was distributed between the Goucher College Library and the Pierpont Morgan Library in New York (now called the Morgan Library and Museum). Goucher received the majority of the collection: more than one thousand books; rare early editions of Austen's novels; a large collection of historical periodicals, scholarly articles, and dissertations; Alberta's ten scrapbooks; and personal correspondence relevant to the collection. The autograph letters and manuscripts went to the Morgan Library, adding to an already strong manuscript collection there.[6]

Even more than the purchased volumes, manuscripts, and autograph letters that the Burkes amassed, the ten scrapbooks of press cuttings and memorabilia best represent the labor of love that was Alberta Burke's obsession for Jane Austen. Henry explained: "Alberta started keeping notebooks where even the most casual Austen reference merited an entry. . . . Anything worth clipping was pasted into the notebooks."[7] Austen scholar

Juliette Wells refers to Alberta Burke as an "Austen omnivore," an apt description. Wells describes the scrapbooks as resembling "the creation of a visionary artist: intricate, time-intensive, and the product of a most unusual mind."[8] For forty years, from 1935 until just days before her death in 1975, Burke clipped and pasted anything and everything that referenced Austen, her novels, or her times even in the most oblique way, and in the process, she documented and curated her own collecting habits. Each scrapbook is titled "*Pride and Prejudice* and other material relating to Jane Austen" and is assigned a volume number. The scrapbooks are not exclusively about *Pride and Prejudice*, but Austen's most famous novel receives the greatest attention throughout. With the exception of one volume, the scrapbooks proceed chronologically, beginning with 1935. The final clipping in the last volume is Alberta's obituary from the *Baltimore Sun*, which Henry must have pasted into the volume sometime after May 24, 1975.

These eclectic and remarkable scrapbooks were created from marbled composition notebooks (9.75 by 7.5 in.), each about 1.5 inches thick. The clippings are not attached aesthetically or with particular care, but they are all given annotations as to origin and date and occasionally include marginalia that offers general or personal context. The scrapbooks include a wide variety of clippings: book reviews of scholarly and non-scholarly Austen-related works; movie magazine stories about the actors to portray Austen's characters on screen; news articles about the actual locations found in Austen's novels, such as Lyme Regis or Bath; lecture and performance announcements; theater programs; book jackets; and print advertisements. The scrapbooks originally housed relevant personal correspondence (now archived in their own folders) that traces the Burkes' collecting and puts it into context. Burke sometimes included copies of her own letters in addition to those she received so as to document both sides of a correspondence when it was important to do so, such as when she wrote to preeminent Austen scholars to inform them of items in her collection about which they might wish to be made aware.[9] To document her book-collecting efforts, she pasted clippings from bookseller and auction catalogs, sometimes circling the items she hoped to procure. In one instance, she circled two items, both early American editions of Austen for sale in 1962, and included the Western Union telegram from the bookseller that indicates the outcome of her attempt to acquire these two volumes. It reads, "Sending item 54, regret 56 sold."[10]

Alberta Burke only kept contemporary items in her scrapbooks; historical clippings and older articles were part of her collection, but they were housed separately. The scrapbooks, then, were not the place she included objects of her collection considered sacred, such as the valuable autograph letters. Yet she viewed the scrapbooks themselves as an important part of the collection. The clippings and ephemera pasted into the volumes, taken as a whole, make each scrapbook special. It is the sum of the parts, the visibility of the labor involved in its creation, and its material permanence that renders each volume a unique and sacred object.

Burke is as present in the notebooks as Austen and in some ways, more so. There is no apparent visual separation or boundary in these notebooks between that which is specifically relevant to Burke and her collecting and that which is related to Austen. Her intention for the scrapbooks was clear: to document all aspects of "Austeniana," as she once referred to it, that appeared in print or on screen, stage, and radio.[11] In so doing, she also managed to document her process and her observations. The scrapbooks present an obsession writ large.

Burke avidly followed radio broadcasts of Austen adaptations in the 1930s and 1940s and pasted into her scrapbooks press clippings that listed broadcast schedules. Next to one such clipping for a CBS radio broadcast on August 29, 1944, of an adaptation of *Pride and Prejudice* by Jean Holloway, she scribbled, "Same as June 13, broadcast—See script for differences noted."[12] In other words, Burke acquired the script from the broadcast company, clipped and saved the broadcast schedule, listened to the adaptation on multiple occasions, and annotated in the script the details that differed from one performance to the next. Burke was keen on possessing scripts of this kind, collecting several broadcast scripts from NBC, the BBC, and even an adaptation made for performance at a British girls' school. Possessing these scripts allowed her to compare different adaptations over time. Moreover, as with all archontic literature, they offered variations on something familiar, allowing Burke the opportunity to read again, as if for the first time, Austen's stories.

A fan can never relive the moment of a first reading or viewing of a favorite book or film yet will strive to find stand-ins for the original experience. In addition to adaptations, several spin-off novels appeared during the years Alberta Burke kept her scrapbooks, offering yet another new way to read about Austen's characters. However, as Joseph Roach suggests of the search for a "satisfactory alternate," the fit is never exact, and therefore, the endeavor is always doomed to fail.[13] Burke herself expressed this dilemma: "I always anticipate these attempts most eagerly, and hope that *this* one will be the perfect adaption, then I end with pursed lips and disappointment."[14] Several of Burke's scrapbooks contain dust jackets taken from spin-off novels, such as D. A. Bonavia-Hunt's *Pemberley Shades* (1949).[15] Being comprehensive, Burke collected both the American and British first editions of this continuation of *Pride and Prejudice.* She removed the dust jackets of both editions, trimmed them to a manageable size, and pasted them into a scrapbook, presumably to display the striking differences between the American and British illustrations and book descriptions.[16] For Burke, collecting this new Austen-themed novel was an ongoing process, punctuated by moments of anticipation and attainment. Her scrapbooks contain articles and reviews announcing the book's publication, in addition to the dust jackets. Burke was driven to create through her scrapbook an effigy for the experience of attaining the novel, which was itself a kind of surrogate for the remembered pleasure of first reading Austen.

Much of what Burke chose to include in the scrapbooks documents Austen-related events in mid-twentieth-century America, including lectures, exhibits, and other happenings. In 1951, the State Teachers College in Frostburg, Maryland, held a Jane Austen Festival, organized by a professor with whom Burke was friends. Burke included in her scrapbook several newspaper clippings regarding the free two-day festival as well as an invitation and copy of the program.[17] These documents reflect the social nature of the event, which included a concert followed by a formal social hour, an English country dance demonstration performed in costume, and a film screening; this was in addition to lectures and other more intellectual offerings. It does not appear that Burke attended the event 150 miles from her home, but she documented it just the same. Having attended some of the comparatively staid Jane Austen Society meetings in

England, Burke may have found the social and lighthearted nature of this American festival intriguing.

Burke's scrapbooks include even the most casual or superficial allusions to Austen. These items reveal how deeply imbued Austen was within the cultural landscape, particularly of an educated upper class. For instance, the fifth volume holds a clipping from the dust jacket of a book completely unrelated to Austen, which Burke deemed worthy because the author's biography states that she owned "a cat named Darcy."[18] Several scrapbook volumes include advertisements such as a Benson & Hedges cigarettes ad clipped from a theater playbill from the mid-1950s that pirates a phrase from *Pride and Prejudice:* "It is happy for you that you possess the art of pleasing with delicacy."[19]

From the first scrapbook volume to the last, the tone becomes more serious. Whereas in the earliest volumes, 1935 to 1944, Burke devoted attention to clippings and theater programs that represent the flurry of adaptations of *Pride and Prejudice* for stage, screen, and radio, the later volumes became gradually more scholarly in nature. As she matured, so did her interests. Burke began to include more articles and book reviews that discussed developments in critical scholarship about Austen and her novels.[20] She devoted the second volume entirely to the 1940 MGM film adaptation of *Pride and Prejudice,* and because it contains more images than any other volume, it resembles most closely the kind of work often associated with fans. These images, which she clipped from more than a dozen different entertainment magazines, such as *Glamour, Silver Screen,* and *Movie Story,* depict glamorous actors, sets, and costumes.[21] Burke tracked Hollywood gossip as the production of the film was under way, such as casting and directorial changes and biographical information on the actors. She pasted into her scrapbooks articles that reveal the story of bringing the film from page to screen. As the tone of the volumes shifts from lighthearted to more serious, the scrapbooks continue to include peripheral allusions that reflect the influence of Jane Austen, and imagined versions of her time period, on culture. From hairstyles to wallpaper fashions, Burke followed the ways that Austen and representations of the Regency era became ingrained in her world, even as she turned her attention more fully to scholarly aspects of her favorite pastime.

Burke wrote two letters to the editor, almost thirty years apart, that illustrate her subjectivity with regard to her collection and reflect the change in tone discernible in the scrapbooks over time. Two days before Jane Austen's birthday in December 1935, when Alberta was twenty-eight years old and had just begun collecting, her letter appeared in the *Saturday Review of Literature*, advising readers that while "all the literate world is celebrating the seventieth anniversary of Rudyard Kipling," it would also be worth remembering Jane Austen: "Since there are no clubs which bear her name, no Jane Austen society to issue learned treatises, Jane Austen's admirers ought to commemorate her birth with some fitting exercise." She suggests this be done "with, at least, a baked apple (baked three times according to Mr. Woodhouse) . . . , and honor at one time 'England's Jane' and the man who gave our cult its most appropriate name."[22]

This clever, lighthearted letter contrasts with the one she wrote nearly thirty years later, in 1962, to the *Times Literary Supplement* (*TLS*, London). This time, she responded to an article by leading Austen scholar Brian Southam in which he amended the dates customarily given for the writing of *Northanger Abbey*, gently correcting an error perpetuated by Austen expert R. W. Chapman.[23] Burke corroborated Southam's deduction, stating that she in fact owned the manuscript that upheld his assertion. Furthermore, she suggested, she had attempted to point out the discrepancy to Chapman in the past: "I have the scrap of notes on the composition of Jane Austen's novel written by Cassandra [Jane's sister]. I purchased the memorandum at Sotheby's in May 1948. Some time in the summer of 1948, when I sent a Photostat of it to Dr. Chapman, I called his attention to the discrepancy between the dates for *Northanger Abbey* in *Life and Letters* and those in the memorandum. In the 2nd edition, 1955, of his *Jane Austen: A Critical Bibliography*, Dr. Chapman corrects one of his statements from the evidence of the memorandum, but in a letter to me, said that he had forgotten about the difference in the dates."[24] Burke then explained how the evidence in the scrap of Cassandra's memorandum could be relied upon. She listed all the items included in the Sotheby's auction lot among which the memorandum was found—a lock of Austen's hair was one—in order to suggest that indeed the provenance of the memorandum was sufficient to guarantee the reliability of its information. This letter illustrates how Burke viewed her collecting: her subjectivity and her collection were inseparable. The letter to the *TLS* is as much about her collection and the act of collecting and corresponding with scholars as it is about the dates when Austen composed *Northanger Abbey*. She concluded the *TLS* letter by describing how, in 1949, she had donated several of the items from the auction to the Jane Austen Museum at Chawton. This point had little to do with the matter at hand, but she could not resist performing her magnanimity. Her passion for her collection was as much about sharing it and making it available as it was about attaining and possessing.

In both letters, Burke displayed her cleverness and knowledge, but it was not until later in her life, after years of serious study and collecting, that her performance of her affinity for Austen took on a much more commanding tone. In the 1962 letter to the editor, Burke and her collection become one: both are serious and replete with information. And in order to put forth a fact, she must tell the story of her collection. Letters like these that Burke wrote to newspapers and prominent scholars appear as part of her scrapbooks. They offer evidence of two modes of performance happening concurrently: Burke performs her knowledge and depth of involvement with Austen by writing these documents; she then turns this act into a performative mnemonic object by putting material evidence of her knowledge into her collection. She documented the performance, creating opportunities for performing anew through her scrapbooks.

Occasionally, Burke annotated her clippings with marginalia. Some of these annotations seem to indicate that she was writing them for and to herself. For instance, beside a book review that compared a new novelist to a "cynical Jane Austen . . . that had been more familiar with Freud than Fanny Burney," Burke notated with exasperation: "If she were familiar with Freud, she would not be Jane Austen!"[25] Other annotations provide brief context, making apparent a self-conscious awareness that these notebooks might be viewed by others at a later time. All of the clippings have penned annotations that give the publication source and date, and they are linked to the numerical index Burke maintained for decades, tracking each entry as though intending the books to be more easily used by others in the future.

It is telling that as early as 1939, after only four years of serious collecting, Burke was making plans with Goucher College to donate her scrapbooks and the bulk of her collection to its library.[26] She knew all along that these scrapbooks would represent her "very happy pastime" for posterity. One of the great concerns shared among collectors is immortality; the collection becomes for them a way of cheating time and death, as the collection lives on. Burke's Austen collection will live on in the archive, keeping her name alive to all who encounter it. The scrapbooks, particularly, offer a glimpse of Burke herself. In her lifetime, they were surrogates through which she kept alive the experience of collecting, and in her death, they have collectively become an effigy of the life and experiences of the woman and collector who created them.

Alberta Burke did not refer to herself as a "fan" of Jane Austen. In one letter, she called herself a "whole-hearted admirer of Jane Austen," and in another, she referred to her friend David Gilson as a "fellow Jane Austen enthusiast."[27] In an earlier letter to Gilson, she wrote: "Do let me know any Jane Austen news you have. I am always very eager to hear from a fellow 'Janeite' (Do you hate Kipling's word, too?)"[28] Her parenthetical question reveals how she felt about the term *Janeite*. Earlier in her life, however, she seems to have been comfortable with words like *cult* and *idolatry* to refer to her mode of relating to Austen and used *Janeite* without the reservation she developed later. Just as her collecting of Austeniana became more serious and more scholarly as she grew older, and her scrapbooks reflect this change over time, the way she chose to describe her habits changed also. All along, though, she readily admitted to an obsession for Austen. To Burke, the word *fan* might have seemed ill suited to encompass the seriousness of her purpose and the thoroughness of her collecting. She did, after all, gather one of the largest and most valuable Austen collections in the world, and she was keen on sharing both her collection and knowledge with others. She would perhaps not have favorably compared herself to contemporary fandoms, such as screaming Beatles fans. Yet her collection and correspondence demonstrate a fervent love for and obsessive commitment to Austen with which self-professed fans today would identify.

Regardless of how Burke may have felt about the term, was she not a fan? It could be argued that she was the paragon of fans. Yet it is more complicated than that: she was also a scholar, even if unpublished. Burke's obsession with Austen was highly academic and intellectual, yet also fun-loving, and was taken up in the pursuit of leisure. Burke possessed the time and financial means to develop her love of Austen fully into a serious avocation, and the archive illustrates how her very subjectivity was dependent on these activities.

Austen bibliographer David Gilson, who had a long, friendly correspondence with Burke (and whose own Austen scrapbook I discuss in chap. 7), described her collecting habits thus: "Mrs. Burke at no time felt impelled to publish on Jane Austen, but devoted herself rather to a more selfless service to scholarship: the formation of a collection of material on which others may work."[29] Many Austen scholars of the twentieth century sought her out; the depth of her collection and knowledge was legendary. Her husband, Henry, also described her habits: "She was also an exceedingly retiring individual, which explains why her letters to friends were brilliant but at no time did she feel an impulse to publish. Perhaps this was one of her links to Jane Austen and the collection itself was the two inches of ivory on which she worked so exquisitely. She was incapable of breaking out of this enclosure just as Jane Austen rejected the allurement of writing about the House of Saxe Cobourg and never in her novels touched on the Napoleonic wars or the class struggle."[30] Henry's description is fraught, being both affectionate and condescending. He admired her, clearly; he goes so far as to compare Alberta to Austen herself, alluding to the oft-quoted "two inches of ivory" metaphor Jane Austen used to describe her own writing with both self-effacement and subtle, ironic boastfulness. Alberta was, by Henry's assessment, "incapable of breaking out of this enclosure," yet her lifelong collecting efforts were worked on "exquisitely."

Both David Gilson and Henry Burke were highly respected professionals—and men—who were also quite involved in a lifelong love of Austen. Henry gave Alberta all the credit for the collecting (and indeed she deserved it), but he, too, was a lover of Austen and conducted most of the actual transactions with entities such as Sotheby's. Gilson, a librarian by trade, spent his life compiling a comprehensive bibliography of Austen, surpassing all prior attempts. Yet both men felt the need to distinguish Alberta's activities from their own, and by *distinguish*, I mean two things: they wanted to highlight her special "selfless service to scholarship" and "brilliant" letters yet also to point out the nonprofessional realm in which she worked in order to distance her work from theirs.

I suggest the key to understanding Alberta Burke's complicated position between fans and academics is through the practice of code switching. She was scholarly when she approached R. W. Chapman to boldly correct errors in his freshly published bibliography; she was a fan when she wrote a letter to CBS to request a copy of the script from a broadcast version of *Pride and Prejudice.* In this letter, she downplayed the seriousness of her collecting in the hopes of convincing CBS to sell her the script. She assured the producers: "My collection is my own private diversion, and is not connected with any sort of institution, public or private. . . . [The script] would be merely a private possession of which I should be extremely proud."[31] These words were to be understood as coming from a fan, not a scholar. To be a fan is not to be something less than a scholar (and vice versa), but at different times, our society values one above the other. Alberta Burke seems to have understood that.

Ten years after Alberta's death, Joan Austen-Leigh asked Henry Burke to provide a paragraph for an upcoming publication that might explain how Alberta came to collect Austen. Austen-Leigh wrote: "It would be interesting to know how Alberta came to have such an obsession for JA. I don't mean to be pejorative by using the word 'obsession' because of course you know I thoroughly approve."[32] Alberta's obsession and exceptional collection were well-known, and her scrapbooks especially demonstrate one woman's passion for Austen while painting a picture of a whole era of Austen fandom, represented by a cross section of press cuttings and memorabilia from both sides of the Atlantic. Serving as both an exemplar and resource, they offer a landscape of the place of Jane Austen in the American cultural landscape and collective consciousness of a certain class, and they represent the practices, pleasures, desires, and energies of one collector.

5

The Scrapbook of Barbara Winn Adams, Book Collector

Born in 1911 in Massachusetts and educated at Wheaton College, where she studied English literature, Barbara Winn Adams (1911–97) was a lifelong book lover and collector. Like Alberta Burke, Winn Adams sustained an interest in Jane Austen throughout most of her adult life, but rather than being an "Austen omnivore," as Burke was, her collecting was more selective, and she collected other interests besides Austen.[1] Together with her husband, Scott Adams (1909–82), a medical librarian for the federal government, she collected thousands of books and periodicals related to various interests. After they were married, in 1935, they lived in New York for several years while Scott pursued a master's degree in library sciences at Columbia University. During this time, Barbara took advantage of the library there in order to conduct bibliographic research on Austen.[2] In 1945, Winn Adams, her husband, and their four-year-old daughter moved from New York to Bethesda, Maryland.[3]

When Barbara Winn Adams passed away, in 1997, at the age of eighty-six, she had been collecting books for about sixty years. She collected novels of the "silver-fork school" and children's books, in addition to works by and about Austen. These collections each found homes at institutions of higher learning as Winn Adams intended. Goucher College received her Austen collection and silver-fork school collection. The Austen collection includes 275 books, plus personal papers and correspondence related to her collecting, and her research collection of essays, articles, journals, and clippings; the silver-fork school collection includes 38 rare books. Her collection of over 2,200 children's books was bequeathed to the University of Southern Maine.[4] Her personalized engraved bookplate by artist Richard Hood, with its layered allusions to Austen's *Persuasion*, may indicate the primacy of Austen in her passion for books (fig. 5.1).

Winn Adams was one of a handful of Americans to join the Jane Austen Society (JAS) in England early in its existence; she remained a member for thirty years. Both Winn Adams and Alberta Burke joined the same year, in 1947, as the JAS made a fund-raising push to save Chawton Cottage, one of Austen's homes. Burke traveled frequently to England and attended a few gatherings of the JAS, but Winn Adams visited Chawton only once, in 1968, so the two women did not encounter each other in this context nor in any other, it seems. In 1979, she was among the first to join the brand-new Jane Austen Society of North America (JASNA), and although she remained a member for at least ten years, she seems to have only attended one gathering of the group, the 1980 Annual General Meeting (AGM). At this event, held in Baltimore, she met JASNA founders Henry Burke and Jack Grey and had the opportunity to see much of Alberta Burke's collection on display at Goucher as part of the weekend's events.

Almost as soon as she began to collect Austen, Winn Adams decided to do the necessary research that could bring Geoffrey Keynes's *Jane Austen: A Bibliography*, published in 1929, up to date through 1940. She worked on creating a selective annotated bibliography, feeling that it would be more useful than a comprehensive but unannotated one because, she said, "many articles sound interesting but upon examination turn out to be slight and sometimes ridiculous." Her goal was to help fellow "students of Jane Austen" more easily find the types of articles they sought.[5] To compile this bibliography, she collected books and periodicals and kept notes about them on three-by-five-inch index cards. These cards served as research toward the bibliography but also formed the organizational indexing system to keep track of her Austen collection. It appears that her bibliography project never advanced past the index card stage. Within the Winn Family Jane Austen Collection at Goucher are seven folders and containers of various sizes and formats, each filled with index cards with handwritten notes, but there is no evidence of a draft of the bibliography.

Comparison between Barbara Winn Adams and Alberta Burke is mer-

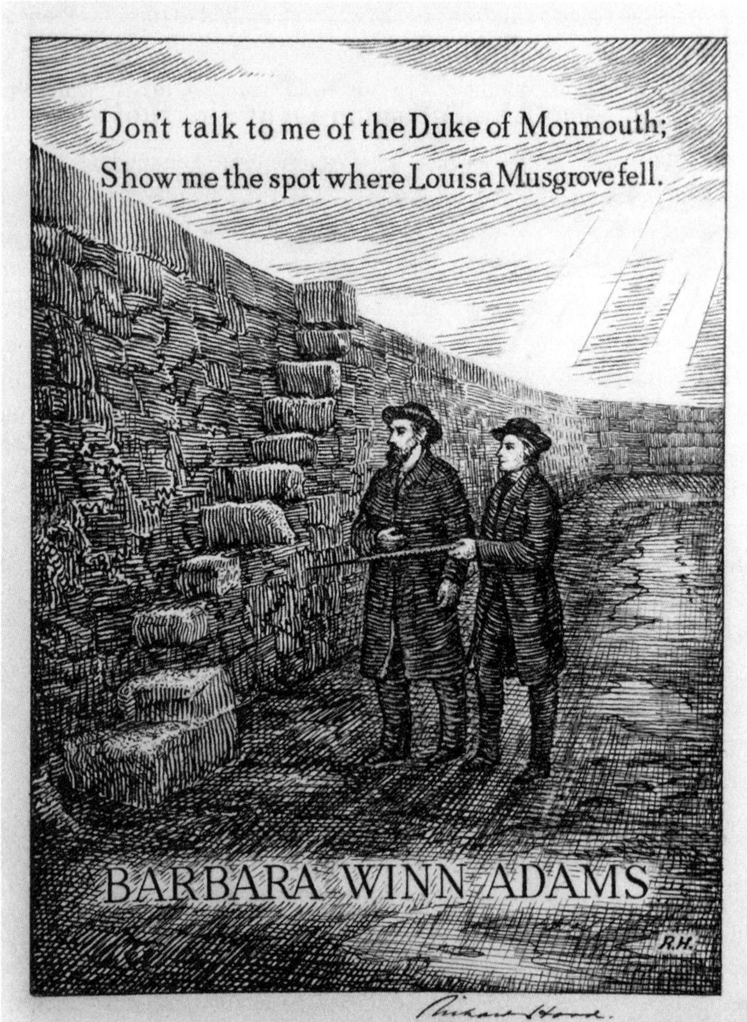

Fig. 5.1. Barbara Winn Adams's bookplate. Original engraving by Richard Hood (1910–95). Alfred, Lord Tennyson, upon visiting the Cobb at Lyme Regis was more interested in seeing the setting of a scene from Austen's *Persuasion* than hearing of British history. He reportedly commented: "Don't talk to me of the Duke of Monmouth; show me the spot where Louisa Musgrove 'fell down and was taken up lifeless.'" Winn Family Collection, Goucher College Library. Photo by author.

ited: they were both remarkable women, born only four years apart, both affluent (although Burke was much more so) and educated, and both spent most of their adult lives living in Maryland, only about forty miles apart. Winn Adams would have been aware of Alberta Burke's collection by 1980 since much of it was on display at Goucher during that year's JASNA Annual General Meeting in Baltimore, which Winn Adams attended.[6] Both women amassed impressive Austen collections over the span of decades; both pursued collecting in a scholarly and methodical manner; both corresponded with R. W. Chapman and David Gilson, the two most prominent Austen bibliographers of the time; both created a card index of their collections, carefully tracking each purchase and its place on their bookshelves; and both collectors created scrapbooks related to their passion for collecting Austen.

For Winn Adams, scrapbooking created a means to hold keepsakes from among the overabundance of print materials she accumulated related to her book collecting, her bibliographic research, and her love of Austen. Of the four individuals discussed in part II, her scrapbooking was the most private and therefore the least overtly performative. Driven less than the others by a desire to share her love of Austen, her habits suggest that she simply desired the personal satisfaction sought through keeping material effigies of past affective experiences.

Winn Adams created only two Austen scrapbooks. One is a purely practical document containing scraps taken from bookseller and auction catalogs from about 1935 to 1948.[7] These dates are approximate because unlike Burke, Winn Adams did not scrupulously notate the dates and sources of all clippings. She used this scrapbook exclusively to keep track of books that had come on the market. This scrapbook contains only a few annotations, such as the occasional seller's address or a year. In one instance, she corrects the date of an edition wrongly listed as 1899, which, she notated, "should be 1894." Unlike Burke's eclectic volumes, this spiral-bound composition notebook is utilitarian, housing tiny cuttings that would have been difficult to keep track of in any other way. She kept other documentation of her collecting habits, such as correspondence with booksellers and records of payment for books purchased, inside the books to which they referred. By contrast, the second scrapbook is more lively and full of articles, reviews, images, and annotations.[8] This scrapbook is housed in a two-ring binder with a substantial leatherette-style black cover. Between roughly 1935 and 1951, Winn Adams added articles, reviews, playbills, research notes, and correspondence to the pages in this binder. The second scrapbook shares many characteristics with Burke's yet bears distinctions that suggest how Winn Adams's scrapbooking practices served desires and needs different from Burke's.

Winn Adams's scrapbook appears to have been meant for her own use alone. There is no title page to introduce the volume, and her name does not appear anywhere in it; instead, there is a clipping of a portrait of Jane Austen centered neatly on the first page, which serves to announce the purpose and content of the book. By contrast, Burke's titles to each volume make clear that she intended them to be seen and used by others. Whereas Burke saved every item she could find that alluded to Austen, Winn Adams was more selective. Considering the collection as a whole, including press cuttings she kept tucked loose inside her books (not pasted into a scrapbook), and based on the notes she penned, it is clear that Winn Adams read articles that she did not include in her scrapbooks. She read a great deal, and she saved much of what she read, but she only included a handful of these items in her scrapbook.

The scrapbook appears to be organized in two halves: the first half resembles a traditional scrapbook, containing newspaper and magazine cuttings that are grouped by theme; the second half contains a few examples of Winn Adams's correspondence, handwritten research notes, articles from the early twentieth century that predate the period in which the scrapbook was created, and theater playbills. In both halves of the scrapbook, the clippings and documents are not presented chronologically but are grouped somewhat thematically. For example, there are several pages near the beginning of the scrapbook that contain miscellaneous clippings that mention Jane Austen from 1939 to 1941; they are followed by an earlier article from a 1933 *McCall's* magazine. Whereas Burke was clipping and pasting mentions of Austen as they appeared and was able to paste them into her books in roughly chronological order as she attained them, Winn Adams seems to have added to her scrapbook more sporadically.

She frequently neglected to annotate the publication information of the articles she included, leaving off the name of the newspaper and date. Furthermore, she did not always clip an entire article but with longer pieces sometimes kept only an excerpt. She seems to have been less interested in the provenance of articles she saved and more interested in what they actually had to say. As an aspiring bibliographer, it is surprising that she did not share Burke's obsession over publication details, but perhaps some of these articles offered something other than purely bibliographic interest to Winn Adams. The differences in habits between the two collectors may simply derive from the fact that Winn Adams's time was limited and her attention divided in ways that were not necessarily the case for Burke, forcing her to be more selective and less thorough.

Like Burke's scrapbooks, Winn Adams's volume of clippings reflects a change in tone over time from more frivolous to more academic. One of the two main thematic sections in the first half of the scrapbook is dedicated to a Broadway production of Helen Jerome's adaptation of *Pride and Prejudice,* which Barbara and Scott saw performed in 1936.[9] The beginning of this section is demarcated by a full-page clipping that depicts sketches of costumed characters from the stage production, and the end of the section is marked by a full-page image of the lead actress, Adrianne Allen, in costume for her role as Elizabeth Bennet. Pasted on the pages between these two evocative images are theater reviews, advertisements for the play, and articles that claim to explain the modern appeal of Austen. The more scholarly second half of the scrapbook includes clippings regarding claims by R. W. Chapman and various letters to the editor written in response. These are of a much more intellectual nature compared to the colorful depictions of the theatrical adaptation in the earlier section. The second half of the scrapbook also includes Winn Adams's notes about discrepancies between her bibliographic research and that of Geoffrey Keynes, which she handwrote on small scraps of paper, filled front and back.

The portrayal of Elizabeth Bennet and Mr. Darcy on stage and screen captured the imaginations of both Winn Adams and Burke. While much of the material in the second half of the scrapbook is more academic, this is also where she placed together a collection of theater playbills, including one from the Broadway production of *Pride and Prejudice* and one from a production at Barnard College, as well as a few pages of clippings about the MGM film. Similarly, in 1949, when *Pemberley Shades,* a spin-off novel that continues the story of *Pride and Prejudice,* first appeared, both women saved clippings related to it in their scrapbooks. These adaptations and continuations offered Austen lovers the chance to renew the experience of reading Austen through familiar yet wholly new renderings. Scrapbooking the book jackets, playbills, and other materials related to these archontic works furthermore served as a means of surrogation for those experiences.

Whereas Burke often wrote to individuals who could benefit from her collection and knowledge, Winn Adams let such opportunities to share with fellow enthusiasts pass by. In 1984, David Gilson wrote to Winn Adams to inquire about *Anna,* an extremely rare German translation of *Persuasion,* of which Winn Adams owned a microfilm copy. She promptly replied to Gilson to explain the circumstances of how she came to discover the existence of *Anna* and acquired a microfilm of the only copy known to exist. She went on to explain to Gilson that nearly twenty years earlier, in 1967, her husband, Scott, had "drafted a letter" regarding the German translation, which he wanted her to send to the Jane Austen Society, but she chose not to send it "because it was not the sort of letter I should write." She also explained, with some chagrin, that when a letter of Gilson's announcing his intent to update and expand the Keynes bibliography appeared in the *Times Literary Supplement,* she "cut it out and fastened it to my refrigerator (a bad American habit)" with the intention of writing to Gilson to inform him about the microfilm copy of *Anna.* However, she says, "the clipping turned yellow with age and I didn't do it!"[10] Although Winn Adams let these opportunities to share her knowledge and collection pass her by, she concludes her letter with a warm invitation to Gilson to visit and look at her collection if he should be in the Washington, DC, area in the future.

The organization and contents of her scrapbook indicate that it was mostly a place for Winn Adams to save items of special interest that did not fit the parameters of her collection yet were meaningful to her. Unlike Burke, Winn Adams created the scrapbook for her own uses, without an intention to share it with future researchers. Her hope had been to write a bibliography; had she succeeded in finishing this endeavor, the published book would have publicly represented her as an exemplary collector and lover of Austen. Although her bibliographic work remained in the form of penciled notes on index cards, never reaching completion, her scrapbook attained permanence through its materiality and offered her the opportunity to participate in literary culture in a meaningful and creative way. Winn Adams's scrapbook was created as a vessel to hold selected meaningful items among the overabundance of print materials she accumulated and as an emblem of her love for Austen that she could return to as one does a favorite book.

6

"A Ready Reference Archive"

THE RESEARCH SCRAPBOOKS OF GEORGE HOLBERT TUCKER

Austen biographer Paula Byrne has said, "The history of Austen criticism and biography tells us as much about the obsessions of her readers as it does about her work and life"[1]—a notion that perfectly summarizes what is significant about the Jane Austen research collection of George Holbert Tucker (1909–2005). Created mostly between 1974 and 1987, the collection comprises 109 scrapbook volumes of meticulously organized research documents, correspondence, articles, and notes that Tucker used in the writing of two biographical works about Austen and her family: *A Goodly Heritage: A History of Jane Austen's Family* (1983) and *Jane Austen the Woman* (1994). Tucker's research scrapbooks, full of details about Jane Austen's life and family background, say as much about the journalist-scholar's obsession with Austen and genealogy as they do about Austen herself. Like fans as well as scholars, Tucker was driven by what Henry Jenkins calls "epistemaphilia"; he desired to be a conduit of knowledge and to share knowledge with other like-minded enthusiasts. His research scrapbooks offer material evidence—particularly through their organizational scheme—of this obsession and desire to share knowledge. George H. Tucker was neither a fan nor a scholar, and yet he was both.

Tucker was born in Norfolk, Virginia, in 1909 and remained there until his death in 2005, except for a stint in the U.S. Navy during World War II. The Great Depression derailed his plans to attend college and shaped his early career. He took a job as an office assistant right out of high school and shortly thereafter worked as a manager for a Works Progress Administration project cataloging early government papers in Norfolk as part of the Federal Archives Project, a post for which he had gained eligibility and experience, having already published a book of genealogical history of the city. Later he took a position at a music store and eventually entered a career writing for the *Virginian-Pilot* newspaper in 1949.[2]

From 1959 until 1977, George H. Tucker wrote a popular column of anecdotal and often humorous tales, known as "Tidewater Landfalls," relevant to the history of the Hampton Roads region in Virginia. The columns included anecdotes of local traditions from the first quarter of the twentieth century, such as Memorial Day celebrations rife with Confederate rhetoric that he poked fun at and tales of memorable figures and moments from Virginia's seventeenth- and eighteenth-century past. Editor of the *Virginian-Pilot* Robert Mason, described Tucker's column as old-fashioned and praised Tucker as a "meticulous researcher as well as a natural depository of tall tales, improbable legends, and robust gossip."[3] He had a knack for finding something rich and pithy in the minutiae of the past and bringing it contextual significance. Tucker was, as his editor described him, "content to relate lively history, spin a fine yarn, indulge in nostalgia, or sketch a memorable personality."[4] He brought all of these traits to his work on Jane Austen.

It is unclear exactly when or how Tucker came to discover his love for Jane Austen. He was known as an anglophile to friends and family.[5] And in a letter to Gale Research Company, he wrote in detail about the influence of his "very bright" history-loving grandmother who taught him to read and to love literature.[6] Moreover, his predilection toward human interest stories, satirical humor, and representations of everyday life in past eras, as evidenced by his Tidewater Landfalls columns, seem to indicate a mind well primed to fall in love with Austen. It was not until his retirement from the *Virginian-Pilot* newspaper, in 1975, that he turned his energies toward researching Jane Austen, his favorite novelist.[7]

In 1983, Tucker published *A Goodly Heritage: A History of Jane Austen's Family* with a small publisher in England.[8] He was the first biographer to conceive of a book on Austen that was organized around essays on each member of her immediate family.[9] He had set out to write a standard biography of Austen but early in his research found that little had been written about Austen's ancestry or close relatives.[10] Tucker was particularly interested in genealogy and skilled in the painstaking research it requires, making him the perfect person to fill this lacuna. As noted by biographer Paula Byrne, *A Goodly Heritage* "paved the way for the approach [taken by the most respected Austen biographers], revealing a sleuth-like ability to nose out obscure but revealing details."[11]

Tucker's research was thorough, and whenever possible, he went directly to primary sources and historical records that others had passed over, collecting vast amounts of research material through correspondence especially with sources in England. His goal always was to avoid repeating errors that past scholars had made and unwittingly perpetuated as fact. For instance, the year of birth for Jane Austen's brother, Edward, had been frequently given as 1768, but Tucker inquired directly about baptismal records of Deane, England, confirming that in fact Edward was born and baptized in 1767, forever setting the record straight.[12]

By the time his first book on Austen was finished and he was working on his second, Tucker had amassed an impressive collection of unique resources, research correspondence, and photocopies of hard-to-find secondary sources, which he sought to give to a research institution for use by other scholars. For instance, Tucker collected several examples of pamphlets and brochures produced in small numbers by British libraries, museums, and historic homes to accompany commemorations or exhibits related to Austen. In 1977, Tucker began to correspond with Herbert Cahoon of the Pierpont Morgan Library in New York, sending Cahoon a handful of materials he had collected in his research and travels as well as some of his own notes on Jane Austen's genealogy. The Morgan Library had already become one of the most important repositories in the world for Austen manuscripts and letters, thanks in part to a bequest of Alberta and Henry Burke. Tucker would have been aware of this, having utilized some of these manuscripts in his own research, and he was actively seeking to complement the library's holdings with his unique research collection. In response to Tucker's gift of a sampling of research materials, Cahoon wrote in 1977: "I have gone over with much pleasure all the wonderful material you have sent us. . . . The documentary material on Austen and kindred genealogies will be important for our files."[13] Cahoon's response was cagey, however, when responding to Tucker's offer to donate the entirety of the research collection to the Morgan Library: "The Director and I have both been away at different times and I have not yet had a chance to sit down and talk with him about your Jane Austen notes. My own feeling is that we would very much like to have them here; the copies we have now show how valuable they are. I will let you know."[14] Nearly ten years later, the collection found a home in the Earl G. Swem Library at the College of William & Mary in Virginia. It seems the Morgan Library was not interested after all; this is unsurprising given that institution's focus on manuscripts and rare books. However, this anecdote reveals how Tucker viewed his collection, feeling it was worthy of the Morgan Library's selective acquisition practices.

In 1987, Tucker's research materials arrived at William & Mary. Although he had no affiliation with the institution, Tucker chose the state school because he was a "Virginian by birth" and held the university in high esteem. He had also been friendly with the man for whom the university's main library is named.[15] Before depositing them, Tucker meticulously organized his materials into scrapbook volumes, which he numbered 1 through 109 and arranged both chronologically and by specialized subject (figs. 6.1 and 6.2). Tucker felt that the volumes of notes, article clippings, photocopied chapters from rare and hard-to-find books, research correspondence, and photocopies of rare documents would "form a solid research tool for scholars who will consult them in the future." Not simply content to have his finished books, *A Goodly Heritage* and *Jane Austen the Woman*, serve the interests of future scholars, he viewed the notes and collected research materials to be the real prize. His cousin Susan Rainwater described to me Tucker's tendency to "let the facts fall where they may" in his research. Regarding his genealogical findings, she described his genuine hope that others would "carry on [his] research in a rigorous fashion" and assured me he would hold no ill will should someone find shortcomings to correct. He was content to allow others to follow behind him and pick up where he left off or even to discover faults in his work for themselves.[16]

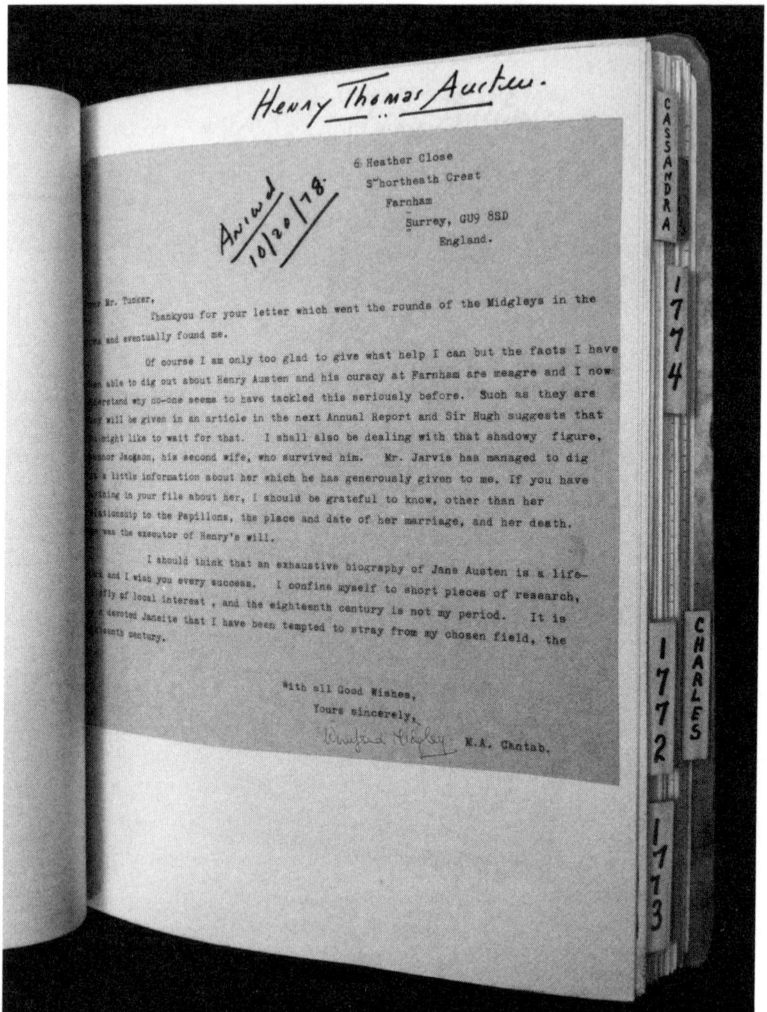

Fig. 6.1. Tucker Collection, vol. 3. Many volumes include correspondence from sources in England verifying genealogical and geographical information. This page shows a response Tucker received from a Winifred Midgely in Surrey regarding an inquiry about Henry Thomas Austen. Note the organizational scheme visible on the fore-edge of the binder. George H. Tucker Jane Austen Research Collection, Special Collections, Swem Library, William & Mary. Photo by author.

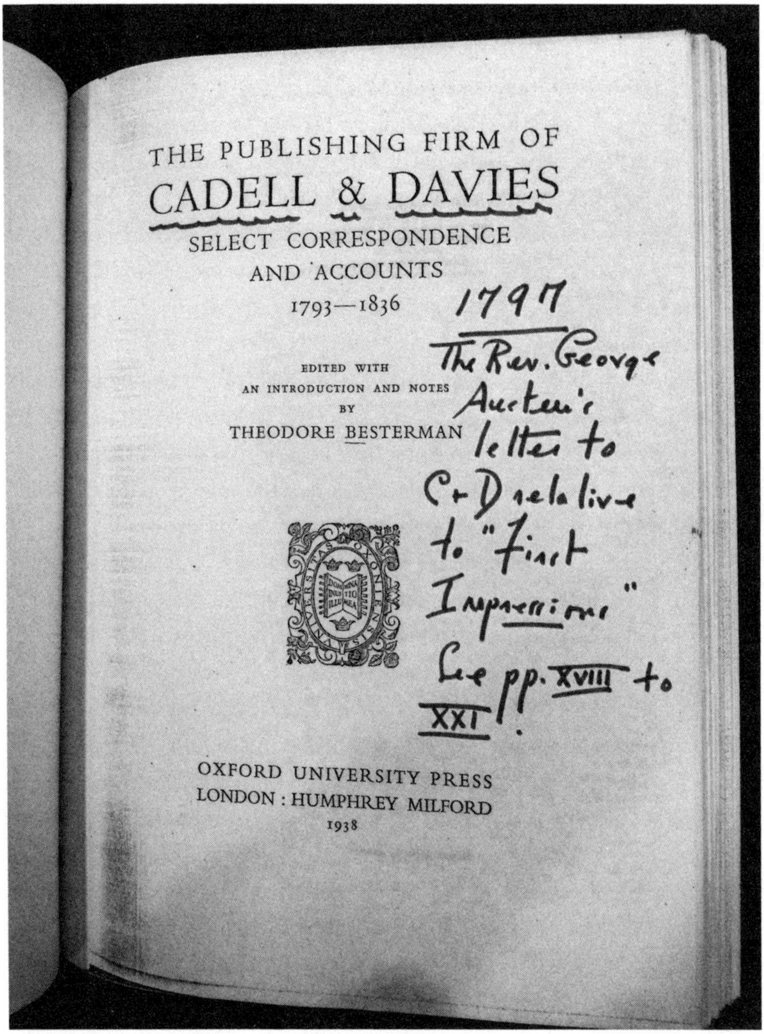

Fig. 6.2. Tucker Collection, vol. 36. Photocopies of pertinent chapters from reference books are found throughout the notebooks. This example relates to correspondence in 1797 between Rev. George Austen and the publishing firm of Cadell & Davies regarding Jane Austen's early version of *Pride and Prejudice*, then called *First Impressions*. George H. Tucker Jane Austen Research Collection, Special Collections, Swem Library, William & Mary. Photo by author.

Ninety-six of the volumes that comprise the research collection are bound with ACCO brand pressboard report covers with adjustable metal prong fasteners; the final thirteen volumes are in metal prong-fastened report folders. The volumes are organized either by year or subject or else by subject presented chronologically. For example, volumes 4–14 are titled "Jane Austen Personal and General Chronology" and cover the years of her life 1775–1817; volumes 37 and 38 are devoted to *Mansfield Park* and *Emma*, respectively; volumes 56–84 address particular topics as they relate to Austen's life and works, such as "Jane Austen and the Theatre" and "Jane Austen and Decorative Arts." The volumes include pages photocopied from books from which Tucker carefully culled details related to particular topics and then organized alongside relevant research correspondence and his own notes and marginalia. In some instances, photocopied chapters and notes appear in more than one notebook when the subject matter overlaps across the timeline or subject matter of more than one volume.

It is evident that Tucker created the organizational scheme specifically for the presentation of these materials to Swem Library, as opposed to having kept them organized this way while using the research notes for book writing. Many of the pressboard covers have several layers of large white sticker labels on the covers, indicating that these covers, with their nonpermanent, adjustable bindings, had been reused many times, each time with a new label placed on top of older ones to explain the contents. Also, some volumes contain photocopied pages from book chapters that Tucker annotated in pen and then photocopied again in the process of organizing the materials into the scrapbooks. In many cases, he cut these photocopies down to a smaller page size and then pasted them onto a loose leaf of paper to be placed in the notebook. The effect of this labor-intensive arrangement is an uncluttered presentation that resembles a finished product. For Tucker, the act of preparing the notebooks for the archive, and the idea of sharing his actual research as a vital resource for others, appears to have been as valuable and gratifying as being published. The notebooks serve as a material expression of his thoroughness, documenting his research process and, more to the point, performing the act of devotion that his research represented.

If the publication of a book is one's goal, then one does not need to go to such lengths to curate one's process; rather, Tucker's intentions and aspirations appear to have been closer to those of a fan and collector than those of a scholar. In the description and index that Tucker provided to Swem Library upon his bequest, he says, "The books are numbered 1 through 96, and should be kept in that order to facilitate easy research." He adds that the collection should "be kept intact . . . as a source for Jane Austen biographical scholars all over the United States. The material is carefully arranged, and should serve scholars as a ready reference archive."[17] The redundancy of these statements illustrates that he wished to put a fine point on the value of the contents as well as the intellectual labor of organizing them for further use. It is telling that he calls the scrapbook volumes "books," as if publishing his research was not actually as important to Tucker as documenting the assiduousness of his process and facilitating the sharing of knowledge by making available the sources he uncovered.

Tucker felt strongly that he was making a substantial contribution to William & Mary's collections, placing the university in the selective company of other institutions with important Austen-related collections, such as Goucher College. He explains: "The collection of notes being given at this time constitutes what is perhaps the best assemblage in this country from original sources of material on Jane Austen and her family connections. It contains hundreds of letters from authorities in England and America on various phases of the ancestry and connections of Jane Austen and is without parallel either here or in England."[18] Sadly, the eight large boxes of materials Tucker gave to Swem Library were acquisitioned and then forgotten; they were never fully processed (which is understandable, considering how thorough his organizational scheme was) and were unused until I rediscovered them. Tucker could not have foreseen that the internet and digital scholarship would make physical collections like his redundant. Much of the material he had painstakingly acquired by mail and then included in his scrapbooks is available now online. Even items such as rare commemorative pamphlets and brochures depicting Austen sites in England can sometimes be found for sale or digitized online. However, all of the wonderful correspondence with Austen scholars and fans and with English registrars, librarians, and mayors remains unique. Most of these individuals were quite genuinely pleased to help an American with his research and touched by his interest in their minute corner of the Austen landscape. Their letters will remain a unique and important part of the Tucker collection.

Being an independent scholar with no formal training in history or biography—and indeed, no college education—it appears Tucker struggled to get his Austen research published. Six years elapsed between finishing his manuscript and seeing it in print. He was a professional writer, but without the credentials typical of other Austen biographers, he labored to attain respect. He found it vital to attain for each of his books a foreword by a vaunted scholar or person of scholarly rank to lend credibility to his work. The books do not include biographical information about the author and his credentials. The back cover of *Jane Austen the Woman* says simply that Tucker is the "author of *A Goodly Heritage*," the reputation of his previous book serving as the strongest available recommendation for the current one, and that he is a "retired reporter and columnist for the *Virginian-Pilot* and *Ledger-Star*."

In a letter to Tucker written just prior to the publication of *A Goodly Heritage*, Joan Austen-Leigh, a descendant of Jane Austen living in Canada and founding member of JASNA, wrote that she longed to hear news of his book: "It does so *deserve* to be published. It's awful the way Brian S[outham]. & Co. have JA sewn up as if she were some sort of limited company. And that business of plagiarism of *your* discovery was shameful."[19] Given her emphasis of *your* and her expressed aversion to what she perceived as scholar Brian Southam's monopoly on research, it seems she was aware that Tucker had been seeking a publisher without much success and was taking his side.

It is revealing that Tucker included this rather personal letter in a scrapbook volume, as it holds statements by Austen-Leigh that she might have found embarrassing should they be made known. That Austen-Leigh, a direct descendant of Austen, had written spiritedly in support of his worthiness for publication and offered a personal vote of confidence in his work must have been particularly significant for Tucker. It is perhaps the type of letter that a scholar might rather exclude from a collection intended to become a rare and important—and public—research collection. Yet how could Tucker resist including a letter in his research scrapbooks that validates his work and the collection itself? The content of the letter adds little to the scholarly value of the scrapbook but certainly lends credibility to his process and offers the cachet of a direct connection to Jane Austen through one of her descendants.

Like Alberta Burke, Tucker deemed no detail too insignificant to be included in his scrapbooks. For instance, in the volume for the years 1807–10 on "Austen's General and Personal Chronology," Tucker includes several photocopied sections from R. A. Austen-Leigh's *Jane Austen and Southampton* (1949), including a chapter on the Austen's neighbors, one of whom, William Fitzhugh, was a naval acquaintance, according to a marginal note by Tucker. The chapter describes how Mrs. Fitzhugh was a devoted admirer of the actress Mrs. Siddons and would "encamp herself in the actress's dressing-room at the theatre and help to dress [her]."[20] This colorful description is precisely the type of minute insider knowledge that fans crave and enjoy sharing. And in this case, the reference itself is about a type of fandom.

The scrapbooks contain several examples that both reveal how Tucker went about researching obscure details and illustrate the pleasure he took in sharing knowledge. In his biographical work *Jane Austen the Woman* (1994), Tucker lays to rest a false (albeit minute) assumption found in earlier biographies of Austen: that Austen did not have a pianoforte during the period of her life between 1801, when she left her childhood home at Steventon, until 1809, when she moved to Chawton Cottage. This is a small point but one of great interest to those fascinated by Austen's lifestyle and affinities. Tucker points out in *Jane Austen the Woman* that two pages from an account book from 1807 survived that prove she rented a pianoforte while living in Castle Square, Southampton, and references an article about this fact printed in the Jane Austen Society (UK) Annual Report of 1980 by Patrick Piggott.[21] Yet in scrapbook volume 11, which documents a chronology of Austen's life for the years 1807–10, Tucker included a photocopy of the manuscript account book pages provided to him by the Morgan Library, offering the original evidence.[22] Although he possessed a copy of the primary document that proved Austen's access to a musical instrument, a detail that had been missed by previous biographers, he supported his argument with a secondary resource by a scholar who had come upon the account book pages at around the same time as Tucker. Furthermore, he was not content with collecting only one resource or the other but went to the trouble to ensure he included both the primary source and the article by Piggott in his collection. This example demonstrates Tucker's thoroughness as well as his inclination toward a cooperative circulation of knowledge like that found in fandom.

When Tucker had the good fortune to receive a copy from a fellow scholar of an unpublished poem by Jane Austen's nephew James Edward Austen-Leigh, he was eager to share it. He sent the poem to others who he felt would appreciate having access to a previously unavailable piece of Austenalia, even if it was a terrible, almost embarrassing piece of writing. Joan Austen-Leigh wrote thanks to Tucker for sending it to her: "My goodness—it is long and rambling and pretentious, isn't it? More Victorian than Georgian. What an out-pouring. . . . Anyway I am most interested & glad to have it—thank you very much." Austen-Leigh did not particularly care for the poem, but she was nonetheless happy to have it. The "having" of unique items as well as knowledge is central to the fan's experience and pleasure. There is the thrill of the chase that collectors experience, and then there is the joy of sharing the spoils with those who will appreciate them. Moreover, Tucker included not just the poem but also Austen-Leigh's letter of thanks in his notebook collection, making material the experience of both having and sharing.

George Holbert Tucker was a scholar without formal training whose research on Austen represents both the recognized, institutionalized labor of academics and the pleasure-seeking labor of love of fans. Through their scope and organizational fastidiousness, his research scrapbooks perform the rigor of his research, his obsession with Austen, and his love of sharing knowledge that motivated his work. Tucker organized his research materials into scrapbooks specifically to make them accessible through a research institution, revealing his desires and the pleasure he took in this labor.

7

The Jane Austen Scrapbook of David Gilson, Bibliographer and Correspondent

David John Gilson (1936–2014) was a librarian at the Taylor Institution Library, part of the Bodleian Libraries at Oxford University, for over thirty years. In 1964, he noticed gaps in the 1929 Jane Austen bibliography by Geoffrey Keynes and felt there might be "room for an article" to fill them.[1] He soon discovered one thing after another, and upon bringing his findings to Keynes, the elder scholar suggested that Gilson collaborate with him on compiling an expanded second edition of the bibliography. Eventually, Gilson's work took on its own life, becoming the 877-page *Bibliography of Jane Austen* that he published in 1982 and reissued in 1997.

Although he was not an American Austen fan like the others, I include a chapter on Gilson for two reasons. First, he corresponded with each of the other Austen enthusiasts discussed in part II. His letters to Alberta Burke, Barbara Winn Adams, and George Tucker—penned in neat, tiny script on blue airmail paper—can be found in the personal papers and scrapbooks of all three Americans.[2] Second, like the individuals discussed earlier, Gilson created a scrapbook that embodies his passion for Jane Austen.[3] From correspondence with Nancy Magnuson, former college librarian for Goucher, I learned that this was the only Austen scrapbook created by Gilson but that he also made scrapbooks of French and English fine and decorative arts of the eighteenth and nineteenth centuries. These remain with Gilson's family. In 2013, the Austen scrapbook arrived at Goucher College, to "dovetail with Alberta's scrapbook collection."[4]

David Gilson, like George Tucker, did less collecting than Alberta Burke or Barbara Winn Adams; instead of amassing things, he collected knowledge. Gilson monitored other's collecting and researched the whereabouts of rare editions of Austen and other books of interest. He relied on the generosity of other collectors and experts who were willing to open their collections to him for his research. By sharing the riches of their collections and knowledge with Gilson, these collectors ensured yet another avenue to immortality for themselves and their connection to Austen—by being included in his *Bibliography.* Alberta Burke received a hearty note of gratitude in Gilson's acknowledgments in the front matter of his book, and her letters to the *Times Literary Supplement* supplying information about items in her collection were included in both Gilson's *Bibliography* and his scrapbook.

The pages of Gilson's scrapbooks demonstrate in equal measure his desire to contribute intellectually to the field of Austen studies through a much-needed bibliography and his personal affection for Austen's novels and her world. The juxtaposition of different types of cuttings throughout the scrapbook and the clues provided by his marginalia and annotations offer a glimpse into Gilson's imbricated experience of both intellect and sentiment regarding his Austen-related pursuits. As a librarian at Oxford, he had skills and predilections suited to bibliography, yet the decades of labor he devoted to his mammoth *Bibliography of Jane Austen* were peripheral to his professional life. Gilson's scrapbook may have helped him impose order on a long-term, large-scale project.

The scrapbook, bound by a black textured cover (10.25 by 12 in.) stamped in gold with the words *Cathedral News Cuttings Book,* holds 120 neat and organized pages, each filled front and back.[5] It seems likely that Gilson began working on the scrapbook in the 1960s, when he became interested in conducting bibliographic research. The scrapbook includes cuttings from as early as 1920 and as late as 1972. Gilson's bookplate appears on the inside cover. The center of the first page features a collectible cigarette card of a small, color portrait of Austen,[6] around which are arranged several images of the church at Steventon where Jane Austen's father was rector and clippings from 1934 related to her early life there. The first page establishes the topic of the scrapbook and sets the tone, sentimentally surrounding the small cigarette card portrait of Austen with images of the places she called home for the first twenty-five years of her life. This page is representative of much of the scrapbook: most of the pages in the book are organized around a theme, and many include images of places and objects from Austen's life or which celebrate her life.

As one might expect of a librarian and bibliographer, many of Gilson's annotations of the press cuttings, postcards, and photographs included within the scrapbook were thorough, giving the date and publication information and occasionally offering context. In several instances, however, he neglected to include annotation, leaving the cuttings to speak for themselves. This inconsistency suggests that in certain instances it was not the source of the material that mattered to Gilson but what it evoked. Moreover, the juxtaposition of carefully annotated cuttings correlated to his *Bibliography* and unannotated ones intended to delight or amuse illustrates how Gilson's subjective attachment to Austen was both industrious and affective. In some cases, the items left unidentified seem to have been included for aesthetic reasons or purely for fun. On a page containing article clippings from the 1930s, which he carefully annotated with publication information, he also included several very small cuttings without date or attribution. These brief, scathing, and sometimes humorous quips appear to have been letters to the editor, in which Austen fans expressed objection to an offhand remark in a recent article dismissive of Austen's popularity. One stated, "I wonder why your Liverpool correspondent describes Jane Austen's novel *Pride and Prejudice* as 'now practically forgotten,' and whether he can offer any evidence of such widespread forgetfulness." Gilson tacked this pithy commentary from knowledgeable Janeites onto the bottom of a page of otherwise dry articles, the juxtaposition suggesting in material form the overlay of labor and pleasure integral to Gilson's devotion to Austen.

Dozens of reviews and articles listed in his published *Bibliography of Jane Austen* appear as cuttings in the scrapbook. Gilson seems to have included in his scrapbook things that held personal interest for him or which he found somehow amusing. When he annotated cuttings of pieces listed in the bibliography, he seems to have written the date and publication information at the time he pasted the clipping into the book, and later, in pencil or a different ink color, he added the corresponding entry number from the bibliography. Presumably, these later annotations were added around 1982, when the *Bibliography* was published. By taking this extra step, he linked the published bibliography to the scrapbook in a personally meaningful way. For example, he included "The Chawton Letters," a piece of epistolary parody from *Punch*, from June 1963, written from the perspective of various characters from Austen's novels who weigh in with advice for a gentleman about a peculiar matter. An annotation beside the clipping says, "Gilson L33," indicating the number he assigned this entry in the list of miscellaneous works in his *Bibliography*.

Whereas many of the cuttings relate directly to Gilson's bibliographic research, others do not but, rather, seem to have been included for their personal significance or purely aesthetic interest. One page holds colorful facsimile frontispieces and title pages of a late-nineteenth-century edition of *Sense and Sensibility*, removed from a copy of Keynes's bibliography. Among the final pages of the scrapbook are several cuttings that concern radio and television adaptations. One page holds a complete set of clippings from three consecutive weeks in October 1972, related to a four-part adaptation of *Mansfield Park* for radio. The final page of the scrapbook is covered in press cuttings related to the 1971 BBC television serial adaptation of *Sense and Sensibility*, including images of the actors in costume. Whereas Burke and Winn Adams were both captivated by MGM's 1940 rendition of *Pride and Prejudice*, Gilson, of a later generation, seems to have been taken with the more accurate retellings and period-appropriate costumes of the later adaptations.[7]

Living in England, David Gilson had the advantage of being able to visit Austen-related sites more easily than the American collectors discussed here. Yet his proximity did little to quell his desire to include images of Austen lore in his scrapbook. Two pages include a portion of an article from the British magazine *Women's Realm*, from July 1967, which is composed of mostly color images. It is apparent that he only clipped the portions of the article that contained images and understandably did not bother to include the remaining fatuous text. The images depict places familiar to Austen in Bath, including the Royal Crescent, Assembly Rooms, and the house where Austen lived as well as pictures from Chawton and an illustration from a book that evokes the clothing style and manners of the period. In contrast with the majority of the scrapbook, the inclusion of this color magazine spread reveals Gilson's appreciation for the aesthetic of Austen's era, beyond his academic interest in supplying the world with a comprehensive bibliography.

Of the four Austen enthusiasts in this chapter, Gilson is the most scholarly by traditional standards. His association with Oxford University and the immense success of his bibliography are testament to his abilities as a scholar and his professionalism as a librarian. Because of this, it may seem most incongruous of all to discuss Gilson within the context of a discussion about scrapbooking as an activity of fandom. Yet due to his credentials and the seriousness of his bibliographic undertaking, his scrapbook—which reveals the same serious devotion mixed with lighthearted fascination as the others—underscores my argument best. Gilson's Austen scrapbook embodies the academic labor he undertook and the love for Austen that drove his ambition. The scrapbook, like the others discussed here, is an effigy, a tangible representation of his labor of love, to be cherished, shared, and eventually entered into the archive, achieving immortality for the object and the man. The scrapbook is a representation of a life's work that performs for its audience something of the creator, making permanent the punctuations and ephemeral moments in a lifetime of researching, discovering, reading, and loving Austen. It is no coincidence that these four individuals felt the need to create material objects that lent permanence to an otherwise ephemeral experience.

Epilogue

LOVE STORIES

Cultural theorist Jean Baudrillard viewed collecting as narcissistic and imbued with a desire to see in oneself an "absolutely singular being" by possessing objects that are singular.[1] Baudrillard saw collecting as ultimately isolating and antisocial, with the "idiom" of social discourse created by the collector being too closed to have value for others and the discourse of the collection only capable of orientation toward oneself.[2] The correspondence of these four Austen collectors and the interconnectedness of their worlds belie Baudrillard's claim. David Gilson corresponded with all three American collectors. Alberta Burke and Barbara Winn Adams never met, but Winn Adams, Henry Burke, and George Tucker were all present at the 1980 Annual General Meeting of JASNA, the first full AGM to follow the organization's inaugural meeting in New York in 1979. Jack Grey, a founder of JASNA and another Austen collector, wrote a letter to Barbara Winn Adams in 1982 that neatly illustrates the connections between these individuals: in it, he praises David Gilson's bibliography, expresses a wish to see Barbara's own bibliographic work covering 1929–41, and says: "I long to peruse Alberta Burke's scrapbooks at Goucher. So—when that happens we may meet and compare notes. I know that you will compare notes with David for the period that your work encompasses and I hope that you would share any discrepancies with me. And him, too."[3] These individuals were connected to each other through their love of Austen; even when not sharing their enthusiasm socially, they were engaged in friendly and mutually beneficial sharing of knowledge and resources. To counter

Baudrillard's more pessimistic view of the isolating nature of collection, I offer the words of Henry Burke: "I think all collections, particularly book collections, are necessarily love stories."[4]

The collections and intellectual labor of Burke, Winn Adams, Tucker, and Gilson were documented in their respective scrapbooks. Scrapbooks, historian Katherine Ott says, "turn a mere existence into a life" by giving it shape and order through a core narrative.[5] The scrapbooks of all four individuals share a core narrative of the celebration and love of Jane Austen through the pursuit of material objects, articles, and books and the garnering of knowledge related to Austen. Each individual used his or her scrapbook(s) as a creative way of participating in literary culture through thoughtful reuse of print material. The scrapbooks are purely the work neither of academics nor fans. Their materiality lends them authority, being similar to published books, and yet they can be kept private if desired. Like academic research, which requires diligence and sustained interest, these scrapbooks were maintained over long periods of time. Yet as scrapbooks, they are understood as the product of a labor of love. These individuals filled leisure hours with scrapbooking about Austen as a way of both intellectually and emotionally engaging with the beloved author, and while all four were quite serious in their obsessive pursuit of all things Austen, their scrapbooks—qua scrapbooks—cannot be viewed as purely academic or literary. Each of the scrapbooks discussed in part II can be understood as a reflection of the unstable movement these individuals negotiated between subjectivities as fans, connoisseurs, and scholars. Ultimately I suggest these scrapbooks are most indicative of the practices, desires, and habits of fans.

Performativity in fandom occurs both in everyday life and in liminal spaces apart from the quotidian. Part II has shown how material creations of fans such as scrapbooks offer opportunities for performance in everyday life through interaction with and creation of these objects, which act as surrogates for ephemeral lived experiences now passed. Austen fans engage with the repertoire of Jane Austen in material ways as a course of everyday life, and this interaction offers opportunities to relive and revive affective engagement and experiences.

In part III, I explore a mode of fan activity that functions much as scrapbooking and the collecting of material objects do. The writing (and reading) of fanfiction and the rich engagement with adaptations enabled by recent digital media such as Tumblr and YouTube offer a way of engaging with the beloved text within everyday life and curating that experience. Like the scrapbooking described here, these activities are performative and are a means of seeking a surrogate to keep alive meaningful, affective experiences of a more ephemeral and/or liminal nature. Just as 1940 was a significant year for Austen lovers, with the release of the first major film adaptation of *Pride and Prejudice*, 1995 was likewise a watershed moment, thanks to the release of the BBC television serial adaptation of the novel staring Colin Firth as Mr. Darcy. With that beloved adaptation occurring simultaneously with the rapid growth and accessibility of the internet, Jane Austen fandom was poised for a surge. Scrapbooking was to the twentieth-century fan what FanFiction.net, Tumblr, and YouTube have become in the internet age. Now digital, the format and media of collected and curated fan creations have changed, but the impulse remains the same, and the habits of engagement remain remarkably similar.

III

SENSE AND VISIBILITY

Digital Fandom and Archontic Works in the Internet Age

Prologue

In 1998, the front cover of the newsletter for the Jane Austen Society of North America, *JASNA News*, boasted the existence of "Fifty-Six and Counting" sequels to Austen novels.[1] Of those listed, fifteen were published in only three years, between 1995 and 1998; countless more were soon to follow. While readers have long thirsted for more stories about the beloved characters and circumstances found within the novels of Jane Austen, sequels and spin-offs have exploded since the BBC brought Andrew Davies's adaptation of *Pride and Prejudice* to life in 1995. Colin Firth's wet shirt moment has been called the "Big Bang" of Austenmania.[2] From then on, Jane Austen fandom escalated and intensified in ways never before seen, thanks to the ubiquity of screen adaptations. With six different Austen adaptations appearing in 1995 and 1996 alone, visits to Austen tourist sites such as Jane Austen's House Museum at Chawton began to increase significantly.[3] This moment was propitious for Austen fans, as it was also poised on the cusp of widespread access to the internet, which brought digital resources to fans, enabling them to expand their practices and widen their reach in unprecedented ways.

In part I, I introduced three categories of fan activities visible in nineteenth-century literary fandom. Here I return to the creation and circulation of archontic works that include spin-offs and fanfiction but which also include visual culture creations of a similar nature. Fan creations that manipulate footage from screen adaptations into visual archontic works share a great deal with fanfiction.[4] Moreover, I recognize the influence visual culture exerts on archontic literary works. Fans create, read, view, and share these works as a means to engage with their favorite texts. I suggest the influence of visual culture on these creations enhances fans' affective experiences. By embracing a broad understanding of archontic works to also include fan-created, intertextual visual creations like those circulated on social media sites such as Tumblr, we can better understand how visual culture in the age of the internet is crucial to fan practices and affective experiences.

New media scholar Abigail De Kosnik introduced the term *archontic* to describe fanfiction in place of terms such as *derivative*, which typically carry a negative connotation.[5] As discussed in chapter 3, she adapted *archontic* from Jacques Derrida's notion that the text is an archive, a world forever expanding and never truly closed. *Archontic* is a useful term even if its boundaries are unstable and difficult to pin down. It emphasizes the intertextuality at the heart of works that creatively seek to take part in the world of an original text.[6] It does not differentiate between amateur fanfiction and professional spin-offs, instead recognizing that they share a common set of practices and genre conventions. It carries a less negative connotation than words such as *imitative* or *derivative*, and it can be used to refer to a range of expressive media and genre, which includes but is not limited to fanfiction. As a result, the concept tends helpfully to destabilize notions about canon and hierarchy, tools traditionally used to marginalize women's creative work. Fanfiction is predominantly written and circulated by women and other marginalized groups. Understanding fanfiction as part of a larger textual archive and within a varied set of creative practices helps recuperate these practices and recover them from the margins. This is not to claim iconoclastically that Austen fanfiction shares the same lasting value and quality as the original novels but, rather, to suggest that it promotes an understanding that these overlapping texts are important to those who enjoy creating and reading them.

As critic Sheenagh Pugh has argued, there are many forms of writing that do not normally fall under the category of fanfiction but share its features, such as works that draw inspiration from a canon of characters or myths—such as King Arthur or Robin Hood—and recycle tropes and characters throughout various retellings.[7] De Kosnik suggests that a work such as David Henry Hwang's *M. Butterfly*, a play based on Puccini's opera *Madame Butterfly*, should be viewed as archontic. It shares common traits with fanfiction in the ways that it deviates from the original while making clear allusions and citations to the original.[8] Moreover, Puccini's opera was based on a libretto taken from numerous previous sources, making both the opera and Hwang's modern adaptation for theater examples of archontic literature—part of an ever-expanding archive of texts. Placing fanfiction in a wider category of expressive forms offers more useful analytical frameworks for understanding its genre conventions.

The writing of Austen-inspired archontic fiction that began in the nineteenth century has grown into a much broader and more widely accessible set of practices. Today the visual nature of screen adaptations heavily influences these practices. Scholars have given a great deal of attention to the adaptation of literature into film.[9] I explore how visual renderings of literature influence the greater intertextual world of a popular novel and the practices and experiences of fans. Many Austen fans claim they were first introduced to Austen through an adaptation. After falling in love with the characters and story on screen, many fans seek the experience of reading the novels. Some Austen scholars have argued that the novels themselves carry a filmic sensibility with aural and visual components.[10] Adaptations offer readers a common visualization and visual language for imagining settings and characters. They foster fan communities by allowing writers and readers of fanfiction to take pleasure collectively in sharing a familiarity with that visual language.

The internet has made the presence of fandoms and fan communities more widely known and accessible around the world than previously possible, but the practices of fans remain essentially the same today as in the past. Digital media has expanded, providing new means to produce archontic creations—both visual and literary—as well as to share and curate them within a fan community.[11] Today's fan creations demonstrate new ways in which to remix, reshape, and edit existing materials with ease, but the essential urge to manipulate media remains unchanged from past eras. For instance, the material and visual practices of scrapbooking resemble the cutting and pasting of digital scraps enabled today by sites such as Tumblr and Pinterest.[12] I suggest that in function, digital archontic works such as Tumblr posts are equivalent to analog material objects such as scrapbooks in the practices of fans. It is the role of surrogation in fan practices that allows us to trace continuity across time and media environments. Both the creation and reception of archontic forms, including fanfiction and visual creations on Tumblr, are acts of surrogation, a search for a replacement for something now lost. As I have suggested, fans seek ways of reengaging with beloved texts. For Austen fans, these acts of surrogation—through the creating, sharing, or curating of fan works—aim to nostalgically preserve what they love about Austen even as they remake it as well as to preserve what they love about the experience of reading and watching Austen.

As mentioned, fandom has been described as taking two predominant forms: transformational and affirmational. Whereas transformational fan practices attempt to subvert intended meanings, affirmational fandom restates the source material, observing canonical rules and norms regarding characters and the central concepts of the text.[13] Fan studies scholars tend to celebrate transformational works over affirmational ones; however, I have found that Jane Austen fans employ a dynamic set of affirmational practices that seek to restate Austen's core narratives, rarely challenging them, even when adapting and modernizing Austen through archontic creations.

Archontic works, whether created by fans or as products of the culture industry, and whether affirmational or transformational, are created for an audience with deep knowledge of the beloved text and engagement in the intertextual archive the text inhabits. Soon after the 1995 BBC adaptation of *Pride and Prejudice* brought to life the idea of Mr. Darcy emerging from a lake wearing a wet, clinging shirt and breeches, spin-off novels and films began to appear that depicted not only Austen's world but also the lives and desires of Austen fans. One scene, in particular, from ITV's television miniseries *Lost in Austen* (2008), illustrates the rich imbrication of visual and literary culture in today's vast body of Austen-related archontic works. After twenty-first-century heroine Amanda Price and Mr. Darcy have finally professed their mutual love, Amanda asks Darcy for a favor: that he remove his cravat, coat, and waistcoat and submerge himself in Pemberley's ornamental lake for her amusement. He complies, standing waist-deep in water in a clingy, wet, white shirt; she watches in wonder, saying, "I am having a bit of a strange postmodern moment here." In this moment, Amanda, an Austen fan who has attained the love of the "real" Mr. Darcy, has him imitate the actions of Colin Firth's Mr. Darcy. Like Amanda, the audience has seen the BBC *Pride and Prejudice,* making this a postmodern moment for them as well. This adaptation quotes a key visual aspect of the earlier adaptation, relying on the audience's knowledge and playing into its members' fantasies.

This use of intertextuality in *Lost in Austen* relies on an audience that has seen other available adaptations, even if they have not read the novels. An archontic work's reception requires an audience with the knowledge to understand and appreciate the allusions and playful nuances that simultaneously set the work apart from and align it with the original. Being an audience to fan works through reading fanfiction or viewing Tumblr blogs is as important to fan practices as creating these archontic works. The reception of such works becomes a means for fans to perform their love of a text and their subjectivity as fans and to display their competence within the fandom's knowledge community. In many cases, such performances by fans take the form of creating more archontic works, themselves adding to the archive.

In the following three chapters, I consider archontic literary and visual works that share several characteristics: they rely heavily on Austen's novels; they are notable for a reliance on intertextuality; and they carry a prominent and unique visual culture component. Distinctions between the material, visual, and literary have become increasingly blurred within the creative practices of Jane Austen fans, thanks to the impact of internet culture on fandom and the prevalence of screen adaptations. In chapter 8, I explore how visual creations by fans found on Tumblr rely on long-established practices. Although they take digital form, the ways in which these creations are archived and shared greatly resemble scrapbooking practices. Moreover, continuity from analog to digital archontic practices is legible in both the impulses these practices represent as well as in the role archontic works perform in fans' engagement through surrogation. The Tumblr platform and its unique characteristics have made space for a dynamic online Austen fandom. In chapter 9, I discuss the YouTube web series *The Lizzie Bennet Diaries* (2012), a narrative adaptation that utilizes visual culture conventions of the internet as well as intertextual allusions to other adaptations of *Pride and Prejudice*. This serial adaptation illustrates how fan activities have influenced visual culture and how visual culture has influenced fan culture. The final chapter in part III turns to Austen-related fanfiction, paying special attention to visual aspects employed by writers and the responses of their readers found in online comments. All of the archontic works discussed in this chapter rely on a complicated intertextuality between Austen's novels and their adaptations. Throughout part III, I focus on works related specifically to *Pride and Prejudice*, which has received the most attention from fans over the years. Whether regarding the visual or the literary or a combination of the two, the topics in part III share a connection to the world—or archive—of Jane Austen and a common means for fans to connect to that world through creation and reception.

8

Pride and Polyjuice

THE VISUAL CULTURE OF INTERNET FANDOM

Tumblr is a veritable internet playground where one can find everything from *National Geographic* photography to quilting patterns, cute animals, web comics, and, until recently, pornography. Tumblr is an essentially archontic space: itself an archive of sorts, fans use Tumblr to create, curate, and share visual and textual works. It provides a space where original source material—including novels, films, television series, and comics—come together with fan creations and adaptations, interacting in new ways and adding to the archive of the original text. Henry Jenkins has claimed that the internet has helped fandom diversify and move away from a cult status toward a cultural mainstream.[1] Tumblr is evidence of this trend; the platform was not created for fandom specifically but has organically become a space for fan cultures. Furthermore, Jenkins suggests that recent changes brought about by internet culture have made possible an online lifestyle for many that make it easier for fans to remain connected to each other and to constantly circulate new information. Whereas fandom was once a "weekend only world," in which fans could connect only in person a few times a year, they can now interact daily or even hourly.[2] Tumblr is a platform that makes this possible, and it is an archive, continually documenting the entire milieu.

With over 435 million individual blogs, Tumblr touts itself as a platform for "the world's creators."[3] Unlike other social media such as Facebook or Pinterest, the Tumblr platform allows users to customize in infinite ways (including by writing code), so they can be creative with the style of their presentation as well as their content. Similar to "liking" or "friending" on Facebook, a Tumblr user "follows" other users. Posts from followed blogs appear on a user's dashboard, which presents a never-ending scrolling page of recently posted items. Blog posts can take one of several possible formats: text posts; sets of photos and/or GIFs (graphic interchange format images), with or without text captions;[4] quotations; links to content such as fanfiction hosted on other platforms; chat posts, which allow users to present imagined or real conversations in a pithy way; audio files; or videos. This range of post types makes for great variety, yet the platform's uploading protocol makes posts appear fairly uniform when presented on a dashboard. The interface is therefore appealingly tidy and uncluttered. The platform is easy to use, and its policies are clearly stated. For all these reasons, and because of its especially visual nature, Tumblr has become a playground of fandom.

These days, however, not all fandoms play on Tumblr as they once did. On December 3, 2018, Tumblr announced a ban on all things pornographic, and two weeks later, it implemented the ban. In response to Tumblr's declaration against adult content, many bloggers promised they would abandon the site on principle alone.[5] Outraged fans who had spent years building communities and sharing content (some of which is now disallowed) declared they would jump ship for other platforms, and it seems many have. Within only two months of the ban on adult content, Tumblr's web traffic dropped by nearly 30 percent.[6] As I write this, it is too soon to tell what the long-term impact of this highly controversial decision will be on the fan communities, artists, and sex workers who relied on Tumblr as an affirming space (much of the adult content was distinctly feminist and LGBTQ-friendly) and, in some instances, for a livelihood (artists and sex workers made safe spaces for themselves in which they controlled their own content and business model).[7]

Yet if 30 percent of traffic to Tumblr has evaporated, 70 percent still remains, and I suspect that many who have stayed on the platform belong to communities such as the Jane Austen fandom. Of the Austen-related Tumblr blogs I studied for roughly six months, beginning in fall 2014, those that remained active in 2019 seem unchanged in the aftermath of the adult content ban. The corners of Tumblr that tend to be more affirmational than transformational also tend to be less pornographic and therefore seem to have been unscathed by Tumblr's strike against free expression.

Although the Tumblr platform can be used in a variety of ways and users can share many types of blog posts on any conceivable topic, I will focus here on visually based blog posts, which consist mostly of photo and GIF sets created by bloggers who self-identify as fans. Fans also post an array of "fanart," original art inspired by beloved texts. Since it is relatively scant compared to that generated by other fandoms, I do not address Austen-inspired fanart here; I focus, instead, on how bloggers recirculate graphics taken from screen adaptations, adding to the archive of archontic works. The fan creations found on Tumblr, based heavily on the visual appeal of the world of Austen on screen, are neither purely visual nor purely textual, and the conventions at work are influenced by the conventions of fanfiction.

Usually a blogger's username (which also constitutes a blog's URL) and blog description (found in the blog header) reveal that person's interests; for instance, the blog "Fuck Yeah Janeites!" describes itself as being "dedicated to the one and only Jane Austen, whose stories and words still resonate with us all."[8] Many bloggers describe their page as "multi-fandom," such as user hulksmashsmaug, who claims, "This blog is mostly Marvel, Tolkien, some Hunger Games & Harry Potter, and its cast. Plus, anything that I find interesting & funny."[9] Blogs such as these display numerous pages of posts depicting sets of screen-captured images, called "caps," and GIFs created from film and television. These frequently include text and captions that offer context or commentary, including quoted text or dialogue taken from the represented scene or quotations from song lyrics or poetry that evoke an aspect of the captured images.

In general, posts by Austen fans fall into several categories, including posts in appreciation of handsome men and elegant women in beautiful settings; posts that capture moments from the novels that are emotionally poignant, heartrending, funny, or painfully awkward; posts that draw attention to and show appreciation for ways the original novels have been adapted; and posts that create juxtapositions between Regency era sensibilities (as depicted on screen) and the contemporary vernacular culture of the internet. These categories often rely on GIFs to visually express a central idea or narrative. Because of file size limitations, GIFs are very short and contain no sound. Because they repeat automatically and continuously, the internal narrative of the post is readily apparent within moments, and the meaning can be ascertained almost instantaneously, especially when one is familiar with the source material, whereas when watching a video or reading a passage of text, an elapse of time is needed for meaning to be revealed or emotions felt. Fans use GIFs as a flexible medium that allows them to play with digital material to form creative works of visual culture.

In *Camera Lucida*, Roland Barthes describes the ontology of a viewer's experience with a photograph as one that is necessarily emotional as well as intellectual, highly personal, and subjective. Barthes is interested in how photographs bring before our eyes something or someone lost, past, or even dead. The moment in time captured, too, is gone forever. Throughout *Camera Lucida*, Barthes alludes to ways in which photographs are inextricably connected to ideas about mortality and death; photographs remind us a person once alive is now dead or that a person still living will one day be gone.[10] Yet paradoxically, photography also engenders a fantasy for the spectator that the photograph might yield that which it represents: the thing that has been.

The photograph, Barthes says, contains a single, essential moment in time, but in cinema, the moment is denied, swept away in the passage of time.[11] Cinema spectators have long sought means of capturing those elusive moments from a film that most affect them using production stills and the like. While photographs snatch a moment out of the flow of time,[12] short clips of moving images such as GIFs snatch several moments out of that flow—an expansive moment, if you will. The viewer of a GIF becomes caught up in the moment, and because the GIF repeats endlessly, it offers the illusion—but only briefly—that the moment can evade termination and, hence, that the emotion or action it carries can be continually accessed and experienced.

Barthes describes the *punctum* as the aspect of a photograph that pierces the viewer, the poignant attribute that the viewer brings to the image and takes away from it.[13] When a fan creates a GIF or screen capture out of a moment from cinema that has pierced her, she is making a way to access the punctum by removing the moment from the context of the film and isolating it. With the repetitious nature of the GIF, she makes it possible to examine details in motion, seeking new information from the images and opening up the potential for new or additional punctum.

The GIF is therefore a shortcut to the moments in cinema that pierce us, that evoke emotion, laughter, or tears. But this moment is not from real life, as Barthes's photographs are, but from a likeness of real life: cinema. A photographic image presents a direct relationship to the referent, or subject;[14] in the case of screen captures or GIFs created from narrative film or television, these images present a direct relationship to a subject that is real (as in it really exists as a film), yet that is also a fabrication and is emphatically not "real life." The film set existed, and the characters were portrayed by real actors, but these are mere constructions that can no longer exist in configuration together. Because of this, the photographic image taken from a film is even less able to conjure and yield its referent than a photograph taken from real life. Therefore, the spectator or GIF creator must continually try again to succeed. Much like acts of surrogation, the attempt to make the image yield the referent is doomed to fail, prompting the spectator to continually seek a better substitution. It is possible through the creation of GIFs to render a single moment from a film in countless different ways; indeed, Tumblr users continually post and repost different versions of a single favorite cinematic moment.

GIFs offer viewers access to both a brief moment and to the punctum of that moment. Furthermore, a GIF has the ability for the punctum to shift in and out of focus or change completely in the passage of a few seconds of time. The impact of the GIF is found in both the content of the moving images and in its change over time (however brief). It is both now, flowing as we watch it in time, and it is past. The loop comes to an end before repeating endlessly, attempting to defy death. Barthes claims that a photograph is an emanation—or ghost—of the referent, which is necessarily past, whereas cinema is not a specter because it flows through time much as life does.[15] I suggest that GIFs can turn cinema into a specter; they let the spectator remember what once existed on screen, allowing the creator or viewer of the GIF to attempt to restore briefly an experience that is now past—the experience of viewing. The appeal of this encounter for fans is undeniable and goes hand in hand with other acts of surrogation found in fandom.

Within fandoms on Tumblr, creating and sharing original material such as GIF sets is valued above simply "reblogging" material that others have created. The majority of posts, however, are "reblogs," in which a user simply shares something they have seen on their dashboard or on another user's blog. When reblogging a post, users have the option to add their own tags and comments, thereby layering on new contexts and meanings. It is possible to trace the lineage of exactly who has reblogged a particular post all the way back to the original creator. The original creator, or "source," of a post is often credited in the upper right-hand corner. These attributions are considered very important, and stealing another user's content without giving credit is understood as poor etiquette. In fact, bloggers frequently neglect to indicate the original film or television source from which their screen caps and GIFs have been created; such a credit is hardly necessary in a community that will instantly recognize the source material from even a thumbnail image. The concern among Tumblr bloggers is not to give credit to Joe Wright for directing the 2005 adaptation *Pride & Prejudice*, but rather, in this fan-made and fan-policed environment, the individual who created a GIF set from the film receives the credit.[16]

Like Twitter, Tumblr relies on a tagging system using hashtags, which act as indexical keywords. Users tag posts with hashtags in order to easily return to them at a later time and so that other users can search for and locate posts pertaining to topics of interest. Because the volume of posts generated and shared is so great, many users create elaborate tagging systems in order to be able to quickly and easily revisit particular items in the future. Hashtags are also frequently used as a place for users to offer pithy commentary, often presented according to certain conventions. Tags can simply indicate a topic (e.g., "#colinfirth"), or they can offer personal commentary (e.g., "#JUSTLOOKATTHOSEYELASHES"); a tag that reads, "I'm just going to leave this here," offers commentary ironically by making no substantive comment.

Many of these conventional modes of sharing, communicating, and commenting on Tumblr take cues from the well-established cultural context that surrounds the writing and sharing of fanfiction.[17] Moreover, narrative conventions from fanfiction have especially influenced the visual culture of posts on Tumblr. Posts often include the use of character pairings that imagine romantic love and sex between characters who are not coupled together according to the canon of that textual universe or perhaps do not even belong to the same universe. Such noncanonical pairings include most famously Kirk and Spock as lovers and, more recently, Sherlock Holmes and John Watson from BBC's *Sherlock*.[18]

Tumblr posts also play with the convention of creating "crossovers," in which characters from different worlds inhabit the same story (e.g., Sherlock helps Harry Potter solve mysteries at Hogwarts), or alternative universe storytelling, "AU," in which fans dramatically augment or erase certain key features of a text or radically alter the setting. Fanfiction writers will often evoke in their descriptions of a character the performance of the specific actor who portrays that character, referencing recognizable mannerisms or characteristics. On Tumblr, because it is primarily a visual medium, this convention of evoking the physicality of an actor's performance is made more readily available for fan manipulation, and opportunities for clever intertextual allusions are rife. In one GIF set, for example, Keira Knightly appears in several frames, each taken from different films (*The Imitation Game; Pirates of the Caribbean; Pride & Prejudice*); these are interspersed with images of David Tennant as the Tenth Doctor (*Doctor Who*). A caption helps the viewer of this compilation of GIFs to interpret these juxtapositions as a crossover AU in which a time-travelling Elizabeth Bennet is the Doctor's lively and witty companion.[19] The Tumblr medium allows fans to visually render the types of imaginative creations found in fanfiction; this is one of the reasons why fans have found the possibilities offered by Tumblr so appealing.

Tumblr posts will often utilize familiar song lyrics and quotations from books, film, and television, which are meaningfully overlaid on visual material. Similarly, fanfiction writers are adept at harnessing such communal materials and can easily expect that their readers will, for the most part, know the allusions.[20] This genre convention, adapted from fanfiction, functions in a similar manner on Tumblr; the imbricated nature of the circulation of images, ideas, emotions, and text relies on an audience that *gets it*.

Tumblr allows for anonymity. Users sometimes provide a brief biographical statement in the description of their blog, in which they might give a first name, age, and general geographic location; in general, users are known by a username only, and most select a user icon that represents their fandom rather than themselves. Yet Tumblr blogs are completely public and internet searchable, so while the platform allows anonymity, it also offers users a public sphere in which to share desires and affective attachments to popular culture. Some of the more prolific bloggers who create posts relevant to larger and more prominent fandoms can garner as many as fifteen thousand followers or more. While Tumblr users can easily follow and be followed by people they actually know, this is not the primary point. Whereas on Facebook the goal is to connect to acquaintances, friends, and family, on Tumblr, users revel in connecting socially yet anonymously with others around the world who share their interests. As one widely circulated text post explains, "My blog is a private thing open to everyone in the world except to the people I know in real life."[21]

Being anonymous allows users a sense of freedom to post and share things they love without needing to reveal themselves. The focus is on the material blogged, not, ostensibly, the person doing the posting. This is significant given that the majority of blogs I encountered in my study of Austen fandom appear to be maintained by young women from all over the world, many of whom identify as queer. Tumblr, as it is employed within the Austen fandom, is a forum in which women, especially, feel they can express themselves as fans. The female gaze is powerful in this space, and women's sexuality is allowed to flourish. Fans on Tumblr—particularly those engaged in more affirmational than transformational modes—are able to curtail some of the negative commenting culture that is so prevalent on Twitter, Reddit, and Facebook. While, to be sure, there are toxic corners of Tumblr, I encountered a preponderance of public communications between users that was positive and self-affirming. While there are ways for users to comment on posts and to send messages to each other, these are kept in check by community etiquette as well as by the ways in which users can control the platform itself. In the affirmational corners of Tumblr, young women and queer individuals can be empowered to share the things they love without fear of the kinds of reprisal or censure encountered across the internet with rhetoric governed by heteronormative, male sexual desires and anxieties. One blogger sums this up perfectly on her blog header: "I need an outlet for my inner nerd :) So I ended up here where I can be a fan girl in peace."[22] The parameters of the platform help allow fans to create and control a mostly safe space, apart from much of the contempt and derision fans might face on other platforms or in public.

The digital—and mostly visual—creations on Tumblr resemble analog material creations of fans such as scrapbooks. Continuity exists between these analog and digital environments in the impulse of fans to clip, save, and arrange media, but the digital realm has enabled new rhetorics for manipulating media. The similarities between Tumblr blogs and scrapbooks readily spring to mind: in both cases, scraps of material from an original source are "clipped" and saved in an organized format, so as to be easily shared and returned to at a later time. What is similar is the impulse fans are acting upon when they create a scrapbook or maintain a Tumblr blog. A key difference between these two forms relates to scope and fungibility. In a digital environment the extent to which scraps of media can be widely disseminated is seemingly limitless, and as scraps circulate in and out of different contexts, they accrue or shed meanings.

Another key difference is found in the way the scraps themselves are manipulated in order to be included in the new format. The visual rhetoric of Tumblr has more to do with conventions of fanfiction than with scrapbooks. Scraps added to a scrapbook are cut out from an original source but are not typically manipulated before they are arranged into the new assemblage, whereas the moving and still images presented on a Tumblr blog are nearly always edited and manipulated.[23] Manipulations include color enhancements; cropping the size and shape of the original image or altering or amplifying the meaning; added textual enhancements, such as film, novel, or song quotes superimposed on images or used as captions; texturing and layering of images; and collage. While it is possible for a scrapbooker to manipulate clippings in similar ways, they often choose not to; the point is not to add color, flair, or layers to the scrapbook clippings but, rather, to save print material and arrange it in a meaningful way but without altering it in a way that would dramatically change the meaning of the content. On Tumblr blogs, however, bloggers strive to alter or highlight the content and/or context of a visual image in unique, interesting, funny, or poignant ways.

Tumblr blogs—and to a certain extent scrapbooks—resemble bricolage, a notion that theorizes the set of processes by which subcultures appropriate elements from the dominant culture, transform the meaning of those elements, and thereby challenge and subvert dominant culture.[24] The term is sometimes misused to describe practices that while they may aesthetically resemble bricolage, they lack the political thrust that the term is meant to encompass; I do not wish to replicate this mistake. Through bricolage, by creating something new from diverse parts, new meanings are forged. For instance, as Dick Hebdige explains, the safety pin was a mundane utilitarian object repurposed as a fashion accessory by punk subculture in order to signify resistance.[25] But repurposing mundane or found materials is not always a case of political struggle as it was for punk subculture. Although they resemble bricolage aesthetically, many fan creations found on Tumblr are distinct from the way bricolage is understood in cultural theory so as to require a new term to describe the processes of manipulation that occur when a fan posts a set of screen caps on her blog. As mentioned, not all fandom is transformational or subversive. In cases where resistance is not the goal, as with Jane Austen fandom, I propose the term *decoction* (in place of *bricolage*, which others have embraced) to describe a process of distilling or extracting the perceived essence of a scrap of film or television to form something new that, instead of rupturing its original meaning, simultaneously condenses and amplifies it. The goal of decoction is to create something that is not entirely new but that gives a new means of access to a moment of film that pierces the viewer, much like Barthes's notion of the punctum.

Decoction can be present in bricolage, but it is distinguished from bricolage in that it does not necessarily hinge on subversion or resistance. In science, to decoct is to heat or boil something in order to extract its essence. On Tumblr, in particular, the processes of manipulation and juxtaposition by which a fan creates assemblages of images (both moving and still) and gives them a new context, is, I propose, a process of decoction, the goal of which is to distill a facet of a text down to that which the creator perceives to be its very essence. This is not to suggest that the film has an intrinsic or indelible essence but, rather, that each individual viewer experiences an essential response to moments within the text and the meanings that they carry for that individual. Through decoction, the creator or viewer of these blog posts gains direct access to a moment within a text and a means of better grasping it—and here I use *grasping* in both the sense of understanding and of holding onto. Through decoction, the fan accesses—and amplifies—the punctum. This is not a disruption of the original intended meaning but an amplification of it. The decoction also allows instant access to a past affective experience—viewing a film, for example—and becomes a mnemonic object, allowing for surrogation.

To illustrate this idea, I offer close readings of several blog posts from the Jane Austen fandom on Tumblr. GIF and photo sets, for instance, extract several moments from a film or television episode and boil them down to the fundamental qualities most important to the viewer. It is often the pivotal, humorous, or poignant moments that fans select for decoction when creating or sharing GIF and photo sets; therefore, it is emotion and affect that is distilled. In many fandoms, but especially in Austen fandom, the moments from film adaptations most frequently captured as blog posts on Tumblr are from scenes that fans would typically want to watch over and over again: the moments that illicit the greatest emotional response. But decocting these moments into a Tumblr post offers fans more than simply the ability to re-watch the moment; it allows them to manipulate it to achieve a desired effect, to share the moment with others, and to revisit the moment, as one does with a scrapbook or other mnemonic object.

A GIF set taken from the 2005 *Pride & Prejudice* starring Keira Knightly exemplifies how one fan has captured a brief but particularly ecstatic moment on screen and through editing has distilled it to condense and amplify the original meaning but without altering it, thereby creating a decoction (fig. 8.1). The scene in the film from which this GIF set is taken focuses on a brief but intense moment of contact between Mr. Darcy and Elizabeth Bennet as he hands her into a carriage. This moment hinges on a close-up of their hands touching, followed by rapid intercuts revealing each characters' expressive reaction to the brief encounter. To extract this moment, the creator of the GIF set cropped and tightened each frame to em-

Fig. 8.1. Tumblr GIF set including cropped images rendered in black and white from the 2005 *Pride & Prejudice* (dir. Joe Wright). DarcyKnightley.tumblr.com.

phasize the intensity and intimacy of the moment and rendered the GIFs in black and white, an effect that highlights the stark contrast between the two characters and their views toward each other. By decocting this moment, the original feeling is captured and reframed to allow viewers to experience the delicious moment of sexual tension in a slightly new way.

In another GIF set taken from this film, Elizabeth and Darcy have accidentally encountered each other for the first time after she has refused his discourteous marriage proposal. The GIF set alternates between the two characters, capturing the end of an endearingly awkward conversation. The dialogue relevant to each frame is superimposed on each GIF to clarify the context and emphasize the thrust of the scene: Darcy wishes to show Elizabeth greater civility and kindness than in the past, and Elizabeth, embarrassed by an awkward chance encounter, attempts to ameliorate the situation through overenthusiastic courtesy. This GIF set is a decoction of this scene, boiling down a socially awkward moment of thwarted romance to its essence in order to amplify it. When viewed on Tumblr, the GIF set brings to mind again this moment, as an emblem of the film, allowing the viewer to relive the moment and access the feelings it evokes. As the GIF loops continuously, the viewer is able to seek out the punctum from each frame.

Fan creations found on Jane Austen Tumblr blogs often document moments and scenes in adaptations of either thwarted or effectuated romance, especially those that are emotionally fraught. A GIF set taken from the web series *The Lizzie Bennet Diaries* applies to both frustrated and actualized romance at once. In six GIFs arranged side by side, it juxtaposes the few brief moments in which Elizabeth and Darcy come in close contact with each other but are kept apart for one reason or another and celebrates the long-awaited moment in which they finally confess their love for each other. The three images on the left side of the GIF set, in which the characters are close to each other physically but are emotionally distant, are rendered in black and white; the three images on the right are taken from the climactic moment of the characters' first kiss and are shown in enhanced color. All of the GIFs are cropped from a much wider shot to focus only on the physicality of the characters and to draw attention to particular details. This GIF set allows the creator and viewers to enjoy these brief and highly anticipated moments in close-up and on never-ending repeat. The emotional impact is immediate, even (or perhaps especially) when removed from the context of the greater narrative.

The creation of GIF and photo sets offers fans the opportunity to be playful with a text, making room for alternate interpretations and meanings or underlining the intended meaning. Capturing another tender moment from the 2005 *Pride & Prejudice*, figure 8.2 shows a GIF set that adds playful commentary by imagining what Mr. Darcy and his sister, Georgiana, are thinking. This set is part of a series of posts created by Tumblr user Garrulus called "Fitzwilliam Darcy's Internal Struggles." The series, which Garrulus created and blogged over the course of more than two years, recontextualizes all of Darcy's scenes from the 2005 film to emphasize the socially awkward portrayal of the character (which many fans find quite appealing) and offer insights to his side of the story. In this scene, Mr. Darcy has invited Elizabeth to Pemberley to meet his sister and hopes to show Elizabeth a better side of his character. The GIF set combines captions that offer the dialogue spoken in the scene (second frame from top), in addition to captions that impart the imagined internal dialogue of Mr. Darcy (third frame from top, with hashtag), as well as the implied reaction of his sister (bottom frame). In the first GIF, Georgiana has just said that her brother had spoken highly of Elizabeth's musicianship, revealing innocently to Elizabeth that Darcy had been inclined to talk about her fondly. This prompts Elizabeth's playful reaction, as seen in the second GIF. In the third frame, Darcy is cautiously pleased by Elizabeth's friendliness. Although the creator of the post has interpreted Darcy's response in a vernacular style using hashtags, it provides a fairly accurate depiction of his reaction: "#oh my she actually genuinely smiled at me! And it is so painfully adorable I might pass out." In the final GIF, Darcy realizes that his sister sees right through him. The first few frames depict Darcy glancing at his sister, with a hashtag caption that reads, "#and this one is on to me." This is followed by several frames of Georgiana looking knowingly at her brother, captioned with the pun, "*going down with this ship*." Georgiana has taken note of Darcy's affection for Elizabeth, and she approves. To "ship" a relationship in fan parlance is to heartily approve of—or even root for—a particular pairing, especially one that has not been

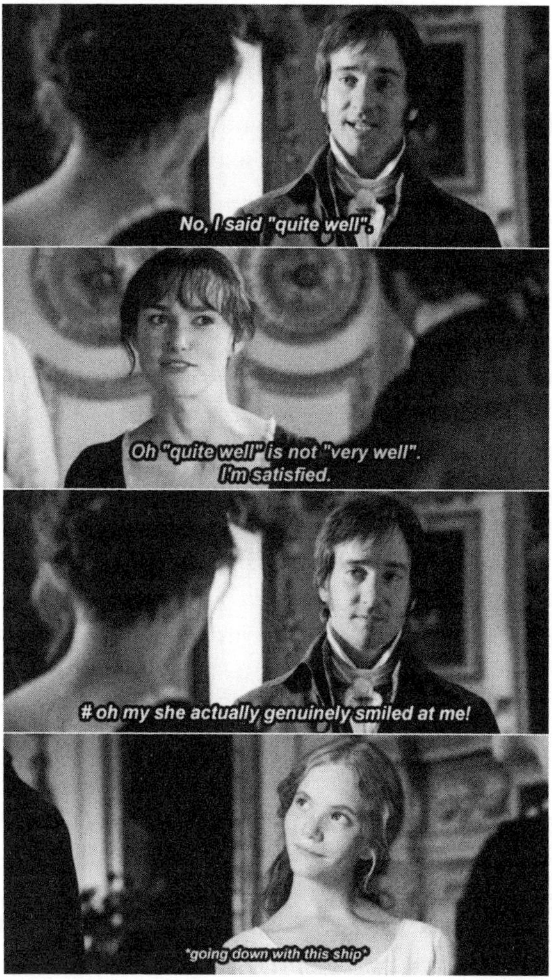

Fig. 8.2. Tumblr GIF set from fan-made series "Fitzwilliam Darcy's Inner Struggles," created by user Garrulus and based on *Pride & Prejudice* (2005). Each set uses multiple captions per GIF to express Darcy's social awkwardness endearingly. Garrulus.tumblr.com.

realized. The creator of the GIF set has brought a playful, idiomatic sensibility to this scene through editing and captioning but without altering the intended meaning. Instead, the meaning is amplified, and the essence of the scene is put on display.

Similarly, a photo set created by alltheladiesyouhate depicts the first encounter between Elizabeth and Darcy at a ball, in which she asks him whether he is fond of dancing, thereby making conversation and obliquely seeking an invitation to dance. It is captioned to capture the essence of the exchange with a pithy colloquial resetting of the dialogue. In the film, Darcy answers Elizabeth's question about dancing with the brusque reply of "Not if I can help it," but appears to immediately regret his tone and his choice of words. In the photo set representing this scene, Elizabeth gets right to the point, asking, "Hey do you wanna," and Darcy simply replies no, before she has even finished her question. The second image in the set depicts Elizabeth's embarrassed yet amused reaction to his rudeness. The final image shows Darcy, alone after Elizabeth has given up and walked away, with a caption implying his sarcastic self-criticism: "Nailed it." As with the previous example, the original meaning of the scene is not altered, but rather, its essence is revealed, using only a handful of images and words to amplify its meaning and significance.

These types of juxtapositions between the Regency manners depicted in the films and the modern sensibilities evoked by the captions are intended to be pithy, funny, and clever. Like most fan creations, they are intended for sharing with an audience that possesses the knowledge to understand and appreciate them. On Tumblr, fans find pleasure in both viewing content and creating and sharing it. Circulating this content offers the pleasure of participating in a mutually beneficial culture of exchange. Tumblr user Garrulus, creator of the "Fitzwilliam Darcy's Internal Struggles" posts, has gained over five thousand followers due to the popularity of these GIF sets, some of which have garnered over four thousand likes and reblogs.[26] Tumblr users live for affirmation and encouragement through positive comments and messages from followers and the reblogging of their content. Fans create and recirculate content to make themselves happy and, moreover, to make others happy. The act of sharing brings joy and pleasure, and the content itself brings access to affective experience, emotion, and meaning.

9

The Lizzie Bennet Diaries

ADAPTATION AND SOCIAL MEDIA

Beginning in April 2012, *Pride and Prejudice* was adapted for the small screen once again, this time reimagined as a fictional video blog, or vlog, told from the perspective of a modern-day Lizzie Bennet and released as a series of short videos on YouTube. A commercial example of transmedia storytelling, *The Lizzie Bennet Diaries* encapsulated the ways in which fan activities have influenced visual culture and how visual culture has influenced fan culture.

Lizzie is a twenty-four-year-old graduate student studying mass communication, living with her parents and constrained not as much by society as by overwhelming student loan debt. Hank Green and Bernie Su of Pemberley Digital, a web production company that adapts classic literature into a multi-platform new media format, created the web series. As its website states, "The company utilizes not only YouTube but other social media platforms . . . to tell an enriched and immersive story that transcends across multiple formats."[1] Released twice per week on YouTube for nearly a year, beginning April 9, 2012, and ending March 28, 2013, the main narrative unfolded in a series of one hundred episodes, each about three to seven minutes long. The story was augmented by supplementary segments and online content that appeared throughout the year, including vlogs made by characters other than Lizzie, Twitter accounts through which the characters communicated off-screen, and websites related to the fictional companies and entities presented in the main narrative. Considered a "groundbreaking multiplatform adaptation," *The Lizzie Bennet Diaries* was the first series on YouTube to win a Primetime Emmy.[2]

The one hundred episodes that reveal the main narrative are set mostly in Lizzie's bedroom and later at her internship office, where she has set up a camera to record herself discussing the goings-on in her life, ostensibly making the vlog for a graduate school project. The scene changes only occasionally, and the only action on screen occurs when other characters come and go from the room and join Lizzie, seated in front of the camera. The camera never moves, and the angle remains constant, so that if a character stands up, her head is no longer in frame, a visual conceit used occasionally to emphasize the awkwardness of interactions between Lizzie and Darcy and to lend the videos authenticity as a vlog, which typically use a stationary, unmanned camera (see, e.g., fig. 9.1). The videos employ a style of editing frequently used by internet video bloggers, in which multiple rapid edits break up a monologue to offer emphasis or comic effect. YouTube provides the platform through which the videos are delivered, but the conventions of its use also dictate the style of the narrative and influence the development of the plot.

The plot of *Pride and Prejudice* is revealed as Lizzie shares her personal accounts of recent events with her internet audience, describing, for instance, visits with the new rich and handsome medical student in the neighborhood, "Bing Lee" (Austen's Charles Bingley), and the social events that occur at which the Bennet sisters get to know "William Darcy" (Austen's Fitzwilliam Darcy). To keep the plot moving and to introduce new characters who have not yet appeared on screen (or in the case of Lizzie's parents, never appear), Lizzie and her two sisters play what they call "costume theater," in which they each don a hat or other emblematic costume prop and portray other characters such as Darcy, represented by a bow tie and tweed cap, or Lizzie's mother, represented by a gaudy church hat, pearls, and a scarf.

In addition to the use of social media, the characters, settings, and plot are Americanized and modernized, through inclusion of ethnic diversity among the characters and the insertion of contemporary feminist views. Many of the plot and setting updates cleverly allude to the original novel: Austen's version of an "accomplished woman" is replaced with a notion of what makes a young woman seem "together"; Lizzie and Georgiana Darcy get to know each other at a karaoke bar instead of at the pianoforte; Mr. Darcy is wealthy because of the success of his family business, Pemberley Digital (which shares its name with the actual production company that created the series); and the threat of poverty that worries Lizzie's mother is not the pressure of archaic entailment laws but financial insecurity and a threat of home foreclosure, like that felt by many Americans following the recession and mortgage crisis of 2008.

Several characters receive feminist revisions, above and beyond the fact that all of the young women are educated and on promising career paths. Charlotte Lu (Austen's Charlotte Lucas), Lizzie's best friend and vlog helper, enters into a profitable business partnership with the annoying Mr. Collins (who runs an internet startup) and, instead of marrying him, gets a much happier ending than Austen gives her: Charlotte becomes highly successful in her career and gains financial independence. Lydia Bennet is ultimately not as careless and foolhardy as she is in Austen's novel. The scandal that befalls Lydia is an internet sex crime perpetrated by George Wickham (a swim coach, not a militiaman). However, Lydia is not disgraced and shamed for her sexualized behavior in this adaptation and, instead, is allowed to have an open sexuality that Elizabeth must learn to respect. This recuperates Lydia's character in important ways; her character matures when she must come to terms with being betrayed by someone she cared for.

The Lizzie Bennet Diaries plays with narrative conventions, social media, and internet culture while referencing Jane Austen's novels and past screen adaptations and commenting on the role of media in daily life and social interactions. Using social media platforms, this adaptation of *Pride and Prejudice* incorporates supplemental bonus features and its own spin-offs that help flesh out the characters and provide a more omniscient narration than Lizzie's vlogs are able to offer with their necessarily limited perspective. The web series creators describe the "Lydia Bennet Channel" on YouTube, featuring vlogs by Lizzie's boy-crazy little sister, as a "spin-off."[3] In her videos, Lydia encourages her viewers to subscribe to her channel as well as to follow her on Twitter, Tumblr, and Facebook. Jane Bennet, Lizzie's kind and beautiful older sister, has a promising career in fashion, which she blogs about on Tumblr and discusses on Twitter, as though she were a real young woman utilizing social media to build a career.[4] These social media accounts appear so authentic that they could easily be mistaken for the creative work of real people were an internet user to come across them without context. Occasionally in the episodes, Lizzie acknowledges comments from viewers on YouTube, and other characters respond to tweets from followers on Twitter. The producers created an immersive experience that fit neatly within viewers' social media browsing habits and newsfeeds.[5] This was particularly effective for viewers who followed the story in real time as it unfolded online.

Following the successful release of the web series, *The Lizzie Bennet Diaries* was made available for sale on DVD, complete with blooper reels, bonus features, and commentary. The production team behind the web series also published a novelized spin-off to the adaptation called *The Secret Diary of Lizzie Bennet* (2014). Like fanfiction, it fills in the gaps in the narrative, offering missing details and exploring Lizzie's inner thoughts and feelings. All of these supplements to the primary narrative are meant to enhance the audience's immersion in the story and to fill in gaps left by the episodic style of Lizzie's linear storytelling. As such, these supplementary elements offer fans precisely what their own creation of fanfiction or other archontic works might offer: the opportunity to imagine scenes left out or to discern the responses of characters not otherwise accessible through the main narrative. Playing into the audience's own habits of creating and circulating archontic works on the internet, *The Lizzie Bennet Diaries* is itself an intertextual archontic work that references other works from the archive of the original Austen text while utilizing multiple platforms that fans themselves are accustomed to using in a similar fashion.

Certain moments, in particular, allow the audience to appreciate the overt intertextuality of *The Lizzie Bennet Diaries*. In episode 2, Lizzie refers to herself as one might in the proverbial singles ad: "I like rain, classic novels, and any movie starring Colin Firth." The reference to Firth immediately alerts the audience—with postmodern irony—that Lizzie, like them, is a fan of the actor who famously portrayed Mr. Darcy, even though it makes no sense within the narrative that Lizzie Bennet could have seen an adaptation of *Pride and Prejudice*. This allusion to Firth's portrayal of Darcy, and subsequent association with *Pride and Prejudice*, aligns Lizzie with her audience while maintaining the illusion that she is a "real" person, simply documenting her life on camera. This conceit returns in episode 4, after Lizzie and her sister Lydia have met a fellow named Darcy. Wondering whether Darcy is his first name or last name, Lydia comments, "Wasn't that Colin Firth's name in that chubby Zellweger movie?"[6] Lizzie responds to this veiled allusion to *Bridget Jones's Diary*, a loose modern reimagining of *Pride and Prejudice*, saying, "I do love that movie." In other words, Lizzie claims to love a movie that is roughly based on Austen's novel and, like *The Lizzie Bennet Diaries*, is constructed as a narrative in the form of a diary. In Lizzie's narrative, it is as if *Pride and Prejudice* does not exist. Although she alludes to an awareness of Colin Firth and *Bridget Jones*, the reference merely offers inside jokes for fans, without violating the closed narrative.

Other episodes make direct references to both the 1995 and 2005 adaptations of *Pride and Prejudice* through the use of dialogue and visual conventions familiar to any viewers who know intimately the earlier adaptations. For example, episode 78, in which Lizzie and Darcy encounter each other at Pemberley Digital for the first time after Lizzie's ardent rejection of Darcy's affections, offers both textual and visual references to the analogous scene from the 2005 *Pride and Prejudice*. In both adaptations, the two characters stand facing each other, profiles to the camera, with an exaggerated amount of distance between them, and speak haltingly to each other (figs. 9.1 and 9.2). In the 2005 film, Elizabeth says, "I thought you were in London," and Darcy lamely replies: "No. No, I'm not." In *The Lizzie Bennet Diaries*, Lizzie says, "I thought you were in L.A.," and Darcy replies, "No, I'm, um, not." Following this exchange, in both adaptations, both characters begin speaking rapidly at once, hoping to dispel the embarrassment of seeing each other so suddenly. In the original novel, no lines of dialogue appear in this scene; therefore, adaptations have needed to translate Austen's description of the characters' astonishment and confusion into dialogue to enact the moment. The writers of *The Lizzie Bennet Diaries* turned to the familiar 2005 adaptation for inspiration. Episode 78 has more in common with Joe Wright's interpretation of this scene in the 2005 film than with the original scene in the novel. Throughout the 2005 *Pride & Prejudice*, close-ups of characters' hands depict a theme expressive of intimacy and intense emotion; Darcy's reaction to certain interactions with Elizabeth, for instance, are expressed with close-up shots of one of his hands, usually shown in contrast against his dark-blue coat, as he grapples with his emotions. While the hand is the focal point of the shot, it does not occupy the entire frame. Similarly, in *The Lizzie Bennet Diaries*, when Darcy and Elizabeth meet unexpectedly in episode 78, both characters' faces are out of frame, and against the background of two dark-blue costumes, Darcy's hands are made prominent, echoing the thematic visual

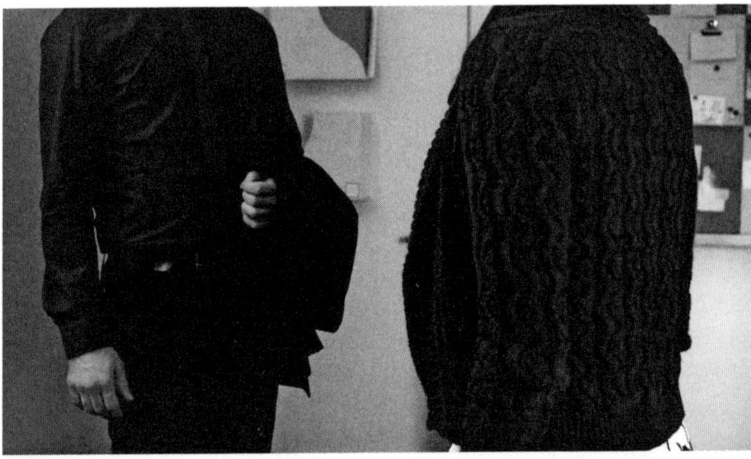

Fig. 9.1. Still, *The Lizzie Bennet Diaries*, episode 78 (2012–13, Pemberley Digital). YouTube.

Fig. 9.2. Still, *Pride & Prejudice* (2005, dir. Joe Wright). DVD.

elements of the 2005 film. Rather than alluding to the novel, the series draws inspiration from one of the many familiar iterations of this popular scene from within the archive of this text.

More often than the other characters, Darcy utters actual lines of dialogue lifted from Austen's novel. As Darcy's demeanor is meant to be viewed as stuffy and uncomfortable, Austen's antiquated language suits him, in comparison to the more modern tone used by the other characters; in episode 7, for instance, when he says to his best friend, Bing Lee, "You're dancing with the only tolerable girl in the room," he echoes Austen's "You're dancing with the only handsome girl in the room." The use of *tolerable* in place of *handsome* references a line later in the same scene from the novel in which Darcy claims, "She [Elizabeth] is tolerable, I suppose, but not handsome enough to tempt me."[7]

In Roland Barthes's *S/Z*, he distinguishes between readerly texts, which leave very little room for the reader to play with interpretation, and writerly texts, which offer a "perpetual present" in which readers can play.[8] Fan studies scholars Karen Hellekson and Kristina Busse claim that if fans are readers "in the Barthesian sense, then serial production is the ultimate writerly text. It invites the viewer to enter, interpret, and expand the text."[9] This is certainly true of *The Lizzie Bennet Diaries*, in which its serial nature drove fans to participate in the unfolding of the story through commenting and engaging in the associated social media sites. The series creators spun a vast web through which fans entered the text and experienced the storytelling.

The Lizzie Bennet Diaries has engendered fanfiction of its own—not fanfiction related to *Pride and Prejudice* per se but specifically related to *The Lizzie Bennet Diaries*. For these fanfiction writers, it is as if the original novel does not exist. When, for instance, these stories describe secondary characters such as Charlotte Lu or Darcy's friend Fitz (Austen's Colonel Fitzwilliam), they do not resemble Austen's characters beyond the role they play in the plot. These characters function in *The Lizzie Bennet Diaries* as they do in Austen's *Pride and Prejudice*, but they have lives and identities independent from those Austen imagined; fanfiction writers have taken these identities and expanded upon them further so that they resemble independent characters that reflect Austen's intentions in only an attenuated manner.

Comments from YouTube viewers reveal both viewing habits and what audiences enjoy most about *The Lizzie Bennet Diaries.* In addition to Lizzie's wit and charm and the clever modern twists that make sense of a familiar story in a new medium, it is the romance and handsome men that viewers most enjoy. Darcy does not appear in Lizzie's vlog until episode 60, more than halfway through the series. The comments from viewers watching the series as it was released show they had been clamoring for him to appear for weeks. As Darcy's first appearance drew closer, YouTube user Meg Alyssa commented on episode 56, "Seriously we are all dying to see Darcy!!!!!!" (March 22, 2013). Inkasrain commented on episode 55 about how her anticipation was building: "My heart actually skipped a beat when I saw Charlotte's shadow, I thought she was Darcy for sure" (February 9, 2013). Liz Wang commented: "Omg I'm dying to meet Darcy. . . . I see the videos with him in it at the sidebar but I don't wanna skip. . . . THE TEMPTATION" (April 25, 2013).[10] Leading up to his appearance, Lizzie acknowledges her viewers' desire to see him for themselves, referring to the comments just as an actual video blogger might. Up until Darcy's first appearance, viewers had only Lizzie's comical portrayals of Darcy's social awkwardness on which to base their opinions of him, and they were ready to see him for themselves. As the comments and view counts reveal, the audience was not disappointed when he did finally appear.

The episodes in which Darcy appears have received a much higher number of views than any others in the series. As of this writing, most of the episodes have received around 700,000 views. However, episode 98, in which Lizzie and Darcy finally kiss and express their affection for each other, has double the average number of views, with over 1,428,000 views. In addition to episode 98, three other episodes with exceptional view counts feature Lizzie and Darcy on screen together and offer iconic moments in their budding relationship: episodes 60, 78, and 83. Only one other video stands out in this way: the episode that represents the climactic confrontation between Lizzie and the analog to Lady Catherine de Bourgh, in which Lizzie exhibits the full extent of her quick intelligence and searing wit. Viewers express in the comments posted to these videos their desire to re-watch these favorite moments. The romantic episode 98, in which the couple declares their love, boasts nearly eleven thousand comments. For comparison, most episodes have received under one thousand comments, and episode 1, the most-watched video in the series by far, with nearly 3 million views, has about three thousand comments.[11] Many of the comments on episode 98 are expressions of joy that the two characters have finally come together. Many avid viewers express their approbation for the episode by describing how many times they have re-watched it. For instance, 2ndRatePatronus comments, "I've lost track of the number of times I've watched this episode," and Gracierobyrdds colorfully claims, "I swear I've watched that kiss so many times over the last eight months that I'm pregnant with their child."[12] This episode is also the most frequently used for the creation of GIF and photo sets by fans on Tumblr.

The ability to comment on individual episodes on YouTube in this way allows the audience an opportunity to turn their reception of the web series into a performance. The audience can respond to the videos, express opinions, ask questions, and enter into dialogue with fellow commenters. By doing so, viewers share a communal act and turn viewing into an engaged, performative experience. Furthermore, the use of social media for storytelling resonates with an audience accustomed to performing subjectivity through these mediums in their everyday lives. The use of these social media platforms is expressly performative, and the creators of the series utilized them so as to encourage the audience to engage with the storytelling in performative ways.

As a means to more personally connect to the storytelling and characters, viewers suspend disbelief, wanting to forget the characters are not real—or, at least, to play along. Transmedia storytelling allows for this in ways that traditional screen adaptations do not. One commenter, addressing Lizzie directly, writes: "I love your dress! :D Where did you buy it?" as though Lizzie herself might respond.[13] Although during the course of the production Lizzie did not reply to user comments on YouTube directly, she occasionally referred (in general terms) to viewer comments within the vlogs. The real possibility that Lizzie *could* respond fueled the suspension of disbelief and desire to play along demonstrated by viewers. Whereas some types of comments from viewers are directed toward the producers, comments are addressed to fellow viewers and are intended to display appreciation and understanding.

By commenting with a display of appreciation for references and allusions to the original novel or to other adaptations, viewers share with others their competency within the knowledge community. In response to the allusion to *Bridget Jones's Diary* in episode 4, one viewer comments: "'Isn't that Colin Firth's name in that chubby Zellweger movie?' Yes! He played Mark Darcy in Bridget Jones Diaries (2001). Awesome reference. I love this show!"[14] Regarding episode 60, in which Darcy first appears, Simsluver491 writes: "Love how this entire episode is one big quote from the various book [*sic*] and movies of it. It is perfect!"[15] Another user notes: "Just discovered this series through Tumblr, and I cannot stop watching, but! Oh my god this scene is exactly like the 2005 adaptation with Keira Knightley, and that's my favorite version of P&P."[16] Adaptations must, in essence, be intertextual, but especially in the case of a text such as *Pride and Prejudice*, any new adaptation must necessarily be aware of the indelible impression that past renditions have left on audiences. As one commenter says, "I thought I'd hate Darcy in this, because Colin Firth IS Darcy in my mind, but I thought he was brilliant."[17]

Occasionally, YouTube viewers make comments that suggest scenes or moments they would like to imagine or see in the adaptation. This convention resembles commenting practices used on fanfiction sites to encourage and prompt writers. For instance, Talia Bennett commented: "I love imagining what all the characters are thinking and my favorite, for this video, is Darcy. Just imagine it, him watching these videos since Lizzie told him to, and seeing her dance around the office like a maniac. One can just imagine the genuine smile and little dimple on his face to see her happiness and thinking, 'I wish I could make her this happy.'"[18] Comments of this type are directed to fellow viewers as a means of sharing an affective experience, rather than being intended as actual prompts for the producers. Similarly, TheLovingthis comments on a parallel between a scene in which Lizzie dances around and plays with a rolling desk chair and a moment in the 1995 BBC adaptation in which Darcy emerges from a bath and, while toweling off, glances through a window and sees Elizabeth on the grounds playing with a large dog.[19] Another viewer, Becky, agrees with her: "That's exactly what I was thinking. I felt like this would make him love her more because of her just being goofy and being herself, their equivalent of Elizabeth just playing around and being goofy with the dog in the [BBC] miniseries. Now, they just need to show us the clip of Darcy getting out of the shower and watching this with a hint of a smile on his face . . . you know, in homage to the movie, of course. And we need a lake scene!"[20] Making a comment like this not only performs the commenter's affinities but also allows others who are familiar with the 1995 miniseries to appreciate the point being made.

As these comments reveal, the visual aspects of this adaptation—both real and those supplied by fans' imaginations—are as crucial to the audience's experience with enjoying this telling of the story of *Pride and Prejudice* as in other adaptations, despite the fact that *The Lizzie Bennet Diaries* is rather visually static because of its setting as a vlog. For fans of this web series, the roughly eight hours of videos offers elements readers love about *Pride and Prejudice:* humor, romance, Lizzie's cleverness, Darcy's awkward yet handsome appeal. Fans re-watch, create GIFs and make screen captures, and they write fanfiction, making archontic works to complement this already archontic adaptation. Fan studies scholars are frequently concerned with the question of what delineates the boundaries of fanfiction. A text such as *The Lizzie Bennet Diaries* challenges traditional understandings of fanfiction: it is an adaptation, but it is also its own text, which has both added to the archive of Austen's *Pride and Prejudice* and is now involved in the ongoing creation of a new archive. This is an archontic creation that has taken on a life of its own.

For the viewers of *The Lizzie Bennet Diaries* who are familiar with this well-worn story, engaging with an adaptation like this one is a means of surrogation. For viewers familiar with Austen from past iterations, this new adaptation offers the chance to audition a stand-in for the original text as well as for the pleasurable experience of affective engagement with that text. YouTube comments from viewers for whom *Pride and Prejudice* was unfamiliar reveal that re-watching the episodes and seeking out Austen's novel or other adaptations, or reading *The Secret Diary of Lizzie Bennet*, became acts of surrogation. For these Austen initiates, *The Lizzie Bennet Diaries* would become the original for which they would forevermore seek a substitute.

10

Fanfiction and Visual Pleasure

If you want to know what Miss Austen's mind was like, see the histories of Miss Fanny Price, Miss Catherine Morland, and Miss Elizabeth Bennet. No man could have invented these girls. . . . But the difficulty about even the realistic heroines of women's novels is that they are touched up. Like Jane Bennet, they smile too much. They know the male eye is upon them, and behave accordingly.

—A. B. WALKLEY, *Still More Prejudice* (1925)

As early as 1905, Henry James complained that publishers and purveyors of the "twaddle of magazines" had found Jane Austen "infinitely to their material purpose, so amenable to pretty reproduction in every variety of what is called tasteful, and in what seemingly proves to be saleable, form."[1] More than one hundred years later, this complaint against the commercialization of Jane Austen continues to resonate with those who bemoan what they see as the cheapening of classic literature through spin-offs, rip-offs, and even zombifications. Many recent literary adaptations of Austen have enjoyed strong commercial success, including, notably, *Pride and Prejudice and Zombies* by Seth Grahame-Smith (Quirk, 2009), and P. D. James's *Death Comes to Pemberley* (Knopf, 2011). Within only a few years, screen adaptations of both these works appeared: Grahame-Smith's zombie remake featuring katana-wielding Bennet sisters received a big-screen release that coincided with Valentine's Day in 2016, and a two-episode rendition of P. D. James's mystery sequel to *Pride and Prejudice* aired on PBS Masterpiece in 2014. This trend of adapting not only Austen's novels for the screen but even the spin-offs may simply be due to Jane Austen's reliability in the eyes of the film and television industry as a product sure to attract a predictable audience. However, I suggest more significantly that archontic works of literature such as those listed here result in screen adaptations because of the imbricated nature of the visual and literary in the enjoyment of these works.

Watching adaptations—of both the original novels and spin-offs—helps to stimulate the affective sensibilities found within literary fandom and influences the conventions of fanfiction and other fan practices. In this chapter, I consider contemporary fanfiction against the backdrop of the screen adaptations that have fueled audiences' imaginations since 1940. Media and performance scholar Francesca Coppa has suggested that to write fanfiction is "to direct a living theatre in the mind."[2] Fanfiction writers trust their audience's familiarity with the visual language of screen adaptations, including settings, costuming, and, in particular, the idiomatic movements and gestures of the actors. Through imagination and fantasizing, fans form stories in the mind that take shape, so to speak, in pictures. When this imagining emerges as fanfiction, it takes on a form of expression that relies on a complicated relationship to the visual: it uses either evocative language that depicts in detail familiar visual elements taken from screen adaptations or perfunctory descriptions lacking detail that rely, instead, on the reader to supply already familiar imagery while reading. Screen adaptations supply both readers and writers of Austen fanfiction with a common visualization of settings and characters, which fosters understanding and community among fans.

Similar to Abigail De Kosnik's idea that texts belong to an ever-expanding archive, Karen Hellekson and Kristina Busse assert that any text is necessarily a "work in progress," as it moves from finished product (i.e., a book for sale in a bookstore) into the hands of readers who will take up the work and make it new through reading and imagining.[3] This nature of texts as always in progress is central to the discourse among readers and writers of fanfiction, with their never-ending renegotiations and reworkings of meanings and scenarios. Fanfiction, always being added to the archive of the original text, ensures that the work is always in progress, with new fanfiction forever igniting new ideas and fantasies.[4] An act of surrogation for both readers and writers, this process can never end;

it is a search for a substitute that is always doomed to fail because the fit can never be just right, and so one must always continue searching. The reading and writing of fanfiction offers fans something intimately familiar yet completely new.

In recent years, two general approaches to studying fanfiction have emerged: one foregrounds the community context in which fanfiction is created and shared, and the other approaches fanfiction as a literary genre.[5] Hellekson and Busse argue that both approaches are valid, suggesting that fanfiction is defined by both its engagement with the source text and by the community context in which stories are disseminated.[6] I agree with this combined approach; more specifically, I investigate the genre conventions of fanfiction that rely on influences from visual culture and use online comments from readers to shed light on these conventions. Regarding a *literary* fandom, it is important to acknowledge that fans enjoy engaging with the beloved text through screen adaptations (sometimes exclusively) and that the visual, embodied nature of these adaptations inspire and infuse fan writing.

Coppa claims that although many fans "maintain at least a (ritual) allegiance to print over film," two of the largest recent fandoms based on literature—*Harry Potter* and *The Lord of the Rings*—became prominent only following the release of film adaptations; she concludes that it's the "dramatic, not literary material" that generates fanfiction in these instances.[7] Although I agree that the dramatic embodiment of characters found in screen performances is a compelling factor in the creation of fanfiction, I would also suggest that the visual nature of these dramatic presentations unavoidably influences the conventions employed by many fanfiction writers. Whether intentionally or not, these writers manipulate point of view and the role of the gaze in their stories in ways that directly reference adaptations, and they introduce visual elements into their stories inspired by the sets, costumes, and actors on screen. The visual nature of this fanfiction opens up a means for Austen fans—mostly women—to subvert traditional ways of looking and being looked at, even in writing that affirms rather than resists the traditional mores and central concepts found in the original texts.

Many scholars view fanfiction as an oppositional strategy for women and marginalized groups to express dissatisfaction with both society's traditional structures and expectations and with media's deficiencies in representation.[8] Some genres of fanfiction, such as slash fiction, serve this function by altering texts to pry open space for alternative ideas and desires.[9] Such transformational fanfiction has received a greater share of attention from scholars privileging what they view as acts of resistance. However, there is a large body of affirmational fanfiction—including Austen fanfiction—that upholds the text by filling in gaps or revisiting favorite scenes without making radical changes to the original or to the mores or worldview represented therein. Although not overtly resistant, affirmational works employ their own set of tactics and strategies worthy of consideration.

Affirmational fanfiction resembles the visual fan creations found on Tumblr. Like GIF sets, these works are intended to prolong a moment in a narrative that imparts a punctum; the writer edits, crops, and manipulates the moment to suit personal taste and desires, augmenting certain aspects of the text and erasing others. These stories retell familiar moments, reworking them into new contexts or altering point of view or voice. These tactics suit the needs of fans by offering affiliation with a text and making space for fans to feel connected to the text. The majority of Austen fanfiction provides readers a sense of affiliation with Austen's world and a means of entering that world through the use of language influenced by the visual culture of adaptations. This fan writing demonstrates readers' cooperation with the source material and its norms yet still allows fans to reorganize meaning and make room for new perspectives without completely rupturing existing perspectives.

Austen fans are frustrated by two themes, which they most frequently attempt to remedy through reading and writing fanfiction: first, that there is not enough Austen to read; and second, that there is not enough lovemaking between favorite pairs of characters, whether mildly sensual or fully pornographic. Neither of these themes provides pure resistance to mainstream readings. Although Austen's world is at odds with fanfiction that includes explicit expressions of sexuality, I do not feel that including sex scenes is particularly oppositional since the behaviors and mores explored in these scenes are not at odds with mainstream modern sensibilities. The majority of Austen fanfiction retains canonical pairings, and slash fiction is conspicuously absent from most of the online fanfiction repositories.[10] Moreover, sex scenes commonly frame the sexual encounter as occurring only in a dream, tempering the deviance of premarital sex in Austen's world with playful nostalgia. Most Austen fanfiction serves the affective sensibilities of fans who revel in nostalgic representations of romance, courtship, manners, and the idea of a simpler society, in which prescriptive notions of class and hierarchy preside.

Even as they reaffirm the original text and adhere to nostalgia, Austen fanfiction writers employ tactics that enable them to more completely identify with the character and insert themselves into the world of the text. Influenced by the visual nature of film adaptations, these writers—predominantly, if not exclusively, women—shift the emphasis of the female gaze in order to take pleasure in the way the male characters gaze at the female characters with whom they identify. This tactic has been directly shaped by film adaptations. As Laura Mulvey has established, traditional cinematic values privilege the "active" gaze of men over the passive "being-looked-at-ness" of women: "In their traditional exhibitionist role women are simultaneously looked at and displayed, with their appearance coded for strong visual and erotic impact so that they can be said to connote *to-be-looked-at-ness*."[11] In this hegemonic cinematic context, women are the spectacle and, by extension, the commodity of cinema. But in fanfiction, writers have the chance to disrupt this power dynamic. Austen fans are encouraged to do so by the cinematic coding of Austen film adaptations, which, made mostly for a female audience and focused on a female narrative, tend to employ a visual coding that privileges the female gaze more than most mainstream films. Both recent screen adaptations of *Pride and Prejudice* contain scenes in which male characters look at female characters in such a way that their gaze conveys an emotional state pivotal to the plot and in which the camera codes the female viewer as identifying with the object of the male character's desire. This approach gives the viewer the potent affective experience of gazing at the handsome man on screen while feeling herself as the object of his gaze.

In the 1995 *Pride and Prejudice*, for example, Elizabeth gives Darcy a sympathetic and caring look from across a room as she kindly aids his sister in the midst of a painful social moment; Darcy returns the look, gazing at Elizabeth for much longer than necessary, thus giving the audience the pleasure of a prolonged look at Mr. Darcy with a rare smile in place of his usual scowl. Darcy stares toward the camera, positioning the audience to receive his gaze from Elizabeth's perspective. In the plot, this moment is pivotal for Darcy as it gives him sudden hope that Elizabeth's look may signal her improved opinion of him. In case the audience has missed the import of the moment, it returns as a flashback shortly after the end of this scene, as Darcy fondly recalls the meaningful exchange of glances.

Austen screen adaptations present an alternative, if not an outright challenge, to what Mulvey has referred to as the phallocentric nature of mainstream Hollywood-style cinema, in which the woman is the spectacle to be looked at and consumed; instead, Austen film adaptations offer women pleasure through a narcissistic voyeurism—the pleasure of identifying with the beautiful heroine pursued by the handsome, cravat-wearing rich man who must be in want of a wife. However, the women of Austen adaptations remain a spectacle, in a sense, as the display of beauty and social graces (or lack thereof) is in fact integral to the stories. Yet the beauty on display is not that typically championed by mainstream Hollywood; the dress and decorum of the Regency resist contemporary beauty standards in ways that prove important to many Austen fans. As the epigraph to this chapter suggests, Austen's heroines were very much aware that they were being looked at and scrutinized by their society, and as fanfiction reveals, today's readers and viewers resonate with this idea.

Fanfiction has grown exponentially as a phenomenon since the advent of internet platforms that facilitate finding and sharing stories. Recent scholarship on fanfiction is only beginning to scratch the surface of what has become a vast network of millions of stories dedicated to a wide range of interests. The field of study is so vast, in fact, that it becomes easy to speak in generalities when discussing trends in fanfiction and theorizing its praxis. What I describe is by no means a monolithic explanation of Austen fanfiction or of fanfiction in general; instead, I provide a glimpse into the ways many archontic works of Austen fans resemble fanfiction practices generally and yet embrace a relationship to the source material that tends to be more affirmational than recent scholarship on fanfiction would seem to suggest.

Two early spin-off novels, *Old Friends and New Fancies* (1913) and *Pemberley Shades* (1949), supply historical perspective on the characteristics of today's internet fanfiction. Like much Austen fanfiction today, both works pay homage to the novelist rather than revising her. *Old Friends* was written prior to the existence of screen adaptations, and *Pemberley Shades* appeared just after the first film version of *Pride and Prejudice* was released; comparing these spin-offs illustrates the impact of visual culture on archontic works.

Old Friends and New Fancies, by Sybil Brinton (1874–1928), is a pastiche, bringing together characters from all six novels in an "imaginary sequel" to *Pride and Prejudice* that presents the "after-adventures" of Austen's characters.[12] Brinton, the daughter of a member of English Parliament about whom very little is known, took inspiration from J. E. Austen-Leigh's memoir of Jane Austen, in which he recalled her habit of discussing among family the future lives of characters from her novels. Austen-Leigh explains that his aunt Jane "took a kind of parental interest in the beings whom she had created, and did not dismiss them from her thoughts when she had finished her last chapter. . . . She would, if asked, tell us many little particulars about the subsequent career of some of her people."[13] Austen-Leigh recorded examples of these particulars in the memoir—including hints about the futures of Kitty and Mary Bennet (of *Pride and Prejudice*) and small details that occur within the scope of the novels but are left unsaid. Brinton took these up as a starting point for *Old Friends*.

Printed by a vanity publisher in 1913, the sequel predates screen adaptations by nearly thirty years and therefore lacks the reliance on readers' knowledge of the visual traits found in adaptations so prevalent in later fanfiction. Brinton describes the physical appearance and movements of the characters in detail in order to convey personality traits and to explain the interactions between characters within each scene. For example, the narrator describes Lucy Steele, whom a reader familiar with Austen would recognize as a conniving and simpering young woman from *Sense and Sen-*

sibility, as "being rather thin, small in stature, and very elaborately dressed in the height of the fashion. . . . [She] might have been considered pretty, but for her sharp, almost shrewish features, restless eyes, and the discontented, irritable lines which had formed themselves in her face."[14] This rather evocative description is distinctive from those normally found in fanfiction today, which are less specific and rely on peculiar traits of actors seen in adaptations. Similarly, Elizabeth's younger sister, Kitty, is described as "a slender, blooming young girl, and pretty without being very striking."[15] This description helps the reader understand the place of the character within her social circle but without naming specific traits like those found in contemporary fanfiction, such as "mousy brown hair" or "wide-set eyes." However, the most familiar characters in *Old Friends*—Darcy and Elizabeth, for instance—receive very little physical description. In a preadaptation imagining of Austen's world, these favorite characters take form without the benefit of actors' portrayals and physicality to augment them, instead being supplied by the writer's and readers' ready imaginations and thorough knowledge of their actions and character traits.

Pemberley Shades, another continuation of *Pride and Prejudice*, was written by D. A. Bonavia-Hunt (b. 1880) and published simultaneously in the United Kingdom and the United States in 1949.[16] In the United States, it received a second and third printing in consecutive months, indicating that it met with a market ready for more. Like much fanfiction, this novel attempts to contrive clever explanations for details left unexplored in *Pride and Prejudice*. According to Bonavia-Hunt, Miss Ann de Bourgh (Lady Catherine's ill-favored daughter) was jilted in love at a tender age, which left her unsocial and sickly. In some cases, these types of details are shared so that the reader will feel she is "in" on an inside joke or understanding. For instance, when Elizabeth Bennet learns of this gossip about Miss de Bourgh's sad past, Elizabeth's response is in alignment with what a Janeite's response might be. Elizabeth says: "I think that if what you tell me is true it explains much that has hitherto suffered a wrong construction. . . . If her feelings suffered such a blow in her early youth as would appear, it [her indifference] is hardly to be wondered at."[17] Furthermore, Elizabeth states something that many readers have likely thought: "In any circumstances to be the daughter of such a mother must have been a severe trial" (101). A reader with knowledge of Austen would well know that Elizabeth herself had a tiresome mother, even if not one as mean-spirited as Lady Catherine.

The novel also contains several intimate moments between Elizabeth and Darcy intended to make a Janeite swoon. When they are alone, she affectionately calls him "Fitz" and caresses his hand when they talk. Darcy speaks poetically to his wife in admiration of her beauty, saying, "You will never know how you look to me, to me especially—or to others. The best part of you is banished from your own vision, for it is in self-forgetfulness, in speaking, in listening, in looking upon a rose, upon your child that you are most beautiful" (107). Herein lies the very thing at the heart of the visual nature of Austen fanfiction today: a fantasy enjoyed by these women writers is to look at desirable men in a certain way and, more important, to be looked at in a way that is distinctive from modern tendencies that make women into a spectacle and women's bodies into a commodity. In this way, Austen fans vitally disrupt hegemonic norms; in all other respects, the fandom tends toward a conservative nostalgia even when championing feminism. Written just a few years after the immensely successful MGM film adaptation of *Pride and Prejudice* and in the midst of a decade of stage and radio performances that made Austen's novel a perennial favorite, *Pemberley Shades* represents a precursor of the type of visual culture infiltration apparent in much of today's fanfiction.

Jane Austen–related fanfiction can be found in several places on the internet: an Archive of Our Own (also referred to as "AO3") is maintained by the Organization for Transformative Works, a nonprofit group started in 2007 to support the work of fans; FanFiction.net is the largest single archive of fanfiction online; the Republic of Pemberley hosts fanfiction amid other Austen-related resources and articles; and Austen.com hosts the Derbyshire Writers Guild, established online in 1997. As Sheenagh Pugh has noted, some fandoms tend to uphold very stringent community principles regarding canon. Among the more canon-focused is the Jane Austen fandom, especially that represented by the Republic of Pemberley's writing archive, "Bits of Ivory."[18] The site's prescriptive guidelines ask writers to respect Austen's original intentions for the characters and uphold the decorum of behavior expected in the Regency. This is not a place where readers will find works the fanfiction community affectionately refers to as "smut." And with no reviews or other community-oriented features, this archive of fanfiction is intended solely to celebrate Austen and her legacy; it does not invite writers to form community or overtly utilize adaptations as inspiration.

In order to delimit my study of *Pride and Prejudice* fanfiction stories, or fics, I opted to consider writing found on FanFiction.net for several reasons: the site is accessible and nonrestrictive of its users; it is by far the largest archive of fanfiction and covers the widest range of topics; and it is user-friendly, offering searching mechanisms to help users find the kinds of stories they want to read based on genre and differentiated by categories of source material. Within the category of fics based on books, *Pride and Prejudice*, with over 4,600 stories, is ranked twenty-fifth among the most frequently written about texts. Topping the list are two multi-book sagas: *Harry Potter*, with 803,000 stories; and *Twilight*, with 220,000 stories. Others at the top of the books category include *Lord of the Rings*, with 57,000 stories, and *The Hunger Games*, boasting 45,700 stories.[19] Notably, of the twenty-five books to inspire the most fanfiction, only two have not been adapted for film or television.

Of the 4,600 *Pride and Prejudice* fics on FanFiction.net, 3,300 of them are tagged as belonging to the romance genre; very few are listed in more subversive genres such as horror (8) or genres that foster an alternative universe such as sci-fi (20). Relatively few (471) are rated for a mature audience. In order to narrow the field of options, I limited my search to stories in English that were listed as "complete" rather than still in progress. I left open the filters for genre and rating, allowing the widest possible range of stories. This left 2,300 fics, which I narrowed to those tagged as featuring Elizabeth and Darcy in a pairing (991). Of these, I surveyed several dozen stories during the fall of 2014. I discovered that the conventions of fanfiction, more often than not, rely heavily on the visual rhetoric of screen adaptations.

In a scene early in the 2005 *Pride and Prejudice*, Elizabeth makes a quip about men, to which her sister Jane responds, "One of these days, Lizzie, someone will catch your eye and then you'll have to watch your tongue." Moments later, Mr. Darcy enters the room, and the pair lock eyes for the first time. In one fic, *A Dream of You,* the writer captures this moment in particular, latching onto the focus of the scene, the movement and direction of the gaze: "Quickly he fixed his gaze as she dropped a curtsey with the women around her, eyes lowered. Then as though she sensed his disquiet, she looked at him directly. He shifted his gaze ahead hastily, barely able to contain a bombardment of emotion."[20] The gaze—the idea of looking and being looked at—is a trope used throughout the 2005 film and is woven into the fanfiction inspired by it.

Dusk, by Snowberryrose, is a 3,600 word one-shot "inspired by the scenes toward the end of the 2005 movie."[21] In the film, Darcy paces briefly in a golden field outside the Bennet home, gazing from a safe distance toward the house; in this fic, "he found himself standing in the field, his eyes fixated on *her* home."[22] Not knowing he is nearby, Elizabeth escapes the house and sits on the roots of a great tree, an image taken directly from the 2005 film. In *Dusk,* instead of Darcy leaving before encountering Elizabeth, he finds her there in the waning light of dusk, where they resolve their past differences and become engaged. Throughout the story, Darcy's gaze is highlighted, whereas the focus of Elizabeth's gaze is rarely alluded to.

The trope of Darcy looking at Elizabeth, or even gazing from a distance at her house, opens up space for fans to imagine more of what is happening for the characters emotionally in the interval of that gaze. Readers' comments attached to this story show how evocative the scene from the film is and how pleased they are to see the two characters encounter each other, instead of missing an opportunity for early reconciliation. One comment reads: "I love the 2005 movie and in that scene when Elizabeth sits by the tree and Darcy turns to look back at Longbourn, I always scream—Go Back! This is a perfect alternate ending."[23] Another reader expressed that *Dusk* captured the feeling of the 2005 film better than most other stories she had read: "I could hear their voices as I read, and I loved how you used past conversations in their current discussion. . . . I'm always looking for someone to write on the movie and yours is one of the few that is done well."[24] Reader LotsOfLaundry was pleased to find a story that filled in a scene she had just been musing over, writing, "This particular scene of Elizabeth sitting under the tree—with the roots sticking up—was just in my head the other day and here I find your one shot and it makes that scene just right!"[25]

Just before the imagined encounter between Elizabeth and Darcy, *Dusk* opens with internal monologues of both characters. Embellishing the sentiments presented by the original script, the internal monologues reveal the characters' emotional states, having both realized their blunders and feeling certain that their love for the other is doomed. The descriptions of their struggles resemble those portrayed in brief facial expressions and glances on screen, but in the fic, these gestures are lingered on, rendered with great detail. Darcy paces, remembering with shame some of his rudeness to Elizabeth, and "in his mind's eye he could almost see his father's disappointed gaze."[26] Darcy remembers encountering Elizabeth earlier in the day, highly aware of controlling his gaze as a means of restraining his emotions: "He had kept his eyes fixed on Miss [Jane] Bennet, no matter how much his heart yearned for a glimpse of *her*. . . . When *she* had spoken to him, he could not resist the temptation any longer and turned to meet her gaze."[27] The writer's insights reveal her concern with the gaze and the visual nature of the actors' portrayals she is so closely following as she tells her story.

A Dream of You, a seven-chapter romance of over 30,000 words rated "M" for sexual content, follows the premise that Darcy has dreamed of Elizabeth before he has even met her and is unsettled by seeing her for the first time; he realizes that the woman in his dreams with "the finest eyes he'd ever beheld" is real and not simply a figment of his sexually explicit imagination. Author Caprittarius'Rising describes the moment Darcy first sees Elizabeth: "As he swept his eyes casually to the right, the absolute last sight he expected to behold caught his attention."[28] This chapter retells in detail the analogous scene from the 2005 film, relying on its dialogue and mise-en-scène, with only a few supplements added to flesh out the interactions. Mostly, the focus is on Darcy's inner turmoil and the machinations of his mind. This story is described as "*seen through the eyes* of Mr. Darcy, following the story line from the 2005 movie."[29]

Sweet Torment, written by Fredrica, recounts the moment at Pemberley from the 1995 BBC series in which Darcy and Elizabeth share a meaningful look, which Darcy later reflects on through flashback: "After his guests had retired, Darcy stole back down to the drawing-room and sat in the darkness surveying the pianoforte, imagining Miss Elizabeth singing there once more."[30] This description conjures for the reader an image of Colin Firth with a candlestick in his hand, leaning against the mantle in a darkened parlor, gazing once again toward the piano, and recalling the earlier scene. Several other scenes in *Sweet Torment* also allude directly to the 1995 adaptation, many of them dealing with moments of looking and being looked at. For instance, "On Tuesday, Darcy encountered Miss Elizabeth in a shady avenue when exercising his horse. He stopped dead a good 50 yards from her, unable to think of anything to say. She stopped also, and glanced around as if wishing to escape. He tipped his hat to her and cantered off, cursing himself under his breath."[31] This is an embellished version of a brief scene in the 1995 adaptation that does not occur in this manner in the novel.

A Sense of Obligation, by Aureader, alludes to a moment from the 1995 adaptation in a new context. Lydia and Kitty's antics at a party interrupt a conversation between Elizabeth and Darcy: "Their tête-à-tête was interrupted by Lydia dashing through the supper room with an officer's sword above her head, shrieking with laughter and shamelessly flirting. Kitty followed hard on her heels, taunting another officer by refusing to return his gloves."[32] In both the fic and the adaptation, Elizabeth has cause to be embarrassed by the behavior of several of her family members at this party: her mother talks loudly of inappropriate subjects; her sister Mary gives a cringe-worthy performance at the pianoforte; and her father tactlessly embarrasses Mary in front of her audience. All of these blunders are found in Austen's prose, but Lydia cavorting with a sword is an invention for Andrew Davies's adaptation, which conveys briefly but effectively how out of control Lydia is in her infatuation with militia officers. With no analogous moment in the novel, this fic writer employs Davies's sword visual to represent Lydia's character. It is a visually iconic moment that most readers will instantly recognize and knowingly interpret.

Francesca Coppa refers to the "extratextual" presence of actors' bodies and voices within fanfiction. I feel that her use of *extratextual*, instead of *intertextual*, belies a sense that embodied performances on screen are somehow separate or apart from the text. Rather, the bodies and voices of actors on screen become conflated with the text and an audience's experience of the text. At the end of *Sweet Torment*, in emulation of the final moments of the BBC adaptation, the writer describes, "It was at this time, that all the ladies present realized just how handsome Fitzwilliam Darcy was, when his face lit up in a beautiful smile and he finally displayed his two dimples."[33] These dimples are not out of Austen's imagination but, rather, are inspired by Colin Firth's visage.

Comments from readers reveal what they desire to gain from reading a story. Often they want more of a story they are enjoying, and they write reviews in order to ask writers to update and expand. In response to *Mr. Darcy's Lucky Stairs*, a reader suggests the writer consider expanding the one-shot beyond a mere twenty-two hundred words by "detailing changing emotions and thoughts of each character."[34] Another comment expresses a similar fascination with the inner turmoil of characters' thoughts and emotions but also reveals a fascination with the role of the gaze: "I love how their thoughts are almost obsessively focused on each other, trying to read into every expression and word that was said between them, trying to interpret every look."[35] Frequently, comments display rhetoric influenced by the visual culture that permeates the stories: "I love *seeing* all the family together again!"[36] Following another fic, *I Hate You, Most Ardently*, a reader comments that the story helped them relive "the K[eira] Knightly movie again. Wonderful,"[37] and "Loved the vivid pictures your words inspired."[38] As Anne Jamison has suggested, fanfiction is "no longer just writing stories about existing characters and worlds—it's writing those stories for a community of readers who already want to read them, who want to talk about them, and who may be writing them, too."[39]

Writers fill roles, casting idealized actors; readers imagine the embodied action of these actors. As with dramaturgy, in fanfiction there is always an awareness of the original text as well as an additional awareness of other past performances of that text. Like theater, in which the visual element of a staged performance is key to the mode of storytelling, much fanfiction today relies on a complex relationship with visual culture representations of stories with which fans are necessarily familiar. Engaging with archontic works—fanfiction, Tumblr blogs, adaptations—through reading, viewing, and sharing, as well through creation, is a performative act.

As Henry Jenkins has suggested, fans seek a utopian dimension within popular culture around which to build an alternative culture and form communities in which they can share a chosen utopian vision.[40] Fans of Austen read and reread, watch adaptations, write and read fanfiction, and create digital and material works that celebrate and re-access the beloved text, reclaiming it and its universe for themselves in innovative ways. As I have demonstrated, the archontic creations of Austen fans tend to be less oppositional than those of many other fandoms; instead, Austen fans employ tactics that reaffirm and restate the source material and a nostalgic vision of Austen's world.

Whether a fan seeks to affirm or transform, the tactics she employs become acts of surrogation. These acts are performances, or what Roach calls "invisible rituals of everyday life." Fanfiction and other archontic works resemble theater and performance: they provide an opportunity to play within the realms of memory and forgetting. For many Austen fans, this means selectively taking up and exploring romantic notions of courtship from the past that offer pleasure and leaving aside those that do not. As Roach explains, "Performance . . . stands in for an elusive entity that it is not but that it must vainly aspire both to embody and to replace."[41] Each new fic or archontic creation attempts to stand in for the original text to both embody and replace it, and yet it will never be able to do so. For readers, reading these stand-in stories becomes a way of attempting to revive the original experience of reading or viewing the text, to relive a text and reenter a world they enjoy inhabiting, but always in new ways and never quite in the way the original text allows.

IV

IMAGINING JANE

Literary Pilgrimage and Jane Austen Fandom

Chawton, in Hampshire, is the shrine to which all devotees of Jane Austen make pilgrimage.

—JOAN AUSTEN-LEIGH, "Chawton Cottage Transfigured," 1982

Prologue

Ever since fans such as Anna Waterston first endeavored to connect to Jane Austen's world through pilgrimage to the handful of then-accessible Austen sites, the predilection for such journeys has grown, and opportunities have expanded. As illustrated in part I, Americans of means were already beginning to make journeys to Austen-related sites in the 1850s. Literary pilgrimage to Britain became a strong impulse in the nineteenth century for Americans eager to connect to a nostalgic English heritage. Those unable to afford pilgrimage could always travel vicariously by reading pilgrimage essays, which had become ubiquitous within the pages of American newspapers and magazines in the second half of the nineteenth century.[1] Today American fans with a sizable travel budget can bring themselves closer to the Austen they love by choosing from a variety of experiences on English soil as well as communal celebrations of Austen in North America.

Deborah Yaffe's *Among the Janeites*, part travel memoir, part journalism, recounts her sojourn in the Jane Austen fandom, attending the Annual General Meeting of the Jane Austen Society of North America and joining a JASNA-sponsored tour of English sites. A lifelong Janeite who had never been particularly involved in the fandom, Yaffe weaves throughout the book her saga of acquiring her first Regency gown to wear at a JASNA function. After a great deal of time, effort, and expense, she is disappointed with the results: "I resemble nothing so much as a small blue refrigerator. I don't feel like a princess, a Jane Austen heroine, or an authentic Regency lady; I feel like a twenty-first-century woman who's about to appear in public in precisely the wrong dress." She discovers that being dressed up in gown and corset is "remarkably uncomfortable," but when a JASNA luminary offers a moving toast to Jane Austen and the three founders of JASNA, she finds herself teary-eyed "because suddenly none of the bad stuff—the faulty corset or the unflattering dress or the cheesy commercialization—matters as much as being part of a community of people bound together by a love of books."[2]

As I have suggested, performativity in fandom takes place both in everyday life and in ritual, liminal spaces, away from the quotidian. In the following two chapters, I turn to these spaces that exist apart from the everyday. In a liminal space, such as a JASNA gathering, meaning is made and remade through marked performances, such as dressing up and playing roles. The performative nature within these spaces offers participants a chance to break away from the quotidian and slide more completely into a sustained illusion of an Other world. This Other world offers the pleasure of temporal displacement and of social, communal discourse. In part IV, I focus on the performances of fans that take place not in everyday life but as a form of escape into an alternative, liminal space. At a convention or Jane Austen costume ball, the performance of the fan's subjectivity qua fan is made explicit, public, and social. These events, as well as the liminal travels of literary tourists, offer features that resemble pilgrimage.

Whereas traditional religious pilgrimage was often considered obligatory, forms of secular pilgrimage today are voluntary and, therefore, understood as a pursuit of leisure. There are two prominent forms of Jane Austen pilgrimage: the social, communal gathering of enthusiasts at a national or regional convention; and the journeys undertaken by literary tourists to visit sites related to Austen. For American fans of Austen, visiting Austen-related sites in England requires a great deal of time and money for travel; many never find themselves able to make such a journey. Attending an event such as the JASNA AGM is more feasible for many Austen lovers living in North America. Indeed, JASNA was formed, in part, to give these fans of Austen a means of convening to celebrate Austen that did not require travel to England. Attending the AGM has therefore become, in a sense, an alternative to visiting pilgrimage sites in England. That is not to say that the experiences are analogous or that one could substitute for the other. While they are distinct, that which the traveler seeks from the journey and the experiences gained in both cases resemble those of pilgrimage.

For a Trekker it is impossible to visit actual *Star Trek* sites, as they do not exist, but this does not preclude the creation of pilgrimage sites. In lieu of any actual locations to visit, Comic-Con or other similar conventions often suffice as pilgrimage destinations. The Harry Potter theme park in Orlando has become a place of pilgrimage for J. K. Rowling fans; it offers a means of experiencing the world Rowling created. New Zealand, where Peter Jackson's *Lord of the Rings* and *Hobbit* trilogies were filmed, has become Middle-earth for Tolkien fans seeking a form of pilgrimage. In addition to seeking out the communal experience of an event such as the JASNA AGM, a Janeite has the option to visit real-life places Austen lived, locations where she set her fictional stories, and even locations used in film adaptations. Pilgrims in search of Austen and her world find these sites frequently overlapping. While a literary pilgrimage to sites associated with J.R.R. Tolkien cannot bring the traveler to Middle-earth, a journey to Bath gives readers access to places where Austen visited and those where her characters cavorted.

A pilgrimage is a quest to seek something outside the familiar, habitual modes of everyday life, by temporarily moving—literally and figuratively—away from an everyday reality and into an alternative form of reality. Through secular pilgrimage, fans seek something apart from the quotidian that may enhance or affirm a sense of subjectivity and cultural identity. Often in the process, like Yaffe, they find an affirmed sense of community.

Pilgrimage can offer a feeling of wholeness or personal completion that can bring one closer to a better world.[3] In the case of Austen fans, that better world is Austen's. Nostalgia for this world sometimes motivates Austen-related pilgrimage, but it is not the sole incentive. While some fans may yearn for a "simpler time" with elegant gowns, refined manners, clear social hierarchies, and men in breeches with homes like Pemberley, it is often more than that. Fans are often motivated by a desire to experience and reexperience the world of the text in new, more material ways and to seek out community. But regardless of fans' motivations, the time travel and temporary escape from the quotidian that pilgrimage provides brings fans in touch with a world—Austen's world—that is not equally welcoming to all. The alternative form of reality Austen's world provides easily makes space for individuals who are white, cisgender, and straight but is less accommodating for everyone else.[4] This is not to say that fans of color or queer fans, for instance, cannot make space in Austen's world to suit their own desires. It is through the liminality of pilgrimage that fans whose identities would be erased—or worse—by the actual circumstances of Austen's historical era are able to make space for themselves. While time travel to Austen's world feels more welcoming for some than others, all time travelers rely on performativity and liminality to make their experiences in the Other world possible.

The following chapters possess three main goals: first, to explain how Austen-related pilgrimage can be understood as a performative phenomenon; second, to demonstrate how societal anxieties over appropriate behavior for fans is mitigated by performativity in these liminal spaces; and third, to explore how this type of fan activity has been represented in various forums—fiction, the popular press, film, and academic scholarship—revealing how representations of pilgrimage help to inform the actual practices of fans.

11

Literary Pilgrimage and the Jane Austen Society of North America

Once, calling yourself a Jane Austen fan seemed to signify a truly refined taste, the ability to appreciate biting irony and subtle characterization. Today, it's just as likely to signify a healthy lust for handsome Brits in tight breeches. Merely calling yourself a Janeite is no longer enough to mark your superior powers of discrimination. Now you have to spell out what kind of Janeite you are.

—DEBORAH YAFFE, *Among the Janeites*, 2013

As Henry Jenkins has suggested, the increase in technologies allowing opportunities for fans to commune online has altered the dynamic between the everyday and the out-of-the-ordinary in fandom. Before the internet made daily, or even hourly, interactions possible for fans, they sustained their communities only occasionally at conventions and other gatherings.[1] The internet, social media, and related technologies have helped blur the line between quotidian and liminal activities. Yet even with ubiquitous access to fan communities and their creative output online, individuals still desire the unique experiences and social intercourse found at conventions and other special events, evidenced by the continued popularity and proliferation of these gatherings. Fan conventions have become big business; Wizard World Comic Con alone currently holds conventions in two dozen cities across the United States each year. Not limited to comic books, cons such as this are inclusive of many genres of popular culture, including television, film, and fiction, both mainstream and cult.

In her study of *Star Trek* conventions, Jennifer Porter convincingly argues for a clear lineage connecting modern secular pilgrimage to the tradition of religious pilgrimage. Drawing on Victor Turner, she suggests that both secular and sacred pilgrimage share characteristics. Particularly, both offer the experience of "communal belonging," or what Turner calls "communitas," as well as a feeling of "freedom from everyday statuses and roles" found within these liminal encounters. These characteristics are central to participants' experiences at conventions, where the participant is temporarily freed from quotidian constraints and takes part in a rich social encounter. That is not to say that encounters in online communities are not also rich but, rather, to distinguish pilgrimage from experiences within the course of a fan's everyday life, which lack liminality and do not require a physical journey. As Porter says, the convention creates a framework in which "fans are free to be fans without apology." Fans can adopt a "liminal persona" that allows them to explore those aspects of their subjectivity "repressed or ridiculed in mainstream social contexts." The framework of the convention creates a liminal zone, making space for performativity and playfully interrupting normative social structures, thereby enabling participants to explore subjectivities. Moreover, in pilgrimage to fan conventions, the fandom itself provides a shared social category that coheres participants, a necessary component of liminality.[2] At a convention, everyday statuses and roles are made temporarily irrelevant, and fans are unified by their passion and their status as fans.

The fandom, then, becomes a normative, collective identity within the liminal site of the convention. Porter claims the communitas, or communal bonding, that develops tends to stress equality and comradeship, yet these sites also allow varied, heterogeneous discourse; since fandom is never monolithic, this aspect of communitas is crucial to the success of the experience for participants.[3] Turner suggests that the liminality of pilgrimage offers a framework through which differences between individuals are tolerated, and while they are not erased, they do not cause schisms as they might in the quotidian world.[4] Ultimately, though, despite the development of communitas among pilgrims, the alternative or idealized social order of the pilgrimage is temporary, and participants return to normal life having reaffirmed their original roles in society, thereby also reaffirming any differences implicit in societal structures.[5]

In the context of the JASNA Annual General Meeting, many individuals work to distinguish themselves as either fans or scholars yet stress equality and comradeship. Whereas in regular life they might exist in mutually exclusive circles, fans and scholars can coexist at the AGM. As Deborah Yaffe says of the experience to be had at the AGM, "Our love for Jane Austen unites us, and yet sometimes it seems that we all love something, or someone, different."[6] Fans and scholars come together to celebrate Austen and to experience communitas, yet there remains a concern among many attendees at the AGM to, as the epigraph to this chapter suggests, "spell out what kind of Janeite" they are. Therefore, ultimately, the liminal experience shared by Austen lovers reinforces the differences between distinctive modes and practices used in the appreciation of the novelist and her world.

In 2011, the BBC released a one-hour documentary, *The Many Lovers of Miss Jane Austen,* written and presented by English Austen scholar Amanda Vickery to explore "the story of how an anonymous minor novelist in her own lifetime became celebrated today as our very best loved writer."[7] Vickery begins the documentary from within a domestic space that could easily serve as a set for a BBC Austen adaptation: "This is the world of a Jane Austen novel, an elegant Georgian drawing room. I can just imagine Emma Woodhouse taking tea, Anne Elliot reading poetry, or even Mr. Darcy warming his breeches before the fire. It seems a safe domesticated landscape, and it's the setting for her stories of the courtships of intelligent, polite, and privileged young ladies." Vickery embraces a common rhetoric found in descriptions of literary pilgrimage—a rhetoric of imagination. The image she conjures of Mr. Darcy "warming his breeches" alerts the viewer that Vickery's approach to Austen may not solely be in admiration of her literary genius. She introduces herself as an "unashamed fan," yet throughout the documentary, Vickery presents a complicated and not wholly positive picture of Austen fans, seeming to indicate that, in fact, there are some aspects of fandom that warrant embarrassment.

Vickery demonstrates the global appeal of Austen by portraying scenes from JASNA's AGM held in Fort Worth, Texas, in 2011. She refers to the

AGM as a "gloriously eccentric hotel convention." Employing terms usually deemed derogatory, she points out displays of what she feels represents "the rampant commercialization of the world Jane Austen made." Vickery shows off examples of the "astounding array of merchandise" available for sale at the AGM, including spin-off novels and a wide range of DVDs. She explains that while the AGM demonstrates evidence of the commercialization of Austen, the people in attendance are "committed readers"; yet the documentary makes a spectacle of bustling Austen consumers in bonnets, omitting any indication of the other activities going on at the AGM. For Vickery, the dichotomy on display is not that between scholars and fans but between lovers of literature and consumers of things; she explains that at the AGM "the Jane Austen commercial brand dances hand in hand with an appreciation of Jane Austen the serious novelist."

She acknowledges that amid the commercialization at the AGM, there is "incredible intellectual fire power." She discovers that "doctors, judges, teachers, and journalists" mix together with "ordinary readers and fans." Yet here her words betray her bias: Vickery makes a distinction between "ordinary readers and fans" and those of the professional class, who although they may not be Austen scholars, she considers intellectual and, therefore, superior to other sorts of readers. By the end of the AGM, Vickery is "moved by the warmth of the community of fans, scholars, and readers, all united by their love for Jane Austen." Vickery finds that "for the 600 delegates, having fun, living the Jane Austen life for a weekend, this is all an attempt to unlock the fiction they love so much." In this statement, she is not wrong; however, her view of the distinctions between different ways of loving Austen is fraught. What Vickery perceives as a distinction between "fans, scholars, and readers" is not inaccurate, but her portrayal of those differences reveals her own anxieties over being misconstrued as the "wrong" sort of Austen fan. Although she seems to recognize the communitas at work, she cannot perceive the ways the everyday roles of Austen enthusiasts (as doctors, judges, teachers, and lawyers) disappear into the collective identity of the fandom. The meaningful distinction at work at the AGM occurs between those viewed as scholars and those viewed as fans, regardless of whatever roles individuals occupy outside the meeting. But even this distinction is more complicated than it might first appear.

The Jane Austen Society of North America began as a nascent idea in 1975 among a handful of Austen enthusiasts from Canada and the United States at the British Jane Austen Society's (JAS) bicentennial celebration of Austen's birth. Joan Austen-Leigh, a Canadian descendant of Austen and cofounder of JASNA, has recounted the tale in JASNA's journal, *Persuasions,* describing how small incivilities, frustrations with stagnant governance, and a general lack of conviviality found at the annual meeting of the JAS prompted a small group to move toward the formation of a new Austen society with a different set of goals and a more democratically based structure of governance.[8] Moreover, while only a few individuals had made the journey to England to celebrate Austen's two hundredth birthday, they knew they could not be the only Austen lovers from their side of the Atlantic and began to wonder just how many North Americans might be interested in joining a new society.[9]

Four years later, in October 1979, about 100 Austen enthusiasts convened at JASNA's first AGM, held as a business meeting and gala dinner in New York City. The organization soon began to grow as awareness of the group spread. Initially, 335 individuals listed as American and Canadian members of the JAS (UK) became members of the fledgling JASNA. Within one year, the membership had risen to 750 members.[10] Regional chapters began to develop; today 76 regions exist across the United States and Canada, many of which host monthly gatherings such as book discussions, lectures, performances, dances, and teas.

Even early on, JASNA experienced a sense of duality: in order to, as Austen-Leigh puts it, "lend an air of credibility to what seemed to us . . . an extremely shaky enterprise," cofounder Jack Grey wrote to several "distinguished academics," hoping to add their names to the organization's letterhead as patrons.[11] As JASNA began producing its first newsletter and started the journal *Persuasions*, already within the first year Jack Grey feared, "I *am* concerned . . . that we are becoming too academic."[12] Keeping just the right balance between fostering serious academic study of Austen and offering light, fun opportunities for fans has been something JASNA has grappled with ever since.

JASNA currently boasts about five thousand members. Yearly seven hundred attend the Austen General Meeting, a three-day event that has grown in scale since the first dinner held in 1979. Registration for the AGM, limited to JASNA members, sells out quickly every year, indicating that more members would attend if accommodations would allow it. Part academic conference, part fan convention, each AGM has a unique theme or topic, sometimes related to the culture of the host city or the timing of the event: the theme in Philadelphia (2009) was "Jane Austen's Brothers and Sisters in the City of Brotherly Love"; the 2011 AGM celebrated the two hundredth anniversary of *Sense and Sensibility;* in 2017, Janeites gathered in Huntington Beach, California, for an AGM themed "Jane Austen in Paradise: Intimations of Immortality"; the 2010 AGM in Portland, Oregon, was titled "Jane Austen and the Abbey: Mystery, Mayhem and Muslin" because it took place over the weekend of Halloween. This AGM celebrated Austen's parody of gothic novels, *Northanger Abbey,* and welcomed discussion of anything macabre, such as the novel *Pride and Prejudice and Zombies,* which had recently been published.[13]

Programming at each AGM includes breakout sessions of intellectual and thoroughly researched academic papers given by scholars from diverse disciplines on topics mostly related to the novels; special interest sessions that include presentations on aspects of Regency society and culture, such as one that offered a detailed explanation of the specific types of carriages mentioned in Austen's novels and what they imply about the social and economic standing of the owner; plenary talks given by prominent Austen scholars and other luminaries, recently including Cornel West, Anna Quindlen, and screenwriter Andrew Davies; and workshops including country dancing, crocheting, and various period and modern crafts such as the making of Austen-themed greeting cards. At any given talk or workshop, as much as one-half of the audience might be dressed in Regency attire. At the ball on the final night, an even larger number appear in their finest period garb. Each host city also offers unique tours to local sites of interest; for instance, the 2013 AGM in Minneapolis offered jaunts to view an extensive Sherlock Holmes collection at the University of Minnesota as well as to Victorian homes and a riverfront historic district.[14] Participants are able to make the journey to the AGM as much about leisure tourism as about Austen pilgrimage.

The language used in the brochures that advertise each AGM evokes the experience many JASNA members seek—one that is both scholarly and lighthearted. The opening text of the 2013 brochure extends a "cordial invitation" to members to join in a "most pleasant and memorable experience." In celebration of the two hundredth anniversary of *Pride and Prejudice,* this AGM aspired "to delight and transport you on a timeless journey back to 1813 via the words of her novel, the knowledge of our speakers, and the ambience created by exquisite fashions, enchanting antiques, the Netherfield Ball, and White Soup. A variety of diversions have been arranged for your entertainment."[15] The description of the 2011 AGM in Fort Worth, Texas, emphasized the attractions of the region, its climate, and the opportunity to witness a "conference where Jane Austen's 'suckling child' [*Sense and Sensibility*] will be discussed, debated, and dissected by the extraordinary plenary, special session, and breakout speakers on the program." The language used in the call for papers for the 2012 AGM, held in Brooklyn, New York, also reveals the hybrid nature of the event, being part scholarly conference, part fan convention: "We welcome proposals that concentrate entirely on Austen's fiction as well as those that make substantial connections between her fiction and other materials/realms. JASNA audiences appreciate inventive and participatory breakout formats as well as traditional lectures that are presented *in a lively manner with a minimum of jargon.*"[16] Academics take note: the norms you are accustomed to at academic conferences will not be welcome here.

The types of practices and activities found at a JASNA AGM are what Juliette Wells has called "extra-literary activities," through which fans experience often very physical engagement with Austen and her world.[17] Through costuming, dancing, taking tea, playing whist, decorating hats, sewing reticules, and other physical and overtly performative means, fans can feel they are connected to, or closer to, the world of Austen, just as they can through pilgrimage to sites associated with the author herself. Unlike the intellectual and emotional experiences of engaging with archontic works such as reading or writing, the things fans do at special liminal events frequently rely on sensory, tactile means to offer access to the text and its world. Wearing stays and other movement-constricting clothing, for instance, gives an individual a sense of what it might feel like to comport one's body in another era. Even basic actions like eating, sitting, or walking are modulated by wearing period costume, giving the participant the chance to feel what a Jane Austen heroine might have experienced—were she real—going about her daily routine.

In addition to the liminality of the setting and the social modes at play, an AGM is coded and experienced as performative, thanks to the importance of the performer-audience dynamic built into the events. I noted several particularly performative moments at the AGM in Portland, Oregon, I attended in 2010. One of them was an informal but scripted performance by two costumed attendees representing characters from *Northanger Abbey*, the heroine Catherine Morland and her chaperone Mrs. Allen. The pair offered the audience advice to prepare us for "our first trip to Bath." This included what not to wear, whom to visit, the best accommodations, and how to behave around young gentlemen. The presentation was crafted from allusions culled from *Northanger Abbey* as well as quotes from Austen's personal letters. This approach created an entertaining conflation of the author with her fictional world. The woman portraying Catherine Morland would offer advice to travelers prefaced with "Miss Austen says," as if the fictional Miss Morland and real-life Miss Austen coexisted in the same society. The role played by the audience in this session was every bit as performative as that of the two presenters. Most of the individuals attending the session—entirely women—were in costume, and their responses to the presentation constituted a crucial part of the performance. They smiled knowingly at the subtle allusions that only a true Janeite would catch, and they swooned on cue when shown an image of the dreamy actor who had most recently portrayed the dashing Mr. Henry Tilney (JJ Feild). The presence of an audience is ontologically essential to what makes a social interaction performative.[18] An event such as this breakout session is framed as a form of play; the interactions between performers and audiences members, therefore, rely on metacommunication, or the sending and receiving of messages through a set of signals, the meanings of which are understood based upon the social context.[19] In the case of this presentation, the audience members understood the appropriate way to respond, gleaning that a display of knowledge and appreciation for the allusions and humor presented was required of them. Through their responses and behavior as an audience, they substantiated the performance. And throughout, good fun was had by all.

These types of performative situations arise even in casual conversations at an AGM, where Austen is never far from anyone's mind. A clever allusion or quotation is always ready to enliven even the most mundane chat. When asked whether I would be dancing at the ball, I explained that I have never learned country dancing but that, as a professional musician, I have sometimes been hired to play to accompany dancing, putting me on the sidelines of the dance floor. "Just like Anne Eliot, then," replied the woman, alluding to the steadfast and selfless heroine from *Persuasion* who always plays the piano so the other ladies can enjoy dancing. Working one's insider knowledge into conversation becomes a means for performative display of enthusiasm and depth of engagement and creates an opportunity for a shared experience that helps build community between fans. The ability to readily impart allusions and to respond knowingly in kind forms a performative dialogue of shared knowledge. It brings the love of Austen out of the personal realm and into the collective.

Knowledge, therefore, is a currency used to distinguish between serious and casual lovers of Jane Austen. The display of knowledge, then, whether speaking from a lectern or nodding sagely from the audience, becomes a performative means to distinguish what type of Austen fan you are. As the epigraph to this chapter attests, some Austen fans feel the need to distinguish themselves as among those with "truly refined taste" as a lover of clever, sparkling prose, rather than as merely an admirer of tight breeches.[20] But the liminality of the situation allows for enough playfulness that even the most staid of scholars can perform a momentary appreciation of tight breeches without compromising status.

JASNA members seem keenly to perceive the distinction between "fans" and "scholars," even as they make an obvious effort to bridge any perceived disparities. In several conversations with AGM attendees, it became apparent that this distinction looms large in participants' experience. Upon asking one woman whether she would call herself a fan of Jane Austen, she hesitantly answered, "Yes, I'm a fan," then explained with more conviction: "I'm certainly not a scholar. I'm an amateur."[21] To her, a

Fig. 11.1. A participant leaving the ball following the close of a JANSA AGM and returning to the real world. Photo by author.

very knowledgeable lifelong admirer of Austen and longtime member of JASNA, it was important to distinguish that, as an amateur, she was not of the scholar's set, as though not wanting to overstep her bounds or offend.

Wearing Regency attire to an event signifies the role the enthusiast is performing (fig. 11.1). While a scholar is not precluded from wearing a costume at the AGM, she will be understood as occupying the role of a fan since Regency attire signifies a particular type of enthusiasm for Austen. This is not to say that a scholar in a gown will be viewed as less than a scholar but that her subjectivity as a scholar will be put aside while she wears attire that signifies visually to those around her that she is in that moment something else: a fan. The distinction between fans and scholars at a JASNA AGM is played out and represented in many ways, informing and inflecting the social performances that take place and forming expectations. Moreover, these performed distinctions at the AGM help to mitigate differences between fans and scholars by making the discrete roles clear during the liminal time when both come together to collectively celebrate Austen.

Lorraine Hanaway, who served as JASNA's president from 1984 to 1988, explained to me in an interview that it was the 1987 AGM in New York when the first ball was held, marking the first time attendees dressed in costume. After that, she said, costumes gradually became an integral part of the AGM experience for many members.[22] Whether or not one chooses to wear Regency attire appears to be an important factor in distinguishing between types of Austen lovers. In a conversation with JASNA past president Joan Ray, a professor of English at the University of Colorado in Colorado Springs (now professor emerita), she made it clear that from her perspective as a professional, dressing up is outside of her purview: "I enjoy reading Jane Austen, but I don't want to get dressed in Regency attire."[23] Joan, from the vantage point of an academic, seemed to feel the need for distinction between fans and scholars within JASNA more than anyone else I spoke to yet was quick to express approbation for the practices of fans. She explained the reason she had been chosen to be president of JASNA for six years: "I talk to the people and I praise them for their love of Jane Austen, and I never talk down to them, because I really do respect them." She refers to the nonacademic members of JASNA as "highly-knowledgeable laypersons." Joan mentioned several individuals she had spoken with earlier that day who work in academic fields outside of literature but who come to the AGM in costume. She characterized these women as highly intelligent professionals, describing their careers and pointing out that although they choose to wear period gowns, they are well-respected academics. Joan emphatically explained to me her efforts to give credit to those in period attire for their dedication and knowledge, as though fearing I might view costumed attendees in a lesser light or perhaps fearing I might assume that a well-respected scholar like her would make that mistake.

When seeking interviewees to speak with about their experiences at the AGM, I had hoped to find individuals with a variety of backgrounds. What I found was that although many individuals choose to identify as either a fan or a scholar along strict lines, many occupy a gray area on the continuum. I spoke to Gracia Ellwood, a soft-spoken woman who holds a doctorate in religious studies and was politically active in the feminist movement in the 1960s. Having had a career in the academy in a discipline different from any that typically inform scholarship on Austen, she seemed reticent to claim a position as a scholar outright, despite having published some articles on Austen. Gracia's approach to Austen is very sophisticated and intellectual, and she wears period dress. She described her stance on the fan-scholar spectrum: "I guess I'm sort of both a fan and a would-be scholar. I've had a couple of essays in *Persuasions On-Line.*" When I asked whether she felt there was anything necessarily dichotomous about being one or the other, she quoted a notion she had heard in a talk earlier that day: "Something about how fans treat characters as real people, and scholars feel they need to keep their distance."[24] Gracia's feeling was that it was important to be able to do both.

Gracia noted that the diversity of offerings at an AGM is one of JASNA's strengths; there is something for everyone, and the coming together of fans and academics is mutually beneficial. She explained, "The level of discourse in the breakout sessions has been quite sophisticated. The fans are welcome and can bask in the atmosphere, and the academics can contribute to everybody's enrichment."[25] Similarly, Lorraine Hanaway, who humbly referred to herself as the "den mother" at the founding of JASNA and had never missed an AGM, commented that from the beginning, it was important JASNA be "an organization that embraced not just academics and people who were studying Jane Austen because it was important to their career." Lorraine explained that JASNA has always worked to include "non-academics who love Jane Austen and like to do research and talk and think about it." Regarding a panel referred to as "Team Tilney" given by faithful admirers of Austen's cheeky hero Henry Tilney (*Northanger Abbey*), Lorraine explained: "Here was a performance yesterday of these true admirers of Henry Tilney, and they had an opportunity to talk. We've always tried to have opportunities for non-academics to take part." She also described how over the years well-respected literary scholars have expressed their enjoyment of coming to AGMs to speak "because they're so different [from regular academic conferences], but everyone here knows the books as well as they do; so there's no worry that people won't know what you're talking about."[26]

Jim Nagle, a gregarious semiretired lawyer from Seattle, Washington, prefers to call himself a Janeite. He explained that *fan* tends to apply to "more of a passing interest," whereas to him *Janeite* connotes something "really hardcore." A few years after retiring from the army in the 1990s, he discovered the BBC adaptation of *Pride and Prejudice* and became hooked. Eventually, he joined JASNA and over the years had attended several of the annual meetings. He joked that as a man attending for himself, rather than in support of an enthusiastic wife, he's an "oddity." In fact, his wife had recently announced, "I'm not going to any more of those Jane Austen meetings." Jim explained that he enjoys the lectures and is inspired by opportunities to connect history and literature to real-world locations. He found visiting the Austen sites in London, Steventon, Chawton, and Bath to be "very moving." Moreover, the AGMs are wonderful, he explained with enthusiasm, because "your horizons are broadened" by the "mind-expanding topics, especially for a lawyer." To illustrate how important the AGMs are for his fellow Janeites, he related to me that there were only two or three registration cancellations for the AGM that came less than a month after September 11, 2001, a time when many Americans were hesitant to travel. "Janeites are a fierce bunch," he explained. "They were going to come, hell or high water." Jim's feeling is that this tenacity is not only about an interest in Austen but, more important, that JASNA and the experience of attending an AGM is "a large part of their social relationships. . . . They like the people, they like the activities, . . . and no terrorists were going to deter them."[27]

In accord with the comments of many others I spoke to, Jim expressed approbation for the impressive level of knowledge and discourse at the AGM. "Boy they know their stuff," he told me, speaking of attendees in general and not differentiating between fans and scholars. As a presenter at the AGM, Jim gave an excellent talk that explained the laws regarding entail of property in Regency England, like those that play a key role in *Pride and Prejudice* and make urgent the need for the five Bennet sisters to be married before their father's death or risk losing their home to a distant cousin. Jim's talk was very well received by an audience grateful to have these arcane and archaic laws explained by someone capable of speaking about the law without obfuscation. "You've got to be on your toes to give a talk here," he told me. "They'll be very kind, but they know their stuff."[28]

Both Gracia and Jim have attended other fan conventions in the past. Gracia was active in the Tolkien fandom in the 1970s, and Jim attended a *Star Trek* convention just prior to the release of *Star Trek: The Motion Picture* (1979). Although he said "it was cool" and it was exciting to be there when Gene Roddenberry was in attendance, he never went back. In comparison to the JASNA AGM, Jim described the *Star Trek* convention, which lacked lectures and panels but emphasized booths selling autographs, as essentially a "money making venture." He explained that if he were to coincidentally be in the same town at the same time as a *Trek* convention, "I think I would go, but I wouldn't go otherwise."[29] For Jane Austen, however, he had traveled to Tucson, Vancouver, Philadelphia, and Portland.

Ultimately, Jim feels that the AGM offers Janeites an opportunity to do something special: "It's kind of important to, every once in a while, step out of your normal routine, your normal rut. And I think people like doing it."[30] For Gracia, she returns year after year because, she explains, "it's nice to talk to kindred spirits."[31] Lorraine commented, "Really it's very important to see your Jane Austen friends again, and once a year you do that." She speculated that one of the draws to joining JASNA is the fellowship that is engendered by attending AGMs: "You know, if you have an interest, very often, you want to share it. I think it's been a surprise to a lot of us that there were other people who felt as enthusiastic about Jane Austen as we did. And I think the fellowship—perhaps that's the word—that we've had is one of the rewarding things about JASNA and the AGM."[32]

However, both Jim and Gracia observed that the topic to be discussed at a regional event or AGM is a crucial part of the draw, not simply that the opportunity exists. Gracia had skipped two AGMs out of ten years as a JASNA member, in both cases because of disinterest in the focal topic.[33] Very active in his local JASNA group, Jim expressed that while there are about one hundred members in the Puget Sound Region, most of them are what he called "mailbox members" who never attend the monthly events. But he is optimistic that eventually "some topic will entice them to come out."[34] So, while an event replete with dancing, lectures, performances, discussions, and camaraderie is itself a draw and offers fellowship, for Janeites, it seems, the specific topic on hand remains crucial to the experience.

Taken together, these observations from JASNA members about the pleasures of the AGM make clear that Austen lovers—whether they consider themselves fans, scholars, enthusiasts, or Janeites—come together to experience the joy of sharing something important in their lives with other like-minded individuals. In so doing, they allow the distinctions between kinds of Austen lovers to become temporarily irrelevant, as all share in deep knowledge and affection regarding Austen and her characters. Within six months of the founding of JASNA, Jack Grey expressed concern that sustaining interest in JASNA and continuing to spread the word of its existence might prove challenging because, unlike England, North America boasts no "shrine" to Austen. He wrote to Joan Austen-Leigh: "It's not the same as Chawton, is it? The cottage is a constant reminder of their [JAS's] existence and we have no such similar hook to hang our hat on."[35] Grey's fears proved to be unfounded. Although North America boasts no historic house where Austen once lived, pilgrims can travel yearly to the AGM to worship her and celebrate her legacy in creative, intellectual, social, and material ways. Perhaps it is the very lack of a shrine that has engendered such energy and momentum in the organization over the years, as JASNA members have had to work with extra diligence to create an event without the benefit of a shrine to "hang our hat on."

The dynamic and active JASNA is viewed as peculiarly American compared with the restrained Jane Austen Society in the United Kingdom. The JAS exists primarily to provide financial support to the historic houses and collections across England related to Jane Austen. Once per year, on the anniversary of Austen's death—which, Joan Ray points out, "is not a happy day"—the JAS gathers to celebrate Austen's legacy with a rather subdued event. The single-day event includes a business meeting, which "they take very seriously," followed by a lunch break, and then in the afternoon a speaker and tea. A special church service is held to conclude the day. By contrast, Joan refers to a characteristic "American energy" that sustains JASNA and distinguishes it from the English society.[36] The English-made documentary *The Many Lovers of Jane Austen* stridently call attention to the perceived Americanness of JASNA. The end credits roll over a performance by two cowboys singing "Happy Trails" to a ballroom full of Janeites, signaling the close of the AGM held in Texas. The artistic choice to end a film about Austen's popularity with singing cowboys points directly to the perception that the JASNA AGM has a uniquely American quality. In part, JASNA's "American energy" arises from the sheer volume of activity the organization encompasses. Seventy-six regions across North America exist to host local and regional events, from book discussion groups to multiday festivals.

In July 2011, I attended one such regional event, a two-day Jane Austen Festival held at Historic Locust Grove, near Louisville, Kentucky, sponsored by the Greater Louisville Region of JASNA.[37] Many of the offerings at the festival focused on period clothing, including an exhibit of Regency fashion on display throughout the historic house, where costumed interpreters were stationed to discuss various styles and social customs of dress. Programming offered under a tent on the grounds included a fashion show and a presentation on Regency hairstyles. One of the most well-attended presentations was a theatrical performance about Jane Austen's life. Other offerings incorporated living history reenactments, such as a gentleman's duel and a historical interpretation from a man portraying the character of a physician who chatted with visitors about period remedies and surgeries. The "Shops at Merryton," which took its name from the village near the home of the Bennets in *Pride and Prejudice*, featured merchants of period-appropriate goods—stockings, bonnets, and trinkets for reenactors—presented under canvas tents. While the annual event, which celebrated its tenth anniversary in 2018, calls itself a Jane Austen Festival, it is in fact more of a 1790s living history event, with a Jane Austen theme.

One very popular presentation at the fourth annual festival, "Dressing Mr. Darcy," involved a young man demonstrating the complexity of a gentleman's wardrobe. He removed each item of clothing one at a time while discussing its purpose and the history of the style. Eventually, he stood barefoot, wearing only his long linen shirt. During his process of disrobing, reenactor Brian Cushing explained that wearing period clothing should not feel as though one is wearing a costume, but rather, one should "get into the mind-set" of understanding what was considered modest in the era represented. This notion is representative of an awareness of performativity felt by many fans and reenactors when donning period attire.

For this program, the front two rows of the tent were mostly occupied with women in their teens and twenties, wearing gowns and bonnets and poised with cameras. At first glance, such behavior might seem mildly prurient. However, Cushing's eventual state of undress would be considered more modest than men's beachwear today; the sight of him was more peculiar than titillating. The women and girls poised with cameras in the front row may have been drawn to the idea of enjoying something prurient by the standards of Austen's era. Moreover, they were perhaps enacting a response prompted by the performer-audience dynamic of the event and expectations of what it means to be a young woman enamored of men in (or out of) breeches.

At this festival, it was difficult at times to tell the presenters from those attending the event in costume. Often the distinction would blur between performer and spectator as the two types of participants came together to interact. Visitors attending in costume were asked to take part in the staged fashion show; frequently, visitors in plain clothes would ask them for photo opportunities. Similar to what is found at comic-cons, audience members in costume are pleased to be asked for a photograph and will stop and pose in character.[38] Once an individual dons a costume, they become part of the performance and an object on the "stage" of an event of this nature. Unscripted, impromptu interactions between participants sometimes occur that draw an audience; this sort of interaction is made possible by the ways such events are framed as liminal. Participants who arrive in costume expect to become part of the performance.

"Today is participatory!" These were nearly the first words spoken to welcome an audience of about fifty Austen lovers to an event hosted by the Southeastern Virginia Chapter of JASNA in March 2013. On a Saturday afternoon in the auditorium of the public library, locals gathered to revitalize a once defunct regional group with an inaugural event open to anyone interested in Austen's novels, era, dancing, or fashion.[39] The event was a pastiche of AGM-style offerings, including a demonstration of period dancing with an opportunity for audience members to learn a country dance with the performers onstage; a "Fashion Parade" in which attendees were "invited to show off and talk about their Regency attire"; and a staged performance in which actors presented "skits taken from *Sense & Sensibility, Mansfield Park, Northanger Abbey,* and *Persuasion*, with accompanying discussion of sibling relationships in Austen."[40]

A brief lecture about the role of dance in late-eighteenth-century society gave insights into the culture of Austen's time but used examples and evidence from Virginia's colonial through Federalist era history. This provided an amalgamation of interest in Jane Austen's world and the local history of the region. The speaker, dressed in a gentleman's silk suit of the late eighteenth century, was well versed in local public history and spoke extemporaneously. The lecture could easily have been an interpretation given in the ballroom of Colonial Williamsburg's Governor's Palace; the speaker quoted from primary sources from the records of Virginia's prominent elite families. His knowledge and interest in local history lent context to his understanding of Austen's world, and his performative interaction with Austen's world through costume and dance provided experiential context to his knowledge of local history.

Here, as in other JASNA-sponsored contexts, the division between performer and spectator was frequently blurred. At the start of the event, everyone in the auditorium in costume was asked to come to the stage to introduce themselves. Those who were to perform in the skits introduced themselves in character; as one costumed woman explained, "I have the honor of being Miss Marianne Dashwood [of *Sense and Sensibility*] for you this afternoon." Members of the audience who were not in costume were also encouraged to introduce themselves, and while the costumed attendees needed little encouragement to stand and be acknowledged, most of us attending in modern clothes were more reticent. This suggests an important distinction between the roles individuals take on while within the liminal setting of such an event. By stepping into the role of performer—whether in costume or not—the individual frames her behavior as a performance. Moreover, framing one's behavior as a performance, such as by wearing a costume, frames the individual as a performer. The result is the mitigation of social anxieties over a practice that might otherwise, in regular society, seem out of place or even deviant. Framing an act as a performance serves to alert spectators that the act is a form of play: it is something real but not real.

The setting of such events helps establish the experience as performative. In the case of this local JASNA event, held in a small auditorium frequently used for chamber music concerts and youth theater performances, the venue cued the audience to understand the event as a performance. However, the division of physical space between auditorium seating and stage made the desired participatory nature of the proceedings difficult to fully achieve. Whereas the open spaces of the Jane Austen Festival in Louisville allowed for and encouraged a breakdown of the fourth wall between performers and audience, with its role as a historic site and museum used for interpreting early Kentucky history lending that venue an air of performativity, the auditorium space at the smaller local event enforced certain conventions of distance between presenters and spectators. It was in participatory moments such as the fashion parade and dancing lesson that the boundary between performers and audience became most fluid.

Regional event coordinators desire to emulate presentations and interactions that take place at the AGM when implementing a local event, providing format and content that resemble those at the national event. Regional events are framed in the same way and offer similar experiences as the AGM, harnessing performativity to present a welcoming space for fans. These smaller events offer an opportunity to recapture the unique experience of the AGM, where liminality creates a special moment, apart from the everyday world. Were an Austen fan to sit in a Starbucks or do her grocery shopping in full Regency attire, she might raise a few eyebrows, but at a special event like those described here, she is able to put on the role of the fan (whether in costume or not), commune with other like-minded fans, pay homage to Austen, and seek a connection to the sentiment of her novels and the experience of reading them.

Making the journey to the AGM requires the greatest commitment of time and money of the three types of JASNA events. The effort required makes attending the AGM seem closer to a true pilgrimage than merely driving to one's local library for an afternoon. However, the experience gained at both events remains the same; the difference is merely one of scale. Attending these special occasions allows fans to enhance or affirm a sense of subjectivity and cultural identity. Participating in leisure activities of this type signals an adherence to certain cultural values of the upper classes associated with education and privilege. Moreover, the ways in which Austen fans choose to identify with the manners, customs, and styles of the upper classes of Austen's world signal affluence and leisure. Perhaps pilgrimage to Austen shrines in England provides the ultimate version of this type of cultural identity performance.

12

Representations of Literary Pilgrimage in the Popular Imagination

In the BBC documentary *The Many Lovers of Miss Jane Austen,* Amanda Vickery visits several of the major Austen sites in England, including Bath, Chawton, and Steventon. She uses the locations as backdrops to a discussion of how Austen has been revered historically by different types of readers since her death. Throughout, she employs rhetoric common to descriptions of literary pilgrimage that contains a hagiographic tone, embraces imagination as a vehicle for affective experience, and relies on the promise of getting closer to the author, her life, and her writing process. Vickery begins with Winchester Cathedral, where she kneels at Austen's gravestone to read aloud the words inscribed upon it in a reverent tone and with evident emotion. Her visit to Steventon requires a heavy reliance on imagination: "This is the site of the vicarage. . . . It is all nettles and cow-paths today so you have to use your imagination to fill in the blanks."[1] At Jane Austen's House Museum, Vickery discusses the overlay of truth and mythology found there, seeking, as pilgrims to this site often do, to discern clues about what Jane Austen was *really* like. This rhetoric of literary pilgrimage is apparent throughout representations of pilgrims' experiences in print and on film and informs the expectations and practices of fans who undertake such journeys. Fans learn from representations of pilgrimage what to expect and how to act so that when the time comes for their own journey into the author's world, they are primed to make the most of the experience.

A close relationship exists between the traditional, sacred journeys of pilgrims and fans who undertake journeys to sites from popular culture.

Both temporarily leave behind a familiar, everyday world in the hopes of obtaining an enriching experience that contrasts with normal life before returning home to the familiar.[2] Although the terms *literary tourism* and *literary pilgrimage* are sometimes used interchangeably, there exists an important distinction: *pilgrimage*, whether sacred or secular, is specifically related to sites associated with "heroes and saintly figures," whereas *tourism* more generally refers to excursions to places that do not necessary hold an association with specific people, real or imagined.[3] I prefer the term *pilgrimage* for its specificity, especially regarding Jane Austen fandom, which so clearly reveres the woman behind the beloved novels. Moreover, *pilgrimage* connotes the search for tactile, material connection to something not normally experienced in a substantially physical way. For religious pilgrims, the journey to a sacred site is a manifestation of faith and an experience of something usually left to the nonphysical realm of feeling and thought; likewise, for a literary pilgrim, the journey provides a manifestation of affective experience.

It is the absence of physicality—which exists at the very heart of reading—that drives the literary pilgrim to seek a physical reality through pilgrimage. The study of tourism to sites associated with authors, characters, and texts provides important insight into the pleasures and experiences of readers. Amateur readers seek a sentimental experience, hoping the pilgrimage site will return them to the text; they are driven by a nostalgic desire to recapitulate sentiment—the characters' emotions, the sense of a world within the text, and the feelings engendered by the act of reading.[4]

Yet scholars disagree over the potential for success in these journeys. One academic view claims that ultimately the pilgrim is disappointed, discovering a sense of absence upon visiting physical sites. The journey ends with the reader feeling compelled to return to the text by her disappointment in not having experienced the sentiment sought through physical reality. In this view, the experience is one of absence and lack. The shrine cannot be the place the tourist wishes it to be; it is inevitably lacking because what is sought cannot truly exist.[5] Cultural geographer Mike Crang and Austen scholar Claudia Johnson conclude that while tourism to Austen sites can be moving, it is fraught with a sense of absence and disappointment. Johnson claims that a sense of "thwarted longing" is at the heart of literary tourism.[6]

In contrast, others suggest that literary pilgrims can indeed find something meaningful and inspirational from their journey, a position supported by my own observations. Juliette Wells demonstrates that with some effort, the pilgrim's imagination has the capacity to fill in lacunae and repair absence. Drawing from her ethnographic research, Wells conjectures that many tourists truly do gain a deeper perspective on Austen's novels and sense of connection to Austen and her world, just as guidebooks, brochures, and conventional wisdom would have us believe is possible. Wells concludes, "A traveler's own goals, inclinations, and imaginative investment determine her response to visiting Austen places today." A great deal of what tourists take away from the experience of visiting pilgrimage sites is derived from the imaginative work that tourists perform, rather than from the interpretive work physical spaces and objects perform. Wells finds that ordinary tourists find their visits to Chawton satisfying, not insufficient or lacking.[7] I would add that pilgrims to literary sites arrive prepared for an experience they have seen modeled on screen and described in the popular press; these representations of literary pilgrimage inform the practices and experiences of fans and fuel their imaginations.

An example of nineteenth-century didactic literature models ideas about literary pilgrimage as a legitimate and important extension of reading habits yet intimates that pilgrims should expect to be necessarily disappointed unless they can deploy their imagination to salvage the experience. Published in 1886, *What Katy Did Next*, by Susan Coolidge, was written as a response to fans of *What Katy Did* (1872) and *What Katy Did at School* (1873), her earlier books about a young American girl who suffers a debilitating accident and must overcome challenges by learning patience, kindness, and generosity. In the dedication to *What Katy Did Next*, Coolidge writes, "This story is dedicated to the many little girls (some of them grown to be great girls now), who, during the last twelve years, have begged that something more might be told them about Katy Carr, and what she did after leaving school."[8] In this example of what might today be considered meta-fandom, Coolidge satisfies Katy fans' desire for more stories by writing about Katy's own fannish adventures in literary tourism.

In *What Katy Did Next*, the titular character seeks traces of her favorite authors and stories in England. Katy visits Jane Austen's tomb (124), happens upon a street mentioned in Austen's *Mansfield Park* (113–14), and eats muffins like those found in a Dickens novel (108–9). Katy is excited by the idea of visiting sites associated with books she has read and authors she loves, but as Nicola Watson would expect, Katy's experience of literary tourism falls short of expectation and is circumscribed by a sense of what is lacking. Upon recognizing a site from *Mansfield Park*, Katy is overjoyed but becomes quickly bewildered: "'Wimpole Street!' she cried suddenly, as she caught sight of the name on the corner; 'that is the street where Maria Crawford in *Mansfield Park*, you know, opened "one of the best houses" after she married Mr. Rushworth. Think of seeing Wimpole Street! What fun!' She looked eagerly out after the 'best houses,' but the whole street looked uninteresting and old-fashioned; the best house to be seen was not of a kind, Katy thought, to reconcile an ambitious young woman to a dull husband. Katy had to remind herself that Miss Austen wrote her novels nearly a century ago, that London was a 'growing' place, and that things were probably much changed since that day" (113–14). Upon first tasting gooseberry jam with muffins—food that sounds delicious in Dickens—Katy finds the muffins to be "tough and tasteless, with a flavor about them as of scorched flannel," and the jam, she feels, "isn't half as good as the jams we have at home." Katy finds herself repeatedly disappointed by her literary quest, concluding, "Books are very deceptive." Her companion Mrs. Ashe agrees: "I'm afraid they are. We must make up our minds to find a great many things not quite so nice as they sound when we read about them" (108–9). The rhetoric apparent in Coolidge's fictional example of literary pilgrimage supports the claims of some scholars that such experiences are fraught with disappointment. More recently, however, real-life pilgrims' expectations are informed by rhetoric found in the various genre that offer representations of literary tourism, such as travel writing in periodicals, fiction, narrative and documentary film, and literary scholarship. Today these representations employ a uniform rhetoric that champions the use of imagination as integral to the success of one's literary journey. Without imagination, the experience is likely to be "tough and tasteless," as Katy's was.

More recently, novelist Charlie Lovett, writing for the *New York Times*, described his experience "seeking inspiration" from Austen-related sites using tropes and language common to literary pilgrimage writing. In typically hagiographic rhetoric, he describes Chawton village as "a mecca for Janeites." With an embroidered impression of the setting of Austen's first home, he emphasizes the central role imagination plays in a rewarding pilgrimage: "Standing in the Steventon churchyard on a September morning, the dew glistening on the closely mowed grass between the gravestones . . . I could imagine Mr. Bingley and Jane or Eliza and Mr. Darcy bursting through the doors, arrayed in Regency wedding garb. . . . I had come to Hampshire hoping to soak up some of Austen's world in preparation for writing my next novel."[9] Nostalgically, Lovett finds that Steventon "feels as isolated now as it was in 1775." Representative of the desire to be brought closer to Austen, he describes a walk through Chawton village as "stepping back in time," where it became "easy to imagine . . . Miss Austen enjoying long walks through this landscape."

The pilgrim's physical movement within a sacred landscape is fundamental to the experience and figures prominently within such descriptions. There is nothing static about visiting these sites; visitors *walk* or *trace* the paths. Moreover, when describing a moment in which movement is paused, such as sitting upon a bench to gaze at a building or object, rhetoric demands that the pilgrim detail what was being imagined in that moment of repose. The sight of Austen's small walnut table moves Lovett especially, arresting his attention for some time. He says, "I lingered by the table for several minutes, trying to imagine plying the trade of noveling and plying it at Austen's heights, on this modest surface." Here he is momentarily in repose, "lingering" by the relic, an act that allows reflection he feels compelled to explain and share.

Even in a solitary moment, awareness of those who have formerly tread the same path serves as another common aspect found in representations of pilgrimage. The pilgrim is aware that he is part of a long tradition with shared practices. Of his visit to Austen's tomb at Winchester, Lovett writes, "The floor of Winchester's south nave aisle, and the gravestone set into it, are, but for the wear of pilgrims' feet, much the same as when the first mourners paid tribute to Jane Austen." In conclusion of his pilgrim's tale, he says, "I felt I had come a little closer to the great 'authoress.'" The consequence of his pilgrimage is precisely what is expected and hoped for—to come closer to Austen. Contrary to the dominant academic theories about literary tourism, Lovett—like the subjects in Wells's study—does find the inspiration he seeks and is not troubled by absence. He knows what is expected of him and, in turn, represents his performance of these expectations through his narrative so that others, too, might comport themselves as pilgrims ought.

Mainstream representations of pilgrimage such as Lovett's *New York Times* piece have become a familiar genre that propagates expectations of literary tourists today. However, an inspiring or meaningful experience requires keen imagination and effort; it is not to be taken for granted that a visitor to Jane Austen's house will experience what she feels she is *supposed* to without some effort. Representations of pilgrimage both characterize the experience and inform expectations. And yet such representations do not necessarily signify inclusion for all Austen fans equally; notions about the characteristics of a typical Austen fan pervade these depictions. Whiteness is to be assumed, as are certain markers of class, gender, sexuality, and ability. While others can and do participate, representations of pilgrimage assume and promote the notion that this is a pursuit for white people with greater socioeconomic means. Those familiar with the rhetoric of this genre cannot help but be influenced by it, learning exactly who participates and how they are meant to experience pilgrimage and express themselves.

A 1955 article on literary tourism in *National Geographic*, like Lovett's essay, illustrates how the rhetoric of literary pilgrimage has been normalized so as to become perfunctory. The regular use of this rhetoric—in both text and image—within the sphere of the popular periodical has propagated it further. This 1955 article harnesses the notion of imagination as integral to the experience of pilgrimage; furthermore, the illustrations that augment the article depict an idealized vision of how the tourist is meant to enjoy such sites and who those tourists are meant to be (i.e., white and upper class). The author, Leo A. Borah, breezily offers historical anecdotes regarding the locations he visited throughout England associated with literary figures, from Chaucer to Keats. Writing of his time in London, he says the city "contains so many literary landmarks that as we went about I could *imagine* well-loved stories and poems springing to life all around me."[10] Even more evocative of the rhetoric of pilgrimage is the visual representation of such a journey found in the "66 illustrations, 50 in natural colors," that make up the bulk of the article.[11]

The images and illustrations accompanying the story are the lifeblood of the reportage. In the majority of images used to illustrate the pilgrimage sites mentioned in the text, it is people posed as visitors to the site who dominate the shot. Reminiscent of publicity stills for a tourism bureau and featuring well-groomed, affluent white people, the sites are depicted not as mere locations but scenes suggesting to similarly white and well-heeled readers that they themselves could be that smiling tourist. In one image, a young boy holding a cricket bat poses with his hand resting on the knee of a bronze Falstaff; in another, a fashionably dressed woman leans in to gaze at the face of Shakespeare carved in wood on display at Hall's Croft, the home of Shakespeare's daughter in Stratford (299). In both images, the tourist is foregrounded, and his or her pose holds far more animation and interest than the statue. In a full-page illustration, two fashionable young women pause in front of the home of Shakespeare's mother, gazing from the foreground of the photograph at the flowers blooming around the facade of the Tudor home, now a museum (306). The two women occupy the entire bottom left quarter of the image, so that the house and its setting must be squeezed into the frame. Without the women dominating the composition of the photograph, the house and grounds could have been shown more completely and within better context, but instead, the image focuses the viewer's attention on the act of appreciating the site, not the appearance of the site itself. The emphasis is not on the object or place on display or the significance of the location represented but on the idea that people are meant to experience something personal amid these objects and places.

Jane Austen receives fleeting mention with regards to Bath and Lyme Regis. Of Bath, Borah writes, "No other spot in England, London excepted, has so many literary associations," and goes on to name Sheridan's *The Rivals*, Daniel Defoe's *Moll Flanders*, and Dickens's *Pickwick Papers* alongside

Austen's *Northanger Abbey* as novels with mentions of Bath. The illustrations to accompany this literary laundry list picture a staged family of five preparing for an outing, posed in front of the iconic Royal Crescent. The father, in gray suit and sunglasses, leans jauntily on a wrought iron fence post, while his gratified wife observes their daughters arranging a baby doll in a pram. A second image offers a close-up of the children dutifully attending to the baby doll and pram posed by the front door of a residence in the Royal Crescent; however, the location itself is nondescript—it could be any front door. The caption on this inset says, "A little family puts baby to bed at No. 5 Royal Crescent, once the home of poet Christopher Anstey, who satirized local society in *The New Bath Guide*" (335). The photograph implies that more important than the famous architectural landmark of Bath is the scene a family could imagine enjoying there. It suggests that nothing could be more wholesome than visiting Bath to enjoy its literary associations. This *National Geographic* photo essay evokes a visual rhetoric that foregrounds the tourist within the landscape, thereby suggesting that the experience of visiting literary landmarks is meant to be a personal one. The rhetoric is intended to help readers imagine themselves in these scenes, readers whom the magazine assumes either resemble those in the photographs or desire to resemble them. It informs readers' expectations about how to participate in pilgrimage as well as about who gets to have these experiences.

In *Among the Janeites,* Deborah Yaffe devotes one chapter of her ethnography of Austen fans to a description of her journey with thirty-one other American Austen enthusiasts to England on a JASNA-sponsored tour. The chapter's title, "Walking Where Jane Walked," evokes the rhetoric of pilgrimage. When pilgrims tread in literary footsteps, they seek inspiration from the traces of genius left behind.[12] Writing in the style of a travel memoir, Yaffe includes her own observations as well as those of her fellow travelers. She describes the places they visited, offers historical context, and comments about what was exemplary and what she might have preferred to skip over, and she uses the reactions of her compatriots to embellish her narrative. She describes the visit to Steventon much as Lovett and Vickery do: the group's experience relied especially on the role of imagination in the pilgrim's experience. One fellow tour mate "contentedly" comments, "We walked in the same place she walked."[13] The church where Austen's father was rector still stands at Steventon, but the rectory where she lived was razed in the nineteenth century; more so than other Austen sites, visiting Steventon requires imagination. Another woman wishes aloud that she had worn her Regency gown that day; alluding to a scene in *Pride and Prejudice,* she wishes it had been muddy so that she could "pretend like Darcy was down at the bottom of the lane."[14]

Yaffe finds that visiting great houses that have served as film sets for Austen adaptations elicits similar responses. At Saltram House, the location for Norland in *Sense and Sensibility* (1995), directed by Ang Lee, excitement comes from recognizing familiar settings where beloved actors once stood: "Emma Thompson ate in that dining room! Hugh Grant walked down that staircase!" Visiting locations related to Austen solely as backdrops to her novels on film, Yaffe still manages to find Austen's presence. She reflects, "Jane Austen's sharp, ironic voice rings with so modern a sound that it's easy to forget how much the culture has changed over two centuries."[15] The continued circulation of such representations in print and on screen ensures that these notions of literary tourism become naturalized and normalized. The more such representations circulate, the more they propagate similar experiences.

Yaffe concludes that it is the community formed on the trip between the fellow pilgrims—what Victor Turner would call "communitas"—that makes the experience unique and worthwhile. She explains: "Ultimately . . . this trip has been about those bonds [between Janeites]. Solitary fandom has its compensations; I preferred Chawton cottage when I could tour it alone, feeling like the only Janeite in the world. But given a choice, I decide, I opt for community—the company of clever, well-informed people, who have a great deal of conversation." Playfully, she adds: "That's a quote from *Persuasion.* You'll know that if you're a Janeite."[16]

Shannon Hale's novel *Austenland* (2007) depicts one fictional Austen fan's pilgrimage in terms inspired by the rhetoric of pilgrimage but also draws heavily on mainstream stereotypes of unhealthy obsession. Although actual fans of Austen enjoy the air of respectability that tends to deflect such stereotypes, fictional fans of Austen are not always so lucky. *Austenland*'s heroine, Jane Hayes, travels to Pembrook Park, a Regency era fantasyland set in England that offers an immersive experience for those who crave an intimacy with Austen's world—and especially with her male protagonists—and can pay dearly for the privilege. Jane Hayes, an American who becomes "Miss Erstwhile" during her three-week stay at Austenland, is emblematic of a stereotype of fans that circulates in the post-1995 popular imagination. She is portrayed as a seemingly normal professional woman within whom dwells an unhealthy obsession with Mr. Darcy. *Austenland* depicts female fans in a way that is familiar to popular imagination—Regency dress, country dances, visits to period homes—yet resembles actual Austen fans very little, instead insisting on caricatures of fans as silly, childish, obsessive women. This stereotype of contemporary Janeites is easy to lampoon. In the film adaptation of *Austenland* (2013), it is visually represented by the protagonist's "shabby chic," romantic apartment décor littered with *Pride and Prejudice* dolls, dollhouse, and other assorted childlike accessories; a prized teacup collection; and a life-sized cardboard cutout of Colin Firth as Mr. Darcy. Lurking behind this comical caricature of all that is deemed ridiculous about female fans is a problematic and deeply conflicted exploration of fandom that laughs at fans as much as it attempts to laugh with them.

Literature scholar Marilyn Francus argues that more recent spin-offs, such as those by Shannon Hale and Alexandra Potter, are more critical of the behavior of Austen fans than representations found in earlier spin-offs of the 1990s and early 2000s. Helen Fieldings's early *Bridget Jones* novels (1996, 1999) and Karen Joy Fowler's *Jane Austen Book Club* (2004) depict characters enjoying solace in Austen that offers "psychologically satisfying, healthy, healing activity."[17] By contrast, more recent Austen spin-off novels, such as *Austenland*, depict heroines as fans with an unhealthy obsession whose escapist retreat from reality becomes the source of their problems.

Jane Hayes is a woman who clings to the hope that every new boyfriend or crush might just be the one she can picture standing beside at the altar and having children with, something she wants desperately and fears she'll never have. And each time, they fall short of her ideal man: Mr. Darcy. For her, an Austen obsession is something to be ashamed of and to hide from public criticism; as she explains, she "loathes this part of herself."[18] When her DVDs of the 1995 *Pride and Prejudice* fall from their hiding place in a potted plant and are spied by her great-aunt, Jane suddenly feels exposed, as though "she stood there in her underwear" (7). Her aunt astutely sees that Jane has a "guilty conscience" about her Mr. Darcy complex and feels that her niece's thirty-something unmarried state is proof that Jane is living in an unhealthy fantasyland. One wonders whether Jane would have felt so embarrassed by copies of the novels visible to visitors; however, it is made clear that the scintillating, visual nature of the adaptation with Darcy in his wet shirt drives her obsession, not the words on the page. As an almost clinical treatment for Jane's malady, her rich great-aunt obliges her to take a nonrefundable three-week trip to Pembrook Park, also known as "Austenland." By making this journey to a nostalgic past, Jane promises to bury her obsession for good and "become a perfectly normal woman" (20).

At the core of *Austenland* is a sense of anxiety over what constitutes a normal or healthy level of fascination with a fictional character. Early in the novel, as Jane Hayes contemplates her trip to Austenland, the narrator chides, "Seriously, a thirty-something woman shouldn't be daydreaming about a fictional character in a two-hundred-year-old world to the point where it interfered with her very real and much more important life and relationships" (9). In other words, daydreaming is okay, as long as it remains within reason and does not interfere with real life. And yet Jane does daydream, and furthermore, she acts on her daydreams: she dresses up in period costume and travels to England to make believe. Yet within the novel these actions are framed as acceptable because they are in pursuit of a cathartic ritual from which to return "cleansed of entrapping fantasies" (176). Playing dress-up, she experiences a "naughty feeling," a "sinful pleasure" as if playing with Barbie dolls when she "should've been too old" (27). Jane's venture into this childish fantasy experience at Austenland is presented as problematic, yet by entering that world in order to seek redemption she is ultimately rewarded with the love of her very own "Mr. Darcy." The novel implies that while fandom may be bad when taken to an extreme and while fans may be infantile, a fan who follows through on her dreams—and performs her role within the fantasy—will be granted her heart's desire.

As with writers of fanfiction and other archontic works, Shannon Hale relies on readers possessing prerequisite knowledge of earlier texts in order to fully appreciate allusions, themes, and plot twists. In *Austenland*, Jane is obsessed with the Colin Firth Darcy and the DVDs, rather than with Austen's novels; therefore, Hale's readers need familiarity with the BBC miniseries but not necessarily with the original novels. In fact, other than a few minor allusions and mirrored conceits, *Austenland* contains very little that overtly resembles Jane Austen. Rather, Hale expects her readers to be familiar with characteristic ways of being obsessed with Austen and Regency romance. Jane Hayes and the other two elite fans she meets at Pembrook Park love the Regency and men in breeches but seem to know little about the novels. They are "clients" of the themed vacation, consumers of a cultural experience. This role is foregrounded repeatedly throughout the novel each time a client's financial status and the high cost of their experience is discussed (albeit vaguely and without the tackiness of actual figures). Although the narrator explains explicitly that Pembrook Park is not run as a brothel (kissing the actors is only barely tolerated), the fact that these fans are understood as clients seems to liken them to johns, consumers buying something viewed as naughty and not all together moral.

When Jane Hayes arrives at Pembrook Park and takes up the name Miss Erstwhile, she finds she has stage fright, afraid she will not be able to carry on the daring make-believe it will take to live in a fictional, immersive Regency world for three weeks. She worries that in this "ridiculously phony" milieu, the actors playing Regency parts—each a composite of Austen characters—would see that "she was just a sad woman with odd fantasies" (30). And in the presence of the resident Mr. Darcy, here known as Mr. Nobley, she finds herself feeling "naked—not naked-sexy, but naked-embarrassed, naked-he-sees-right-through-my-idiocy-and-knows-what-a-silly-woman-I-am" (54). She is made to feel that her obsessive love for Mr. Darcy makes her a "silly woman" afflicted by idiocy. Yet Jane yearns for the experience to be as accurate and authentic as possible because "the less historical vigor observed, the more difficult it was for Jane to pretend that this whole exercise was anything beyond wish fulfillment" (35). She was there for curative therapy, after all, seeking a cure for her Darcy lovesickness. Insecure and terrified of what the actors and other guests must think of her and her obsession, her journey results in an existential breakdown that ends in her rebirth into a fictional persona.

Even as Miss Erstwhile attempts to lose herself in the fantasy, she feels she must distance herself from an association with the other guests, who she deems are women without restraint and with a misplaced love of the Regency era. The caricatures of Miss Charming, a busty woman well past her pretend age of twenty, whose false British accent and constant misuse of idiomatic phrases render her ridiculous yet affable, and Miss Heartwright, the perfectly mannered, quintessential Regency romance gal, both represent a type of fan that Jane sees as frivolous and inane. These women are fans of their own fantasy; they represent everything that Jane fears to recognize in herself. While Jane's own fandom does not seem to run much deeper than an appreciation for tight breeches, she seeks solace in the notion that she does not resemble these other women.

Throughout the novel, in addition to anxiety about appropriate levels of obsessiveness, Hale reveals conflicted concerns over female desire. When the men of Pembrook are first introduced to Miss Erstwhile and Miss Charming, Jane finds herself completely overwhelmed by their mere presence—cravats, breeches, and all. She fights to compose herself and finds that these men, who appear to have stepped out of an Austen novel, have made the whole experience of being in Austenland suddenly much more real and tangible. Taking in the sight of them, Jane comments to herself that there appears to be "one man of each type for the buffet," likening them to delicacies to indulge in. Jane thinks to herself, confidently, "Don't mind if I do" (39), even while she nervously frets over the awkwardness of her circumstances and worries what others think of her. The men are there for the women to enjoy and ogle, which might read like a fun inversion of the male gaze except that it is tempered by Jane's guilt and inability to relax fully into the role of voyeuress.[19]

Jane Hayes's pilgrimage into Regency fantasyland is portrayed as a travesty playing out in an overwrought imagining of a fictional past in which she must learn to play along and yet is never fully able to suspend disbelief; however, the result of this excursion must, in accordance with romantic plot conventions, lead to Jane's satisfaction and success in love. In the end, to be worthy of a real-life relationship, Jane must feel that she has "buried her fantasy," realizing finally that she could be open "to real possibilities." Only after conquering her obsession by seeing that "fantasy is the opiate of women," and "not practice for what is real," does she win the ultimate prize of true love with the man of her dreams, the very actor who portrayed the Darcy-esque Mr. Nobley (180). As it turns out, he is guilty of escaping into Austenland, too, having worked there to run away from memories of a failed marriage and subconsciously hoping to find his dream girl, someone to fulfill *his* fantasy, among the clients to Pembrook Park.

The representation of Janeites in *Austenland* as childish, obsessed, silly women is as entertaining as it is far-fetched. It aligns with mainstream stereotypes of female fans, but these fans have little in common with the reality of contemporary Janeites, who, while they may indeed appreciate the appearance of a man in a cravat, are much more obsessed with knowledge and appreciation of Jane Austen's literature and history. As a representation of literary pilgrimage, however, it is in keeping with established rhetoric that influences fans' expectations of journeys meant to bring one closer to Austen's world, a world many Austen lovers view as better than their own.

Representations of Austen fans such as those found in *Austenland* and in the documentary *The Many Lovers of Miss Jane Austen* expose the anxieties visible within the Austen fandom over distinguishing between types of fans. In both the fictional pilgrimage of *Austenland* and the actual pilgrimages of Janeites to a JASNA AGM or to Chawton, performance is what mitigates anxieties over perceived distinctions between fans and scholars, serious readers and lovers of tight breeches. Fans display knowledge and affinities while engaged in overt performances such as giving a talk, offering a dance demonstration, or enacting a scene. Moreover, fans perform through their participation within an audience in which they display expected behaviors or knowledge or through social interactions. The representations of pilgrimage discussed in this chapter make visible the ways Austen fans socially and publicly experience the pleasures of momentary displacement from everyday life.

Pilgrimage, like the other modes of fan engagement I have presented—collecting and scrapbooking as well as the circulation of archontic works—is a means through which fans attempt to get closer to Austen and her world. Whereas these other modes allow fans to craft and manipulate objects, visual culture, and ideas as part of their daily lives, pilgrimage allows fans to forge an experience both physical and social that takes place outside the quotidian. As opportunities for literary pilgrimage have expanded, representations of pilgrimage have also become more prevalent. Ubiquitous representations of pilgrimage have served to inform literary pilgrims and influence their expectations and experiences.

Coda

EFFIGIES OF EXPERIENCE

I conclude with a tale of an object—a letter—that exemplifies the modes of Jane Austen fandom discussed heretofore. This letter, describing a pilgrimage to Chawton in 1946, became a cherished object, saved as a prized part of an Austen collection, shared and circulated among those of a mind to appreciate its value, and admired within the pages of Austen scholarship. The letter was a relic of one man's journey to see Austen's home at a time when it was not the museum and shrine it is today but a house lived in by an ordinary family in the post–World War II English countryside. In the letter, written as an act of devotion to his Austen-loving wife, the man described his journey to Chawton and the experience of seeing the house and depicted the setting in detail. The letter, as an object, was venerated; moreover, its contents have been lovingly scoured by many eyes for details and clues about what a visit to Austen's home was like before the careful renovations of recent years and before the footprints of countless pilgrims had become well-worn.

In 1946, Scott Adams (1909–82), husband to Austen collector Barbara Winn Adams (1911–97), was sent in his capacity as a medical librarian for the Library of Congress to Germany to help extract and catalog books that had been stockpiled in salt mines during the war.[1] Scott Adams's ten-page letter to his wife details his travels through parts of Ireland and Great Britain en route to Germany. While stopping over briefly in London, he took a Sunday off to seek out Chawton. The journey through postwar England took remarkable time and effort to reach the out-of-the-way village;

Adams's description reads like an adventure story.[2] Eventually, he reached Chawton and located the house where Jane Austen did most of her writing:

> The house is in fine condition. There is a sign outside "St. Nicholas Club," but I learned from Mrs. Stevens, the tenant, that the war disbanded The Club. . . . Mrs. S. . . . was very pleasant, & not only acceded to my request to photograph the house from all angles, including the backyard, but asked me in. She showed me just the one room "where Jane Austen did all her writing" and I photographed the mantel, which I believe has been done before, as the original. There is a steel engraving of JA on the wall, along with other incognate [*sic*] decor. The front door did open directly into this parlor, but a hall partition had been put up in recent years. . . . There are two oak trees planted by J. A. which I photographed. The backyard is all garden, and, if you think it at all appropriate, I tried to pick some leaves there & got stung. They were nettles.

After feeling he had seen and photographed all there was at Chawton, he took the train toward Steventon to see the site of the house where Austen was born:

> At the first cottage, I met a man out in the yard, who directed me to Steventon Church, & marked the site of the old parsonage "at the first pump in the field where you turn off." I had no trouble in finding the spot. . . . There were cows grazing by the pump, sure enough near the corner of the road. Then the road runs uphill a full half mile through woods, until at last you can see the spire of the church on top of the hill. I photographed the church, including the cherubs on the doors, and the manor. The latter was a strange affair. I treated it most respectfully, just poking open the iron gate & looking in. Then I gathered courage, and finally walked around. It was entirely deserted. It had been used, evidently as a military post, for there were guard houses, a tank of water for fires, a modern barracks & a game room (empty of all furniture). . . . The garden was all grown up; There were dead fish in the pool—a perfect setting for an English mystery story. . . . It was an eerie visit, being late afternoon on a deserted hilltop, and church bells were ringing for vespers down in the village as I left.

Along the way, Scott took note of his surroundings so that he could sketch out maps of the settings for Barbara in the margins of his letter. These charming sketches would serve to orient Barbara to his descriptions and allow her to imagine the experience of moving through the spaces where Austen herself once walked—a visual rendering of the rhetoric of pilgrimage.

The description of the effects of World War II on these sites seems to have especially captured the imaginations of the Austen lovers with whom Barbara Winn Adams made the effort to share the letter. She mailed the original letter to JASNA founder Jack Grey, offering to allow portions of it to be published in JASNA's journal, *Persuasions*. Grey's response was enthusiastic and prompted him to relate his own experience of visiting Chawton for the first time: "How kind of you to have entrusted that wonderful letter to me! It really is quite moving. I figure that your husband must have made his pilgrimage on 8 September, 1946—twenty-one years to the day that I first visited Chawton. In 1967. Unlike his experience, however the weather couldn't have been more glorious. The day was so perfect that I came back to the States and re-read the novels. That was the beginning."[3] Grey explained that he shared the "salient passages from the letter" with Joan Austen-Leigh, the editor of *Persuasions*, with the hope that she might include Scott Adams's pilgrimage in the upcoming volume. Grey corresponded with both Barbara and Scott Adams (then divorced) for the next several months. Scott mailed Grey the photographs taken on his journey. Although these photographs were not included in the *Persuasions* article because of their poor quality, Grey made enough copies to share them with friends and fellow lovers of Austen. These visual and material representations of Adams's pilgrimage to Chawton, depicting the state of the house in 1946, became sacred relics even among people who had since visited the site for themselves. The photographs illustrate an era in the history of the shrine to Austen in which a tenant family occupied the house—a fact both fascinating and dismaying to latter-day Austen devotees. The photographs were taken during a period in which many American readers were enthralled with Austen's novels, falling in love with popular stage and screen adaptations, and yet very few were able to make the journey to England to come closer to Austen and pay homage in person. Scott Adams's photographs offered a unique window into Austen's world. Jack Grey wrote to Winn Adams, "I cannot tell you how much I appreciate your help and interest over the past few months. I know that someday, somewhere, others will be grateful, too, for a glimpse into post-WWII JA territory."[4]

The letter represents an object—a relic of historical fandom—that has circulated in all three of the modes of fandom discussed in this study. The letter itself describes a pilgrimage; it is also an object kept within a collection, serving as a reminder of an experience to be revisited and shared; and the letter was taken up by Joan Austen-Leigh and recontextualized as a piece for the journal *Persuasions,* remaking Scott Adams's story in an archontic fashion. By the time the excerpts from the letter appeared in Austen-Leigh's brief article in *Persuasions* in late 1982, Scott Adams had died. But because of the actions of devoted, assiduous, and industrious fans of Jane Austen, the story and visual documentation of his journey through the English countryside remains as a record of his pilgrimage, now part of the archive.

How does such an object, with its rich history, help us better understand the performativity of fandom? From outside the fandom, an individual might consider the lingering afterlife of this simple letter from husband to wife as somewhat puzzling. What power does it hold that it captivates the imagination of perfect strangers? Why would this artifact continue to hold interest to Austen enthusiasts decades later? Like Austen's own writing desk or the sitting room in which she did her writing or even like a particularly good piece of fanfiction, artifacts meaningful to a fandom bring individuals closer to Austen and her aura. They also bring fans closer to each other, galvanizing the fan community. Scott Adams's letter provided a glimpse into Austen's home just before efforts began to preserve and restore it as a shrine to the author, thereby giving other enthusiasts a unique means of intimately accessing Austen's world. An object such as this letter provides a way to experience something meaningful—knowingly and feelingly—with others who share the singular position of understanding the object's significance.

As I have posited, the objects fans create and share resemble what Joseph Roach refers to as "effigies," the contrivances that enable performance. In his estimation, an effigy evokes something from the past, enabling a dynamic production of memory.[5] Effigies are fashioned through performance but also enable performances through their use. Scott Adams may not have thought of his letter to his wife as a performance, but by recounting his journey and tracing the steps of his pilgrimage in narrative form, he created an effigy to evoke that experience. Other types of writing, such as works of fanfiction, although often not material in form, can also become effigies and are created with that intent in mind. In other words, the writing of a work of fanfiction is the fashioning of an effigy; its creation is a performance, sharing it is a performance, and the subsequent reading of it is a performance. The object is a performance, it enables performance, and its features are performative. The complexity of these layers and shades of performativity in fandom will, I hope, invite continued unpacking in future investigations.

Roach suggests that when people use the word *performance*, the most important meaning the term denotes is that related to surrogation—the notion that it is a "doomed search for originals by continuously auditioning stand-ins."[6] Roach explains that within the idea of performance lies a paradox regarding repetition. Performance theorist Richard Schechner has called this paradox "restored behavior," or "twice-behaved behavior," which he describes as "living behavior treated as a film director treats a strip of film."[7] These strips of behavior are reworked and reused to constitute performance. As Roach explains, "No action or sequence of actions may be performed exactly the same way twice; they must be reinvented or recreated at each appearance."[8] Repetition is as central and inextricable within fandom as it is within performance. Material and digital creations by fans facilitate the enacting and experiencing of restored behaviors. I believe there is much to uncover regarding the role of performativity in the practices of fans, particularly in the ways the *things* fans create and share function as objects of fandom and of performance. I hope that future studies like this one will further probe the entwined roles of repetition and performativity in fandom as a way to foreground the lived experiences of fans.

I am by no means alone in recognizing the usefulness of this approach. In 2001, Kurt Lancaster's *Interacting with Babylon 5* promised a performative turn in fan studies. Studying science fiction gaming and role-playing, Lancaster suggested how "immersion through performance" is key to these experiences.[9] He describes the ways the structures of various types of gaming make space for different forms of performances and inform the rules of engagement. For Lancaster, the performativity present in fandom is a form of participation guided by certain structures and rules of play that facilitate imagination, fantasy, and community interaction, the ultimate goal of which is pleasure.

In his foreword to Lancaster's book, Henry Jenkins expressed his hope that using performance studies as a lens might allow fandom scholars to better recognize "the creative and expressive potential of everyday people."[10] Jenkins recognized that "metaphors of performance" would prove useful for analyzing emerging forms of media consumption that increasingly rely on intertextual, interactive, and immersive modes.[11] Yet for the most part, in the years following Lancaster's *Interacting with Babylon 5*, very few fan studies scholars attempted any robust application of performance theory to the study of fan practices or fan communities.

More recently, in 2015, the journal *Transformative Works and Cultures* (*TWC*) released a special issue that focuses on the relationship between fan studies and performance studies. In it, scholars and fans alike theorize the ways in which fandom is performative and how theories of performance can be used to better understand fandom. This special issue marks a renewed interest in performance studies; however, many of the articles tend to utilize metaphors of performance in limited ways. Several suggest that certain fan practices can be understood simply as performances of fandom. In this model, fan practices are viewed as a kind of social performance of identity. While the idea certainly rings true that fans perform their fandom by strategically representing affinities and associations in public spaces, it is of limited utility. What does it tell us about fans and their practices and desires that we do not already know? Certainly, particular fan practices—cosplay and gaming, for instance—can readily be understood as literal performances involving costuming and role-playing; however, other less literal forms of performativity also exist in fandom and deserve careful attention.

Abigail De Kosnik's contribution to the performance-focused issue of *TWC* suggests that reading fanfiction is performative. I have suggested that the kinds of online comments fans make in response to fanfiction and web series such as *The Lizzie Bennet Diaries* demonstrate a performance of fan subjectivity through a display of competence within the knowledge community. De Kosnik argues that a performance takes place specifically within the imagination of the reader of fanfiction as readers enact the descriptions of action and emotion based ineluctably on familiar restored behaviors of characters and actors represented within the original texts.[12] Her attention to imagination and memory as performative forces within fan practices offers a promising direction for studies of fanfiction. My own investigation of the visual culture influences embedded within Austen fanfiction supports De Kosnik's theories.

Matt Hills has written about the creation of "mimetic objects," such as replica props, which are made in an affirmational spirit and are intended to be authentic representations rather than transformational fan creations. Pushing against the disciplinary understandings of material culture within fandom, he argues that although it is possible to distinguish analytically between material and textual (nonmaterial) fan creations, they share more intersections and similarities than many scholars have acknowledged.[13] The evidence throughout my study of Austen fandom supports Hills's suggestion. For example, I believe Hills's argument particularly rings true regarding an object such as Scott Adams's letter to his wife, Barbara, which is a textual creation and yet has also become a sacred material object through its veneration and reuse over time. The distinction between material and textual fan creations is more permeable than many studies have allowed, and this aspect of fandom deserves further consideration. Whether affirmational or transformational and whether material, digital, or textual, our understanding of fan creations and fan practices will continue to benefit from a performance theory lens.

The creation of objects of fandom such as Scott Adams's letter is performative. The sharing of these objects is performative; their reception is performative. They are used in acts of surrogation. Moreover, they are imbued with an overlay of visual, textual, and material characteristics that derive from the genre and narrative conventions of the original beloved texts. From the visual pleasures afforded by fanfiction to the reliance on textual and narrative conventions of visual creations on Tumblr, objects of fandom evoke and perform the original text as well as the fan's love of the text. There is more to uncover regarding the rich imbrication of textuality, materiality, and visuality within these objects and the ways in which they are themselves performative and enable performances.

Throughout this work, I have given attention to the ontological similarities between different modes of fan engagement and the creations fans produce. In doing so, a picture has emerged of what Jane Austen fans in America have done to celebrate Austen's novels for nearly two hundred years. There is greater continuity than disparity between today's Austen fans and those of the nineteenth century than I supposed when I first began this study. And the discrete modes of engagement that became apparent to me as I researched practices within the Austen fandom also share more similarities than differences. My hope is that future studies of fandom will begin to interrogate those similarities and seek out subtle differences, looking to performativity to better understand the practices and materials of fandom.

Notes

INTRODUCTION

1. *Lost in Austen*, ITV (UK) miniseries, 2008.

2. Several recent books offer explanations for Austen's popularity and continued relevance to modern audiences. See Brownstein, *Why Jane Austen;* Harman, *Jane's Fame;* Johnson and Tuite, *Companion to Jane Austen;* Looser, *Making of Jane Austen.*

3. For literary studies of Austen's audiences see, e.g., Halsey, *Jane Austen and her Readers, 1786–1945;* Johnson, *Jane Austen's Cults and Cultures;* Lynch, ed., *Janeites: Austen's Disciples and Devotees;* and Wells, *Everybody's Jane: Austen in the Popular Imagination,* and *Reading Austen in America.* In *Everybody's Jane,* Wells describes the desires of everyday readers of Austen and highlights particular afterlives of the novels, exploring a variety of ways in which readers engage with Austen; the current study covers similar ground yet is distinguished from previous works on Austen's devotees by a grounding in the theories and methods of fan studies, focusing on cohesive features and practices discernible in the fandom and their continuity overtime.

4. Capra, "Between Tradition and Innovation," 139–49.

5. Sun, "Reception of Jane Austen in China," 55–59, 232.

6. The term *archontic* encompasses derivative literatures such as fanfiction and published spin-offs. I address the usefulness of this term in greater detail in later chapters.

7. Lawrence Grossberg argues in "Is There a Fan in the House?" (50–65) for the importance of understanding the "affective sensibility" of fandoms and how essential it is to fans' modes of engagement.

8. Turner, *From Ritual to Theatre,* 18.

9. In her influential *Gender Trouble,* Judith Butler argued that gender is constituted through performance; in *Limited Inc,* Jacques Derrida expands on J. L. Austin's theory of performativity to suggest that all language is performative and relies on what he calls "iteration," a restating or citation of past language.

10. Another recent study also hinges on performativity but focuses not on audiences and practices as I do, but rather on texts. In *Jane Austen and Performance,* Marina Cano explores

various performative adaptations of Austen's novels based on the premise that the novels themselves are innately performative.

11. "After Many Years," *Boston Journal,* no. 19409, September 10, 1892, 6, America's Historical Newspapers online database.

12. Rosenzweig and Thelen, *Presence of the Past.*

13. Boym, *Future of Nostalgia,* xv, xiii–xiv.

14. *Lost in Austen,* ITV (UK) miniseries, 2008.

15. Boym, *Future of Nostalgia,* xiv.

16. See Crang, "Placing Jane Austen, Displacing England"; Thompson, "How to Do Things with Austen."

17. Levine, *Highbrow/Lowbrow,* 23–24.

18. Pearson, "Bachies, Bardies, Trekkies, and Sherlockians," 98–109.

19. Leavis, *Great Tradition,* 7. Leavis feared a cultural decline and dumbing-down of culture in the twentieth century; he nostalgically felt Austen's novels captured everything lost in the course of modernization and world wars.

20. For various aspects of the publishing history of Austen, see Fergus, "Professional Woman Writer"; Todd, *Jane Austen in Context;* Halsey, *Jane Austen and Her Readers.*

21. In *Distinction,* social theorist Pierre Bourdieu observes the ways distinctions between high and low culture become codified, embedded, and reproduced in society and its structures. Bourdieu proposes that cultural competence related to knowledge and appreciation of culture helps to maintain social distinction and social classes (1–3).

22. St. John's College, "Catalogue Issue: Bulletin of St. John's College in Annapolis; Official Statement of the St. John's Program, Catalogue 1950," *St. John's College Digital Archives,* accessed September 2, 2018, http://digitalarchives.sjc.edu/items/show/183.

23. In "Commodifying Austen," e.g., Kate Bowles describes how the internet is to blame for a "growing horde of fans" and "worse, . . . the self-publication of fan fiction" (16).

24. Fordyce, "Sermon IV, On Female Virtue" in *Sermons to Young Women,* 176.

25. For negative critiques of fans, see Caughey, *Imaginary Social Worlds;* Schickel, *Intimate Strangers;* Burchill, *Damaged Gods;* Caughey discusses fans as having pathological delusions. Film critic Schickel argues that fans' relationship to celebrity has endangered society. British cultural critic Julie Burchill says fans—Americans particularly—have an impulse to deny reality. For a critique of negative stereotypes of fans, see Jolie Jenson, "Fandom as Pathology: The Consequences of Characterization."

26. *Escapism* appears in medical dictionaries to describe a pathological tendency to daydream or indulge in fantasy or entertainment as an escape from daily reality. *American Heritage Medical Dictionary,* s.v. "escapism."

27. Heidi Green, conversation with author, October 30, 2010.

28. Gelder, *Popular Fiction,* 5.

29. In *Reading the Romance,* e.g., Janice Radway argues that women read romance novels as a strategic way to return to daily duties emotionally reconstituted and replenished (184).

Romance readers use the text to go somewhere else, metaphorically, where they can explore mores, frustrations, dreams, and desires.

30. Young, "Subterranean World of Play," 150–51.

31. Jenkins, *Textual Poachers*. Jenkins was determined to show that fans were not misfits, dupes, or mindless consumers, as they were frequently portrayed at that time (1980s) by the media and many scholars.

32. Jenkins, "*Star Trek* Rerun, Reread, Rewritten," 197.

33. Felski, *Gender of Modernity*, 61–90. Felski argues that "woman as consumer" is a common trope of modernity. It represents anxiety and ambivalence about modern modes of consumption.

34. Jenkins, "*Star Trek* Rerun, Reread, Rewritten," 197.

35. Roach, *Cities of the Dead*, 14, 36, 3.

36. Ibid., xi.

37. These terms originated in an online discussion among fans posted on Dreamwidth. The idea is credited to "Obsession_inc." Obsession_inc, "Affirmational fandom vs. transformational fandom," Dreamwidth, June 1, 2009, http://obsession-inc.dreamwidth.org/82589.html.

38. Hills, "From Dalek Half Balls to Daft Punk Helmets," 1.2.

39. Jenkins, *Textual Poachers*, 280.

40. Pande, *Squee from the Margins*.

41. Pearson, "'It's Always 1895,'" 160.

42. Kiefer, "Anatomy of a Janeite," para. 3.

PART I PROLOGUE

1. Alcott, *Little Women*, Modern Library Edition, 98–99.

2. Ibid., 481 n. 4.

3. Shealy, "Louisa May Alcott's Juvenilia," 15–18.

CHAPTER ONE

1. Trilling, "*Emma* and the Legend of Jane Austen," 85. He believed this tendency revealed the human weakness of her admirers, driven by an impulse to "self-flattery."

2. Hills, *Fan Cultures*, ix.

3. Jenkins, *Textual Poachers*, 1–2.

4. Gamson, *Claims to Fame*, 19–22; see also Braudy, *Frenzy of Renown*, 380–89.

5. Braudy, *Frenzy of Renown*, 380–89.

6. Bakhtin, *Speech Genres and Other Late Essays*, 46–47.

7. See Judge, "Kidnapped and Counterfeit Characters"; and Simonova, *Early Modern Authorship and Prose Continuations*.

8. Judge, "Kidnapped and Counterfeit Characters," 38.

9. Nelson, *Market Sentiments*, 215–16.

10. Cavicchi, "Loving Music," 239.

11. Ibid., 223–24.

12. Ibid., 235–46; see also Cavicchi, *Listening and Longing.*

13. Cavicchi, "Loving Music," 239.

14. Lynch, "Cult of Jane Austen," 111.

15. Several scholars have recently addressed literary celebrity and the fannish responses of readers in this period, including Eisner, *Nineteenth-Century Poetry and Literary Celebrity;* Throsby, "Flirting with Fame"; Mayer, *Walter Scott and Fame.*

16. Martineau, "Literary Lionism," 139–50. Further citations of this work are given in the text.

17. Martineau, *Autobiography, with Memorials by Maria Weston Chapman,* 100, 429.

18. Emphasis mine.

19. Robertson, *Worshiping Walt,* 9.

20 Bram Stoker, quoted in Hindley, "When Bram Met Walt," n.p.

21. On fans as activists, see, e.g., Lancaster, *Interacting with Babylon* 5; Henry Jenkins and Sangita Shresthova, eds., "Transformative Works and Fan Activism," special issue, *Transformative Works and Cultures* 10 (June 2012).

22. Hindley, "When Bram Met Walt," n.p.

23. Eisner, *Nineteenth-Century Poetry and Literary Celebrity,* 136.

24. Elizabeth Barrett Browning, from a letter written in February 1842, quoted in Eisner, *Nineteenth-Century Poetry and Literary Celebrity,* 138, 136.

25. Browning, from a letter written in December 1856, quoted in Eisner, *Nineteenth-Century Poetry and Literary Celebrity,* 136.

26. Eisner, *Nineteenth-Century Poetry and Literary Celebrity,* 140.

27. On the rich history of this fandom, see "Sherlock Holmes," Fanlore Wiki, last modified April 11, 2018, http://fanlore.org/wiki/Sherlock_Holmes#History; Jamison, *Fic: Why Fanfiction Is Taking Over the World,* 42–46; Rosenblatt and Pearson, "Sherlock Holmes Fandom, Sherlockiana, and the Great Game"; Saler, "Clap if You Believe in Sherlock Holmes."

28. Martineau, *Autobiography, with Memorials by Maria Weston Chapman,* 100.

CHAPTER TWO

1. Wells, *Reading Austen in America,* 26. Today only six copies of this edition are known to exist, with two of those being recent discoveries by Juliette Wells.

2. Gilson, "Jane Austen's 'Emma' in America," 518, 519, 525.

3. In *Reading Austen in America,* Wells describes this copy in detail, outlining the negative marginalia left behind by early American readers who found *Emma* wanting.

4. Halsey, *Jane Austen and Her Readers,* 110.

5. "Notice," *Atkinson's Saturday Evening Post* 18, no. 919, March 9, 1839, 4, ProQuest American Periodicals. Also listed for sale in this notice are *Pickwick Papers,* and the novels of Scott, Bulwer, and Marryatt.

6. Gilson, "Later Publishing History," 135.

7. Halsey, *Jane Austen and Her Readers*, 112. For a much more exhaustive listing of published American editions and English editions available in the United States, see Gilson, *Bibliography of Jane Austen.*

8. See Lynch, "Cult of Jane Austen"; Johnson, *Jane Austen's Cults and Cultures.*

9. Harman, *Jane's Fame*, 95.

10. Lynch, "Cult of Jane Austen," 112.

11. Wagner, "Mrs. Hubback's *The Younger Sister*," n.p. The earliest sequels include Catherine Anne Hubback's 1850 completion of Austen's *The Watsons* and the attempt by Austen's niece, Anna Lefroy, to complete *Sanditon* in the 1830s. These texts have been written about in other contexts. See Wagner, "Mrs. Hubback's *The Younger Sister*"; Lynch, "Sequels"; Grey, *Jane Austen Handbook.*

12. Price and Smith, *Periodical Literature in Nineteenth-Century America*, 3.

13. Ibid., 5. According to Price and Smith, between 1830 and 1890, the United States saw many transformations that allowed the flourishing of periodical circulation: technological developments in printing; increased distribution made possible by railroad and postal routes; rising literacy rates due to expanded public education; and economic and population growth (3–5).

14. Noonan, *Reading The Century Illustrated Monthly*, x–xi; see also Conn, *Museums and American Intellectual Life;* DiMaggio, "Cultural Entrepreneurship."

15. Ibid., xi; see also Langston, "Sarah Josepha Hale's Rhetoric of 'Mental Improvement.'"

16. "Female Literature of the Present Age," *Atheneum; or, Spirit of the English Magazines* 7, no. 10, August 15, 1820, 472, ProQuest American Periodicals.

17. "Female Authors," *Casket* 4 (April 1827): 145, ProQuest American Periodicals. Also found in *Philadelphia Album and Ladies Literary Gazette*, September 1827; and in *New York Mirror*, September 8, 1827.

18. Allen Cunningham, "British Literature: Biographical and Critical History of the Literature of the Last Fifty Years," *Literary Inquirer* 2, no. 22, June 4, 1834, 172, ProQuest American Periodicals.

19. "The 'Conversazione,'" in [*Godey's*] *Lady's Book* (January 1837): 1, ProQuest American Periodicals.

20. "The Novels of Jane Austen; with a Biographical Notice of the Author," *Gentleman's Magazine* 3, no. 3 (September 1838): 220, ProQuest American Periodicals.

21. "Editor's Table," *Journal of Belles Lettres*, August 21, 1838, 8, ProQuest American Periodicals.

22. "Literary Review," *Ladies' Companion* (October 1838): 299, ProQuest American Periodicals. *Oliver Twist* and *Nicholas Nickleby* each receive fewer than six lines of description; Charles Addison's *Damascus and Palmyra* receives the lengthiest treatment besides Austen's works, with seventeen lines of text.

23. G.F.D., "Jane Austen," *American Review: A Whig Journal Devoted to Politics and Literature* 4, no. 6 (December 1849): 621, ProQuest American Periodicals.

24. "Novels of the Season," *North American Review* 67, no. 141 (October 1848): 367–68, Making of America Collection.

25. "Sparks's *Life and Works of Dr. Franklin*," *North American Review* 59, no. 125 (October 1844): 453, Making of America Collection.

CHAPTER THREE

1. Wagner, "Mrs. Hubback's *The Younger Sister*," para. 2. Austen's niece Anna Lefroy attempted to finish the incomplete *Sanditon*, but it was left in fragments until published in 1983.

2. Abigail De Kosnik first suggested the term *archontic* in her influential chapter, "Archontic Literature: A Definition, a History, and Several Theories of Fan Fiction" (published under the name Abigail Derecho); she has since expanded on this idea in *Rogue Archives* (2016).

3. Derecho [De Kosnik], "Archontic Literature," 65. I return to theoretical concerns regarding archontic works in part III.

4. De Kosnik, *Rogue Archives*, 275.

5. Carlson, *Performance*, 49.

6. Derecho [De Kosnik], "Archontic Literature," 63–66.

7. Miss [Eliza] Leslie, "The Beaux, a Sketch," *Godey's Lady's Book* (January 1842): 19, ProQuest American Periodicals.

8. Two maternal characters from *Sense and Sensibility* and *Pride and Prejudice*, respectively.

9. Wickham is the dashing yet dastardly ne'er-do-well of *Pride and Prejudice*, and Lydia is Elizabeth Bennet's youngest sister, foolish enough to fall for his tricks.

10. Leslie, "Beaux," 19.

11. Austen, *Pride and Prejudice*, 32, Oxford World's Classics.

12. Leslie, "Beaux," 19.

13. Pugh, *Democratic Genre*, 219.

14. Lang, *Old Friends*, 98. Further citations of this work are given in the text.

15. Basu, "Virgilian Fandom in the Renaissance."

16. Jamison, *Fic*, 35. In part III, I explore in greater detail specific theoretical concerns surrounding today's fanfiction.

17. "Recent Books on England," *North American Review* 83, no. 173 (October 1856): 519–20, Making of America Collection.

18. In part IV, I return to literary pilgrimage in greater detail. For a history of literary tourism, see Nicola Watson, *Literary Tourist*. Watson offers historical context for the rise in visiting poet's graves in the mid-eighteenth century.

19. Tuckerman, *Month in England*, 10. Further citations of this work are given in the text.

20. Turner, *From Ritual to Theatre*, 18.

21. Palmer, *Woman's Wit and Whimsy*, 3. In *Reading Austen in America*, Juliette Wells discusses Anna's diaries and brings to light in detail the important role Anna and her family played in Austen's American reception in the mid-nineteenth century.

22. A. C. Waterston [Anna Cabot Lowell Quincy], "Jane Austen," *Atlantic Monthly* 11 (February 1863): 235–37, Google Books. Further citations of this work are given in the text.

23. Quoted in Palmer, *Woman's Wit and Whimsy*, 62, 82.

24. Palmer, *Woman's Wit and Whimsy*, 85.

25. Quoted in ibid., 139. In *Emma*, Mrs. Elton boasts about riding in this particularly expensive style of carriage.

26. Letter from Anna Waterston to James Fields, quoted in Palmer, *Woman's Wit and Whimsy*, 148.

27. Letter from Eliza Susan Quincy to Sir Francis Austen, quoted in Austen-Leigh, *Memoir of Jane Austen and Other Family Recollections*, 114–15. Further citations of this work are given in the text.

28. Howe, *Articulate Sisters*.

29. Quoted in Palmer, *Woman's Wit and Whimsy*, 147. The letter from Anna to Eliza is transcribed in its entirety in Palmer's appendix. For a more detailed description of the ongoing and engaging correspondence between the Quincys and Sir Francis Austen's family, see Wells, *Reading Austen in America*.

30. Mr. Mabie, "Literary Talks," *Ladies' Home Journal* 19, no. 11 (October 1902): 17, ProQuest American Periodicals.

31. "Literature of Today," *Chicago Herald*, December 12, 1891, 12, America's Historical Newspapers online database.

32. "Literary Chat," *Boston Daily Advertiser* 159, no. 82, April 5, 1892, 5, America's Historical Newspapers online database.

33. "Out & About," *Worcester Daily Spy* 132, no. 124, May 4, 1901, 7, America's Historical Newspapers online database.

34. Jeannette A. Marks, "Wellesley Girls in the Play," *Ladies' Home Journal* 17, no. 5 (April 1900): 17, ProQuest American Periodicals.

35. Pugh, *Democratic Genre*, 193.

36. For a comprehensive list of known adaptations and spin-offs through 1999, see Rolf Breuer, "Jane Austen etc.: The Completions, Continuations and Adaptations of Her Novels," http://webdoc.gwdg.de/edoc/ia/eese/breuer/biblio.html, accessed on August 30, 2018.

37. Bennett, quoted in Halsey, *Jane Austen and Her Readers*, 187.

PART II PROLOGUE

1. Goodspeed's Book Shop (Boston) to Barbara Winn Adams, February 20, 1940, Winn Family Jane Austen Collection, container 1, folder 16, Goucher College Library.

2. Alberta Burke to the Columbia Broadcasting System (CBS), November 24, 1940, Alberta and Henry Burke Jane Austen Collection, container 7, folder 4, Goucher College Library.

3. Winn Adams and Burke do not appear to have known each other at this time, or later on. However, Alberta's husband, Henry, would likely have met Winn Adams in 1979 or 1980, as both were founding members of JASNA.

4. Garvey, "Scissoring and Scrapbooks," 212.

5. Jenkins, *Fans, Bloggers, Gamers*, 136.

6. Ibid., 149. I address these more recent fan practices in part III.

7. Belk et al., "Collectors and Collecting," 550–51. For more about collecting, see Martin, *Popular Collecting and the Everyday Self;* Muensterberger, *Collecting.* I engage further with scholarly ideas about collecting in the epilogue to this section.

8. Moreover, some scholars see collecting as regressive, a view redolent of negative critiques of fandom and with which I disagree. Jean Baudrillard viewed collecting as narcissistic, imbued with a desire to see in oneself an "absolutely singular being" by possessing objects that are singular ("System of Collecting," 12). Muensterberger suggests that collecting results from childhood trauma and is reflective of a phallic-narcissistic personality; he claims that collectors "like to pose or make a spectacle of their possessions," which are simply "stand-ins for themselves" (*Collecting*, 13). Narratologist Mieke Bal views collecting as a narrative that allows the collector to develop a sense of self and to display subjectivity to those who view the collection ("Telling Objects," 105).

9. Benjamin, "Unpacking My Library," 60.

10. Stewart, *On Longing*, 151. Stewart has theorized the nature of both collections and souvenirs (including scrapbooks). She views collections as spatial and material rather than temporal and scrapbooks as having a complicated relationship to temporality, having the ability to bring the past into the present.

11. Roach, *Cities of the Dead*, 3, xi.

12. Historian Robin Bernstein has suggested that analysis of uses of material objects can recover "performances of everyday life," from the past (*Racial Innocence*, 8). Although I feel these scrapbooks do not neatly fit Bernstein's useful notion of "scriptive objects," her theorizing of the performativity of material culture has informed my thinking.

13. Garvey, *Writing with Scissors*, 208–14. For histories of scrapbooking practices, see also Tucker, Ott, and Buckler, *Scrapbook in American life.*

14. See Aron, *Working at Play;* Gelber, *Hobbies.*

15. Ott, "Between Person and Profession," 29, 31.

16. Christensen, "'Look at Us Now,'" 181, 179.

17. Garvey, "Scissoring and Scrapbooks," 219.

18. Jenkins, *Fans, Bloggers, Gamers*, 140; Baym, "Talking about Soaps." Baym uses the term *socioemotional* to underscore the affective interactions of soap opera fans.

19. Jenkins, *Fans, Bloggers, Gamers*, 139.

20. A survey of landmark texts on fandom reveals scant mention of scrapbooking. But a quick internet search reveals its prevalence, including blogs that display images of scrapbooks created by *Star Trek* fans over the past five decades and sites that sell *Twilight Saga*–related scrapbooking materials. Furthermore, sites such as Pinterest and Tumblr offer forums for digital curation that resemble scrapbooking. I address these similarities in part III. Recently, Evan Hayles Gledhill has taken up this subject in "Tumblr and the Romantic Sentiment Album."

21. Describing Alberta Burke's scrapbooking and collecting habits in *Everybody's Jane,* Juliette Wells claims that Alberta was "the direct forerunner of post-1995 fans," yet she also suggests that the activities of fans today have changed as they have expanded (59). My reading of Alberta's scrapbooks alongside the others suggests otherwise. Rather, I argue the individuals and their scrapbooks discussed here demonstrate that while the materials have changed from analog to digital, the habits and impulses are not so different from those of fans today.

22. Garvey, "Scissoring and Scrapbooks," 215, 224.

CHAPTER FOUR

Epigraph: Alberta Burke to CBS, November 24, 1940, Alberta and Henry Burke Jane Austen Collection, container 7, folder 4, Goucher College Library.

1. Henry Burke, "Books, Burkes, and Bibliophiles," March 30, 1976, Burke Collection, container 4, folder 24. This was an address to the Baltimore Bibliophiles. For a lengthier treatment of the Burke's collecting habits, see Wells, *Everybody's Jane.* I am grateful to Wells for her thoughtful descriptions of Alberta's collecting which informed my analysis of the same archive. Utilizing some of the same sources as Wells, I offer fresh interpretation that builds on her strong foundation.

2. Henry Burke letter to Charles Ryskamp, Morgan Library, July 1, 1975, Burke Collection, container 1, folder 5.

3. Alberta Burke draft letter to Sarah Jones, Goucher Library, November 22, 1954, Burke Collection, container 9, folder 12.

4. Alberta Burke to Helen Hayes Theatre, November 24, 1940, Burke Collection, container 7, folder 4.

5. Scrapbook, vol. 1, December 1935–March 1944, Burke Collection, container 7, folder 1.

6. Additionally, one particularly fine book on fashion history went to the Walters Art Gallery in Baltimore, and a book once owned by Jane Austen went to Jane Austen's House Museum, Chawton. David Gilson, obituary for Alberta Burke, Burke Collection, container 1, folder 2.

7. Henry Burke to Charles Ryskamp, July 1, 1975, Burke Collection, container 1, folder 5.

8. Wells, *Everybody's Jane,* 49. Wells paints a rich portrait of Alberta's unique subjectivity as an Austen devotee.

9. In addition, David Gilson donated to Goucher the letters he received from Burke.

10. Scrapbook, vol. 7, April 1959–October 1963, Burke Collection, container 9, folders 15, 16.

11. Alberta Burke letter to Dr. David Robertson, president, Goucher College, January 19, 1939, Burke Collection, container 7, folder 2.

12. Scrapbook, vol. 3, April 1944–August 1948, Burke Collection, container 8, folder 6.

13. Roach, *Cities of the Dead,* 2–3.

14. Alberta Burke letter to Eleanor Falley (1941), Burke Collection, container 1.

15. Scrapbook, vol. 4, June 1948–July 1952, Burke Collection, container 8, folder 8. I will discuss this early example of archontic literature in more detail in the next section.

16. Dust jackets were not considered an integral part of a collectable book until the 1950s, so while book collectors today would be horrified by Burke's decision to cut them up and paste them into a scrapbook, in 1949, the jacket was still considered nothing more than an illustrated wrapper used for promotional purposes. See Tanselle, *Book-Jackets.*

17. Scrapbook, vol. 4, June 1948–July 1952, Burke Collection, container 8, folder 8.

18. Scrapbook, vol. 5, August 1952–September 1956, Burke Collection, container 9, folder 11.

19. Items removed from Scrapbook, vol. 5, August 1952–September 1956, Burke Collection, container 9, folder 12.

20. This shift in tone also corresponds to the burgeoning professionalization of literary studies in the mid-twentieth century.

21. Scrapbook, vol. 2, July 1940–November 1942, Burke Collection, container 7, folder 3.

22. Alberta Burke, "Two Anniversaries," *Saturday Review of Literature,* December 14, 1935, Burke Collection, container 1, folder 1. At the time she wrote this, there were indeed no Austen societies in the United Kingdom or the United States. The reference to baked apples is taken from *Emma* and would have been recognized by fellow Austen fans. Burke attributes the name "Janeites" to Kipling's short story of that name about World War I soldiers reading Austen in the trenches. In fact, the term was first coined by George Saintsbury in 1894.

23. B. C. Southam, "Northanger Abbey," *Times Literary Supplement* 3163, October 12, 1962, 800, Gale TLS Historical Archive (EX1200130084).

24. Alberta Burke, "Northanger Abbey," *Times Literary Supplement* 3167, November 9, 1962, 857, Gale TLS Historical Archive (EX1200325867); also found in Burke Collection, container 1, folder 1.

25. Scrapbook, vol. 5, August 1952–September 1956, Burke Collection, container 9, folder 11.

26. Alberta Burke letter to Dr. David Robertson, president, Goucher College, January 19, 1939, Burke Collection, container 7, folder 2.

27. Alberta Burke letter to CBS, November 24, 1940, Burke Collection, container 7, folder 3; Alberta Burke letter to David Gilson, February 28, 1968, Burke Collection, container 1, folder 12.

28. Alberta Burke letter to David Gilson, December 1, 1967, Burke Collection, container 1, folder 12.

29. Obituary for Alberta Burke by David Gilson, Burke Collection, container 1, folder 2.

30. Henry Burke letter to Charles Ryskamp, Morgan Library, July 1, 1975, Burke Collection, container 1, folder 5.

31. Alberta Burke letter to CBS, November 24, 1940, Burke Collection, container 7, folder 3.

32. Joan Austen-Leigh letter to Henry Burke, 1985, Burke Collection, container 3, folder 18.

CHAPTER FIVE

1. Although Alberta Burke's collection has received some scholarly attention (see Juliette Wells, *Everybody's Jane*), Barbara Winn Adams's collection, also housed at Goucher, has been overshadowed. The Burke Collection has been a well-known part of Goucher's holdings since 1975, whereas Winn Adams's collection arrived at Goucher only in 1998.

2. Barbara Winn Adams letter to David Gilson, September 10, 1984, Winn Family Jane Austen Collection, 1815–1991, container 1, folder 4, Goucher College Library; hereafter cited as Winn Family Collection.

3. Scott and Barbara Adams divorced in the 1970s; later in her life, Barbara preferred to be called Mrs. Winn Adams.

4. This collection, the Edith C. Rice Collection of Children's Literature, was named for a children's librarian in Arlington, MA, who inspired Winn Adams's love of reading. See https://usm.maine.edu/library/specialcollections/book-collections.

5. Barbara Winn Adams handwritten notes, Winn Family Collection, container 3a, folder 33.

6. In a letter to Winn Adams in October 1980, JANSA cofounder Jack Grey alludes to Burke's scrapbooks and his desire to see them so that he and Winn Adams might "compare notes," thus implying that she had seen them. Jack Grey letter to Barbara Winn Adams, October 30, 1982, Winn Family Collection, container 1, folder 2.

7. Scrapbook, 1935–48, Winn Family Collection, container 1, folder 20.

8. Binder Scrapbook, Winn Family Collection, container 2, folder 32.

9. The stage production, directed by Max Gordon, opened in 1935 and played at the Plymouth Theatre. Its success and popularity led to the production of the 1940 MGM film.

10. Barbara Winn Adams letter to David Gilson, September 10, 1984, Winn Family Collection, container 1, folder 4.

CHAPTER SIX

1. Byrne, "Afterword," *Persuasions Online* 32, no. 2 (Spring 2012): n.p.

2. George Tucker letter to Gale Research Company, April 5, 1985. George H. Tucker Donor File, Special Collections, Swem Library, College of William & Mary.

3. Robert Mason, "Introduction," in Tucker, *Tidewater Landfalls*, n.p. Many of Tucker's columns were gathered into two volumes published by Landmark Communications, the parent company of the *Virginian-Pilot*, in 1969 and 1975. Tucker also published *Abstracts from Norfolk City Marriage Bonds, 1797–1850* (1934), *Norfolk Highlights* (1972), *Virginia Supernatural Tales: Ghosts, Witches, and Eerie Doings* (1977), *Cavalier Saints and Sinners: Virginia History Through a Keyhole* (1990), and *Bedlam without Bars: A Fanciful Dixie Peep Show* (1991).

4. Mason, "Introduction," in Tucker, *Tidewater Landfalls*, n.p.

5. Susan Rainwater, email message to author, October 11, 2013. Ms. Rainwater is Tucker's second cousin once removed.

6. George Tucker letter to Gale Research Company, April 5, 1985. This letter was regarding his entry submission to *Contemporary Authors* to be published by Gale, in which he was eager to be included. It does not appear that he was included.

7. George Tucker to Gale Research Company, April 5, 1985.

8. This book was revised and rereleased in 1998 as *A History of Jane Austen's Family.*

9. Le Faye, "'Three or Four Families,'" para. 3.

10. George Tucker to Gale Research Company, April 5, 1985.

11. Paula Byrne, "Afterword," *Persuasions Online* 32, no. 2 (Spring 2012): para. 9.

12. Tucker, *Goodly Heritage,* 118; see also Scrapbook, vol. 2, George Holbert Tucker Collection of Jane Austen Materials, Special Collections, Swem Library, College of William & Mary; hereafter cited as "Tucker Collection." Vol. 2 contains biographical information on Edward, including the correspondence from Deane, England.

13. Herbert Cahoon letter to George Tucker, September 12, 1977, Tucker Collection, vol. 35.

14. Herbert Cahoon letter to George Tucker, May 24, 1978, Tucker Collection, vol. 35.

15. George Tucker letter to Swem Library, April 11, 1987, George H. Tucker Donor File, Special Collections, Swem Library, College of William & Mary.

16. Susan Rainwater, email to author, October 11, 2013.

17. George Tucker letter to Swem Library, April 11, 1987. He later added notebooks, which brought the total to 109.

18. Ibid.

19. Tucker Collection, vol. 14. I have been unable to find out what Austen-Leigh was referring to regarding plagiarism or what Tucker's discovery might have been.

20. Tucker Collection, vol. 11. This passage was taken from Austen-Leigh, *Jane Austen and Southhampton,* 46.

21. Tucker, *Jane Austen the Woman,* 42. Piggott is author of *The Innocent Diversion: Music in the Life and Writings of Jane Austen* (1979).

22. Tucker Collection, vol. 11. These photocopies bear a stamp from the Pierpont Morgan Library. These two account pages from 1807 were part of Alberta Burke's collection, which she gave to the Morgan Library.

CHAPTER SEVEN

1. Gilson, *Bibliography of Jane Austen,* ix.

2. Juliette Wells has recently recounted the rich correspondence between Gilson and Burke in *Reading Austen in America.* She describes his book collecting, highlighting similarities and difference between Gilson and Burke (185–203).

3. Nancy Magnuson, email message to author, September 16, 2014. I am grateful to Tara Olivero, curator of special collections and archives at Goucher College, for informing me of the arrival of Gilson's scrapbook and allowing me to look at it prior to processing.

4. Chris Viveash to Nancy Magnuson, Goucher Library, June 15, 2013, David Gilson Accession File, Goucher College Library.

5. David Gilson Scrapbook, Goucher College Library.

6. This card was part of a "Celebrities of British History" series, made by cigarette company Carreras in 1935.

7. The 1940 film made gross changes to the story, and the costumes anachronistically set the film in the 1840s rather than the Regency era.

PART II EPILOGUE

1. Baudrillard, "System of Collecting," 12.

2. Ibid., 24.

3. Jack Grey letter to Barbara Winn Adams, October 30, 1982, Winn Family Collection, folder 3.

4. Henry Burke address to the Baltimore Bibliophiles, "Books, Burkes, and Bibliophiles," March 30, 1976, Burke Collection, container 4, folder 24.

5. Ott, "Between Person and Profession," 34–35.

PART III PROLOGUE

1. "Fifty-Six and Counting!" *JASNA News* 14, no. 2 (Summer 1998): 1. A great deal has been written about Austen spin-offs, continuations, fanfiction, and the like. See, e.g., Dow and Hanson, *Uses of Austen: Jane's Afterlives;* Wells, *Everybody's Jane.*

2. Yaffe, *Among the Janeites*, xiii.

3. Wells, *Everybody's Jane*, 115.

4. In *Rogue Archives*, Abigail De Kosnik recently argued for an expanded use of *archontic* to encompass all fan works, not just textual ones. My findings support this pivot toward this broader understanding of what she now calls "archontic production" (275).

5. Derecho [De Kosnik], "Archontic Literature: A Definition, a History, and Several Theories of Fanfiction," 61–78.

6. Ibid., 65–66.

7. Pugh, *Democratic Genre*, 9.

8. Derecho, "Archontic Literature," 69–70.

9. See, e.g., Cartmell and Whelehan, *Cambridge Companion to Literature on Screen;* Macdonald and Macdonald, *Jane Austen on Screen.*

10. See Monaghan et al., *Cinematic Jane Austen.*

11. Kylie Mirmohamadi has recently explored the online environments of fandom in her study of Austen fanfiction and intertextuality in *The Digital Afterlives of Jane Austen: Janeites at the Keyboard.*

12. Evan Hayles Gledhill has also recently engaged with this idea in the 2018 article, "Tumblr and the Romantic Sentiment Album: Bricolage and the Culture of the Margins."

13. These terms were originally coined in a post by a Live Journal and Dreamwidth user "Obsession_inc," http://obsession-inc.dreamwidth.org/82589.html, June 1, 2009.

CHAPTER EIGHT

1. Jenkins, *Fans, Bloggers, Gamers*, 142.

2. Ibid.

3. "About," Tumblr, accessed on September 22, 2018. All Tumblr URLs referenced in this chapter were accessed multiple times in fall 2014. I gratefully acknowledge the support of bloggers who offered friendly encouragement and granted me permission to reproduce images of their posts.

4. A GIF, or graphic interchange format, is a file format that allows a short clip of digital moving images to repeat in a loop. GIFs do not include sound and are usually only a few seconds long. Most GIFs on Tumblr are grouped into sets.

5. Kaila Hale-Stern, "In a Catastrophically Bad Move, Tumblr Will Ban All Adult Content," *Mary Sue*, published December 3, 2018, https://www.themarysue.com/tumblr-will-ban-all-adult-content/. This article provides a good overview of the principle concerns over the sudden changes to Tumblr; the posted comments highlight the frustrations of Tumblr bloggers declaring they will seek new platforms.

6. Shannon Liao, "After the Porn Ban, Tumblr Users Have Ditched the Platform as Promised," *Verge*, published March 14, 2019, https://www.theverge.com/2019/3/14/18266013/tumblr- porn-ban-lost-users-down-traffic.

7. Hale-Stern, "In a Catastrophically Bad Move."

8. http://fuckyeahjaneites.tumblr.com/. Naming a blog "Fuck Yeah" is a common convention. Sometimes the name is abbreviated to give a cleaner version of this celebratory sentiment, such as "F Yeah Mr. Darcy."

9. http://hulksmashsmaug.tumblr.com/. The blog's subtitle reads, "accio arkenstone," referencing both *Harry Potter* and *The Hobbit*.

10. Barthes, *Camera Lucida*, 96.

11. Ibid., 78.

12. Bazin, *What Is Cinema*, 9.

13. Barthes, *Camera Lucida*, 25–27, 55.

14. Ibid., 5.

15. Ibid., 89.

16. Original work is valued in other genres of fan creations as well. E.g., cosplayers who craft every aspect of a costume themselves from scratch are respected more than those who purchase or are given costume parts or props.

17. Bloggers sometimes post fanfiction on Tumblr, but most use other platforms such as FanFiction.net or Archive of Our Own to share their writing. Occasionally, bloggers use

Tumblr to request from their followers recommendations for fanfiction to read or inspiration and prompts for things to write about.

18. These types of "slash" pairings in fanfiction have been addressed by Henry Jenkins in *Textual Poachers;* Camille Bacon-Smith in *Enterprising Women;* and many others. Noncanonical pairings are frequently homoerotic (e.g., Harry/Draco) but not always (e.g., Harry/Hermione).

19. http://my-thoughts-of-flight.tumblr.com/post/92472117072/au-the-doctor-is-traveling-when-he-meets-the.

20. Pugh, *Democratic Genre,* 43.

21. http://buhaybabae.tumblr.com/post/69668266800.

22. http://serecenhawke.tumblr.com/.

23. Here I am specifically referring to the kinds of Tumblr blog posts that utilize found material, not those that share original art. I would add, however, that in some cases, original art becomes an original source for other bloggers to manipulate, not just to re-blog and share.

24. The concept of "bricolage" was introduced by anthropologist Claude Lévi-Strauss, and later applied by cultural studies scholar Dick Hebdige (*Subculture: The Meaning of Style*) to the study of subcultures. More recently, in "Tumblr and the Romantic Sentiment Album," Evan Hayles Gledhill uses the term *bricolage* to compare scrapbooks and Tumblr blogs; they claim that these are resistant practices and often marginalized. Yet they conclude that "bricoleurs" ultimately end up replicating dominant cultural ideas. While I agree with the assessment that these practices demonstrate continuity across media and time, I would like to suggest that *bricolage* is not the right term to employ precisely because the creation is ultimately not disruptive.

25. Hebdige, *Subculture,* 17–18, 102–5.

26. Garrulus, online communication with author, February 24, 2015.

CHAPTER NINE

1. Pemberley Digital website, http://www.pemberleydigital.com/about/. Pemberley Digital has since released an adaption of *Emma* called *Emma Approved,* Austen's incomplete novel *Sanditon,* called *Welcome to Sanditon,* Mary Shelley's *Frankenstein,* as *Frankenstein M.D.,* and others. Scholars have responded to *The Lizzie Bennet Diaries* and other Pemberley Digital adaptations in a variety of ways, with some analyzing their narrative strategies and digital rhetoric and others criticizing their commodification of Austen. See, e.g., Caddy, "New Media and Transmedia: Jane Austen in the Digital Age"; Russo, "Austen Approved: Pemberley Digital and the Transmedia Commodification of Jane Austen."

2. https://www.facebook.com/pg/LizzieBennetDiaries/about/.

3. https://www.youtube.com/channel/UCRt5wuVdwkFYvZdp7Bglhew.

4. http://looksbyjane.tumblr.com/.

5. Caddy, "Fan Media and Transmedia," 48.

6. Lydia is referring to the fact that actress Renée Zellweger gained weight to portray Bridget Jones in the film adaptation of Helen Fielding's novel, *Bridget Jones's Diary.*

7. Austen, *Pride and Prejudice,* Oxford World's Classics, 9.

8. Barthes, quoted in Hellekson and Busse, *Fanfiction and Fan Communities,* 6.

9. Hellekson and Busse, *Fanfiction and Fan Communities,* 6.

10. Accessed October 26, 2014.

11. It is likely that episode 1 has a higher rate due to viewers who give the series a try but ultimately decide not to watch more. Additionally, many viewers may be clicking on the link to the first episode in order to access the entire playlist, adding to the view count even when attempting to locate a different episode in the playlist.

12. Comments dated October 2, 2014, and October 19, 2013, respectively.

13. Captain Torchwood, February 5, 2013, comment on *LBD,* episode 55.

14. Erin Howarth, November 30, 2013, comment on *LBD,* episode 4.

15. Simsluver491, November 14, 2013, comment on *LBD,* episode 60.

16. Dane Plaza, March 24, 2014, comment on *LBD,* episode 60.

17. The Improbable Squid, February 5, 2014, comment on *LBD,* episode 60.

18. Talia Bennett, January 18, 2013, comment on *LBD,* episode 55.

19. TheLovingthis, October 17, 2012, comment on *LBD,* episode 55.

20. Becky, November 30, 2012, comment on *LBD,* episode 55.

CHAPTER TEN

1. James, *Question of Our Speech,* 62.

2. Coppa, "Writing Bodies in Space," 243.

3. Hellekson and Busse, *Fanfiction and Fan Communities,* 6–7.

4. Ibid. Moreover, fanfiction is often open-ended in the sense that it is posted online one chapter at a time, keeping readers in suspense. Furthermore, writers sometimes abandon stories, leaving them forever unfinished.

5. Pugh, *Democratic Genre,* 10–11.

6. Hellekson and Busse, *Fanfiction and Fan Communities,* 26.

7. Coppa, "Writing Bodies in Space," 229.

8. See Derecho [De Kosnik], "Archontic Literature," 67; Jenkins, *Textual Poachers.*

9. In *Textual Poachers* (162–77), Henry Jenkins distinguishes ten narrative tactics used in fanfiction: recontextualization; expanding the timeline; refocalization; moral realignment; genre shifting; crossovers; character dislocation; personalization; emotional intensification; eroticization. In her influential article "Brownian Motion" (135–62), Constance Penley argues that female fans relate to gay male bodies because their bodies are a political battleground just as women's have always been and that slash fiction offers a remaking of masculinity to suit feminist ideals and needs.

10. Slash pairings and other tropes (e.g., crossovers) that would require fic writers to deviate from Austen's intended romantic entanglements can be found on Archive of Our

Own (ao3.org), but they are still far outnumbered by more affirmational fics. I found virtually no examples of these otherwise common fic tropes and genres on FanFiction.net or any of the Austen-specific sites.

11. Mulvey, "Visual Pleasure and Narrative Cinema," 19.

12. Brinton, "Author's Introduction" to *Old Friends and New Fancies.*

13. Austen-Leigh, *Memoir of Jane Austen,* 118–19.

14. Brinton, *Old Friends and New Fancies,* 9.

15. Ibid., 80.

16. Like Brinton, very little is known about Bonavia-Hunt. Her father was a clergyman and founded Trinity College of Music in London. Laurel Ann Nattress, "*Pemberley Shades:* The Legend of the Lost Sequel," *Austenprose,* September 17, 2008, http://austenprose.com/tag/d-a- bonavia-hunt/.

17. Bonavia-Hunt, *Pemberley Shades,* 101. Further citations of this work are given in the text.

18. Pugh, *Democratic Genre,* 37.

19. As of March 2019.

20. Caprittarius'Rising, *A Dream of You,* chap. 3, para. 13–14. https://www.fanfiction.net/s/7473932/1/A-Dream-of-You. This author, Sheena Monroe, asked that her real name be included in citation. I am grateful to the fic writers who graciously gave me permission to quote their work and warmly offered encouragement.

21. Snowberryrose, *Dusk,* "Author's Note," https://www.fanfiction.net/s/10356340/1/Dusk.

22. Ibid., para. 9.

23. Astonishment, May 17, 2014, comment on Snowberryrose, *Dusk.*

24. Foxy11814, June 26, 2014, comment on Snowberryrose, *Dusk.*

25. LotsOfLaundry, September 1, 2014, comment on Snowberryrose, *Dusk.*

26. Snowberryrose, *Dusk,* para. 4.

27. Ibid., para. 6.

28. Caprittarius'Rising, *Dream of You,* chap. 3, para. 10.

29. Ibid., description and author's note; emphasis mine.

30. Fredrica, *Sweet Torment,* chap. 22, para. 62. Originally, this piece was forty chapters, thirty-five thousand words; it has since been removed from FanFiction.net (the prologue remains) as the author, Fredrica Edward, is in the process of self-publishing the work (correspondence with author, May 2019).

31. Ibid., chap. 14, para. 1.

32. Aureader, *Sense of Obligation,* chap. 6, para. 40. This story has since been removed from FanFiction.net in order to be self-published (Amazon.com) under the name Rose Fairbanks.

33. Fredrica, *Sweet Torment,* chap. 38, para. 28.

34. Gen, June 21, 2014, comment on Gingersnapperr, *Mr. Darcy's Lucky Stairs.*

35. Kmart92, September 17, 2014, comment on Gingersnapperr, *Mr. Darcy's Lucky Stairs.*

36. Kmart92, September 14, 2014; emphasis mine.

37. Dizzy Lizzy.60, October 15, 2014, comment on Anonymouslyme8, *I Hate You, Most Ardently,* chap. 15.

38. Dizzy Lizzy.60, November 8, 2014, comment on Anonymouslyme8, *I Hate You, Most Ardently,* chap. 17.

39. Jamison, *Fic,* 35–36.

40. Jenkins, *Textual Poachers,* 282.

41. Roach, *Cities of the Dead,* xi, 3.

PART IV PROLOGUE

1. Southam, "Jane Austen and Winchester Cathedral," 229.

2. Yaffe, *Among the Janeites,* 220, 221–22.

3. Reader and Walter, *Pilgrimage in Popular Culture,* 9–10.

4. The vast majority of fans discussed here are, in fact, white but not exclusively.

CHAPTER ELEVEN

1. Jenkins, *Fans, Bloggers, Gamers,* 142.

2. Porter, "To Boldly Go," 247, 249–50, 252, 248; see also Turner, "Variations on a Theme of Liminality," 47–48.

3. Porter, "To Boldly Go," 257.

4. Turner, "Pilgrimage as Social Processes," 207–9.

5. Tuner, *From Ritual to Theater,* 29.

6. Yaffe, *Among the Janeites,* 225.

7. Directed by Rupert Edwards. The BBC has released this title on DVD in the United Kingdom, but it is currently only available in the United States on YouTube, thanks to a fan.

8. Austen-Leigh, "Founding of JASNA," 7–13.

9. Lorraine Hanaway, interview with author, October 29, 2010.

10. Austen-Leigh, "Founding of JASNA," 12.

11. Ibid., 9.

12. Jack Grey, quoted in Austen-Leigh, "Founding of JASNA," 12. Taken from a letter, June 1, 1980.

13. JASNA's website lists all past and upcoming AGMs.

14. Brochure from the 2013 JASNA AGM, author's collection. All AGM brochures cited in this chapter are viewable online: http://www.jasna.org/agms/index.html.

15. Ibid.

16. *JASNA News* 27, no. 1 (Spring 2011): 1, 8; emphasis mine.

17. Wells, *Everybody's Jane,* 103.

18. Goffman, *Presentation of Self in Everyday Life.*

19. Goffman, *Frame Analysis.*

20. Yaffe, *Among the Janeites,* xix.

21. Heidi Green, conversation with author, October 30, 2010.

22. Lorraine Hanaway, interview with author, October 29, 2010. Lorraine was one of those few Americans present at the bicentennial Austen celebration at Chawton when the notion of founding a North American society was first discussed.

23. Joan Ray, interview with author, October 29, 2010. Joan retired in 2012 and is now a professor emerita. She is the author of many articles as well as *Jane Austen for Dummies.*

24. Gracia Ellwood, interview with author, October 30, 2010.

25. Ibid.

26. Lorraine Hanaway, interview with author, October 29, 2010.

27. Jim Nagle, interview with author, October 30, 2010.

28. Ibid.

29. Ibid.

30. Ibid.

31. Gracia Ellwood, interview with author, October 30, 2010.

32. Lorraine Hanaway, interview with author, October 29, 2010.

33. Gracia Ellwood, interview with author, October 30, 2010. She explained, e.g., that she skipped the 2005 AGM when the topic was Austen's letters, in which she was less interested.

34. Jim Nagle, interview with author, October 30, 2010.

35. Jack Grey, quoted in Austen-Leigh, 11. Letter dated March 15, 1980.

36. Joan Ray, interview with author, October 29, 2010.

37. Locust Grove is a fifty-five-acre National Historic Landmark that offers living history programs portraying the 1790s and houses a small but well-appointed museum.

38. Costumed fans and reenactors both take a great deal of pride in the craftsmanship of their attire as well as in either the labor or expense borne in producing it.

39. In Williamsburg, where it is possible to make a living in eighteenth-century costume—thanks to the living history museum, Colonial Williamsburg—there is ample interest in the culture of the era and a thriving community of English country dancers.

40. Event description, JASNA Southeastern Virginia Region, Facebook post.

CHAPTER TWELVE

1. *The Many Lovers of Miss Jane Austen,* YouTube (BBC 2011).

2. Reader and Walter, *Pilgrimage in Popular Culture,* 6; see also Turner and Turner, *Image and Pilgrimage in Christian Culture.*

3. Reader and Walter, *Pilgrimage in Popular Culture,* 2.

4. Watson, *Literary Tourist,* 8, 211.

5. Ibid., 12–13.

6. Johnson, "Jane Austen's Relics and the Treasures of the East Room," 219.

7. Wells, *Everybody's Jane,* 104, 123, 129.

8. Coolidge, *What Katy Did Next,* front matter. Further citations of this work are given in the text.

9. Charlie Lovett, "Seeking Inspiration in Jane Austen's World," *New York Times*, December 16, 2014, https://www.nytimes.com/2014/12/28/travel/seeking-inspiration-in-jane-austens-world.html.

10. Leo A. Borah, "Landmarks of Literary England," *National Geographic*, September 1955, 300; emphasis mine. Further citations of this work are given in the text.

11. *National Geographic*, September 1955, front cover.

12. Reader and Walter, *Pilgrimage in Popular Culture*, 20.

13. Sonya Samuels, quoted in Yaffe, *Among the Janeites*, 25.

14. Debra Call, quoted in Yaffe, *Among the Janeites*, 25.

15. Yaffe, *Among the Janeites*, 39, 40.

16. Ibid., 43.

17. Francus, "Austen Therapy," para. 5.

18. Hale, *Austenland*, 20. Further citations of this work are given in the text.

19. Like Stephenie Meyer, author of the popular *Twilight* novels, *Austenland* author Shannon Hale is Mormon. A Mormon sensibility runs throughout the depiction of women as fans in both the novel and the film. In fact, Meyer produced the film adaptation of *Austenland*, and director Jerusha Hess is also Mormon.

CODA

1. Barbara Winn Adams letter to David Gilson, September 10, 1984, Winn Family Collection, series 1, subseries A, Goucher College Library.

2. Describing the course of the morning of his journey to Chawton, he says he got on a train and chose third-class "to see what it was like." He says: "I got into a carriage with a young man, his wife, and very attractive baby, and we fell into conversation immediately. We chatted about rain & food & atom bombs & babies & had a very nice time." Later he crossed a Royal Air Force field, "the concrete runway bisected the road, which bore a sign 'Dead Slow—Airplanes.'" Scott Adams letter to Barbara Winn Adams, September 14, 1946, Winn Family Collection.

3. Jack Grey, letter to Barbara Winn Adams, March 7, 1982, Winn Family Collection.

4. Jack Grey, letter to Barbara Winn Adams, August 21, 1982, Winn Family Collection.

5. Roach, *Cities of the Dead*, 36.

6. Ibid., 3.

7. Schechner, *Between Theatre and Anthropology*, 35–36.

8. Roach, *Cities of the Dead*, 29.

9. Lancaster, *Interacting with* Babylon 5, xxviii.

10. Jenkins, "Foreword," in Lancaster, *Interacting with* Babylon 5, xx.

11. Ibid., xviii.

12. De Kosnik, "What Is Global Theater?"

13. Hills, "From Dalek Half Balls to Daft Punk Helmets," para. 1.1.

Bibliography

Aron, Cindy Sondik. *Working at Play: A History of Vacations in the United States.* Oxford: Oxford University Press, 2001.

Austen-Leigh, J. E. *A Memoir of Jane Austen and Other Family Recollections* (1870). Oxford: Oxford University Press, 2002.

Austen-Leigh, Joan. "Chawton Cottage Transfigured." *Persuasions* 4 (1982): 10–13.

———. "The Founding of JASNA." *Persuasions* 15 (1993): 7–13.

Bacon-Smith, Camille. *Enterprising Women: Television and the Creation of Popular Myth.* Philadelphia: University of Pennsylvania Press, 1992.

Bakhtin, Mikhail. *Speech Genres and Other Late Essays.* Translated by Vern W. McGee. Austin: University of Texas Press, 1986.

Bal, Mieke. "Telling Objects: A Narrative Perspective on Collecting." In Elsner and Cardinal, *Cultures of Collecting*, 97–115.

Barthes, Roland. *Camera Lucida.* Translated by Richard Howard. New York: Hill & Wang, 1981.

Basu, Balaka. "Virgilian Fandom in the Renaissance." In "The Classical Canon and/as Transformative Work," edited by Ika Willis. Special issue, *Transformative Works and Cultures*, no. 21 (March 2016). https://doi.org/10.3983/twc.2016.0683.

Baudrillard, Jean. "The System of Collecting." In Elsner and Cardinal, *Cultures of Collecting*, 7–24.

Baym, Nancy. "Talking about Soaps: Communicative Practices in a Computer-Mediated Fan Culture." In *Theorizing Fandom: Fans, Subculture and Identity*, edited by Cheryl Harris and Alison Alexander, 111–29. Cresskill, NJ: Hampton Press, 1998.

Bazin, André. *What Is Cinema?* Translated by Hugh Gray. Berkeley: University of California Press, 1967.

Belk, Russell W., et al. "Collectors and Collecting." *Advances in Consumer Research* 15 (1988): 548–53. http://www.acrwebsite.org/search/view-conference-proceedings.aspx?Id=6863.

Benjamin, Walter. "Unpacking My Library: A Talk about Book Collecting." In *Illuminations*, 59–67. New York: Harcourt, Brace, 1968.

Bernstein, Robin. *Racial Innocence: Performing American Childhood from Slavery to Civil Rights.* New York: New York University Press, 2011.

Bourdieu, Pierre. *Distinction: A Social Critique of the Judgement of Taste.* Translated by Richard Nice. Cambridge: Harvard University Press, 1984.

Bowles, Kate "Commodifying Austen: the Janeite Culture of the Internet and Commercialization through Product and Television Series Spinoffs." In Macdonald and Macdonald, *Jane Austen on Screen*, 15–21.

Boym, Svetlana. *The Future of Nostalgia.* New York: Basic Books, 2008.

Braudy, Leo. *The Frenzy of Renown: Fame and Its History.* New York: Oxford University Press, 1986.

Brownstein, Rachel M. *Why Jane Austen?* New York: Columbia University Press, 2011.

Burchill, Julie. *Damaged Gods: Cults and Heroes Reappraised.* London: Century, 1986.

Butler, Judith. *Gender Trouble: Feminism and the Subversion of Identity.* New York: Routledge, 1990.

Byrne, Paula. "Afterword." *Persuasions On-Line* 32, no. 2 (Spring 2012). http://www.jasna.org/persuasions/on-line/vo132no2/index.html.

Caddy, Scott. "Fan Media and Transmedia: Jane Austen in the Digital Age." In Malcolm, *Fan Phenomena*, 43–51.

Cano, Marina. *Jane Austen and Performance.* London: Palgrave Macmillan, 2017.

Capra, Eleonora. "Between Tradition and Innovation: Celebrating Jane Austen in Italy Today." In Malcolm, *Fan Phenomena*, 139–49.

Carlson, Marvin. *Performance: A Critical Introduction.* New York: Routledge, 2004.

Cartmel, Deborah, and Imelda Whelehan, eds. *Cambridge Companion to Literature on Screen.* Cambridge: Cambridge University Press, 2007.

Caughey, John L. *Imaginary Social Worlds: A Cultural Approach.* Lincoln: University of Nebraska Press, 1984.

Cavicchi, Daniel. *Listening and Longing: Music Lovers in the Age of Barnum.* Middletown, CT: Wesleyan University Press, 2011.

———. "Loving Music: Listeners, Entertainments, and the Origins of Music Fandom in Nineteenth-Century America." In Gray et al., *Fandom: Identities and Communities in a Mediated World*, 235–49.

Christensen, Danille Elise. "'Look at Us Now!': Scrapbooking, Regimes of Value, and the Risks of (Auto)Ethnography." *Journal of American Folklore* 124, no. 493 (Summer 2011): 175–210. Gale (A269229146).

Conn, Steven. *Museums and American Intellectual Life, 1876–1926.* Chicago: University of Chicago Press, 1998.

Copeland, Edward, and Juliet McMaster, eds. *The Cambridge Companion to Jane Austen.* Cambridge: Cambridge University Press, 2011.

Coppa, Francesca. "Writing Bodies in Space: Media Fan Fiction as Theatrical Performance." In Hellekson and Busse, *Fan Fiction and Fan Communities in the Age of the Internet,* 225–44.

Crang, Mike. "Placing Jane Austen, Displacing England: Touring between Book, History, and Nation." In Pucci and Thompson, *Jane Austen and Co.,* 111–30.

De Kosnik, Abigail. *Rogue Archives: Digital Cultural Memory and Media Fandom.* Cambridge, MA: MIT Press, 2016.

———. "What Is Global Theater? Or, What Does New Media Studies Have to Do with Performance Studies?" *Transformative Works and Cultures* 18 (March 2015). http://dx.doi.org/10.3983/twc.2015.0644.

Derecho, Abigail [Abigail De Kosnik]. "Archontic Literature: A Definition, a History, and Several Theories of Fan Fiction." In Hellekson and Busse, *Fan Fiction and Fan Communities in the Age of the Internet,* 61–78.

Derrida, Jacques. *Limited Inc.* Translated by Jeffrey Mehlman and Samuel Weber. Evanston, IL: Northwestern University Press, 1988.

DiMaggio, Paul. "Cultural Entrepreneurship in Nineteenth-Century Boston: The Creation of an Organization Base for High Culture in America." In *Rethinking Popular Culture: Contemporary Perspectives in Cultural Studies,* edited by Chandra Mukerji and Michael Schudson, 374–97. Berkeley: University of California Press, 1991.

Dow, Gillian and Clare Hanson, eds. *Uses of Austen: Jane's Afterlives.* London: Palgrave Macmillan, 2012.

Eisner, Eric. *Nineteenth-Century Poetry and Literary Celebrity.* Basingstoke, UK: Palgrave Macmillan, 2009.

Elsner, John, and Roger Cardinal, eds. *The Cultures of Collecting.* Cambridge: Harvard University Press, 1994.

Felski, Rita. *Gender of Modernity.* Cambridge: Harvard University Press, 1995.

Fergus, Jan. "The Professional Woman Writer." In *The Cambridge Companion to Jane Austen,* edited by Edward Copeland and Juliet McMaster, 1–20. Cambridge: Cambridge University Press, 2011.

Fordyce, James. "Sermon IV, On Female Virtue" (from *Sermons to Young Women,* 1766). In *Women in the Eighteenth Century: Constructions of Femininity,* edited by Vivien Jones, 176–79. London: Routledge, 1990.

Francus, Marilyn. "Austen Therapy: *Pride and Prejudice* and Popular Culture." *Persuasions On- Line* 30, no. 2 (Spring 2010). http://www.jasna.org/persuasions/on-line/vo130no2/francus.html.

Gamson, Joshua. *Claims to Fame: Celebrity in Contemporary America.* Berkeley: University of California Press, 1994.

Garvey, Ellen Gruber. "Scissorizing and Scrapbooks: Nineteenth-Century Reading, Remaking, and Recirculating." In *New Media, 1740–1915*, edited by Lisa Gitelman and Geoffrey B. Pingree, 207–27. Cambridge, MA: MIT Press, 2003.

———. *Writing with Scissors: American Scrapbooks from the Civil War to the Harlem Renaissance.* Oxford: Oxford University Press, 2013.

Gelber, Steven. *Hobbies: Productive Leisure and the Culture of Work in America.* New York: Columbia University Press, 1999.

Gelder, Ken. *Popular Fiction: The Logics and Practices of a Literary Field.* New York: Routledge, 2004.

Gilson, David. *A Bibliography of Jane Austen.* Oxford: Clarendon Press, 1982.

———. "Jane Austen's *Emma* in America: Notes on the Text of the First and Second American Editions." *Review of English Studies*, n.s. 53, no. 212 (November 2002): 517–25. http://www.jstor.org/stable/3070573.

———. "Later Publishing History." In Todd, *Jane Austen in Context*, 121–59.

Goffman, Irving. *Frame Analysis: An Essay on the Organization of Experience.* New York: Harper & Row, 1974.

———. *Presentation of Self in Everyday Life.* New York: Doubleday, 1959.

Gray, Jonathan, Cornel Sandvoss, and C. Lee Harrington, eds. *Fandom: Identities and Communities in a Mediated World.* New York: New York University Press, 2007.

Grey, J. David, ed. *The Jane Austen Handbook.* London: Athlone Press, 1986.

Grossberg, Lawrence. "Is There a Fan in the House? The Affective Sensibility of Fandom." In Lewis, *Adoring Audience*, 50–65.

Halsey, Katie. *Jane Austen and Her Readers, 1786–1945.* London: Anthem, 2012.

Harman, Claire. *Jane's Fame: How Jane Austen Conquered the World.* New York: Holt, 2009.

Hayles Gledhill, Evan. "Tumblr and the Romantic Sentiment Album: Bricolage and the Culture of the Margins." In "Tumblr and Fandom," edited by Lori Morimoto and Louisa Ellen Stein. Special issue, *Transformative Works and Cultures*, no. 27 (June 2018). https://doi.org/10.3983/twc.2018.1213.

Hebdige, Dick. *Subculture: The Meaning of Style.* New York: Routledge, 1988.

Hellekson, Karen, and Kristina Busse, eds. *Fan Fiction and Fan Communities in the Age of the Internet.* Jefferson, NC: McFarland, 2006.

Hill, Constance. *Jane Austen: Her Homes and Her Friends.* New York: John Lane, 1902.

Hills, Matt. *Fan Cultures.* London: Routledge, 2002.

———. "From Dalek Half Balls to Daft Punk Helmets: Mimetic Fandom and the Crafting of Replicas." *Transformative Works and Cultures* 16 (2014). http://dx.doi.org/10.3983/twc.2014.0531.

Hindley, Meredith. "When Bram Met Walt." *Humanities* 33, no. 6 (November–December 2012). http://www.neh.gov/print/8456.

Howe, M. A. DeWolfe. *The Articulate Sisters: Passages from Journals and Letters of the Daughters of President Josiah Quincy of Harvard University.* Cambridge: Harvard University Press, 1946.

James, Henry. *The Question of Our Speech: A Lesson of Balzac; Two Lectures.* Boston: Houghton Mifflin, 1905. https://books.google.com/books?id=MfBaAAAAMAAJ.

Jamison, Anne. *Fic: Why Fanfiction Is Taking Over the World.* Dallas: Smart Pop, 2013.

Jenkins, Henry. *Fans, Bloggers, and Gamers: Exploring Participatory Culture.* New York: New York University Press, 2006.

———. "*Star Trek* Rerun, Reread, Rewritten: Fan Writing as Textual Poaching." In *Close Encounters: Film, Feminism, and Science Fiction,* edited by Constance Penley, 171–204. Minneapolis: University of Minnesota Press, 1991.

———. *Textual Poachers: Television Fans and Participatory Culture.* New York: Routledge, 1992.

Jenson, Joli. "Fandom as Pathology: The Consequences of Characterization." In Lewis, *Adoring Audience,* 9–29.

Johnson, Claudia L. *Jane Austen's Cults and Cultures.* Chicago: University of Chicago Press, 2012.

———. "Jane Austen's Relics and the Treasures of the East Room." *Persuasions* 28 (2006): 217–30.

Johnson, Claudia L., and Clara Tuite, eds. *A Companion to Jane Austen.* Chichester, UK: Wiley-Blackwell, 2012.

Judge, Elizabeth. "Kidnapped and Counterfeit Characters: Eighteenth-Century Fan Fiction, Copyright Law, and the Custody of Fictional Characters." In *Originality and Intellectual Property in the French and English Enlightenment,* edited by Reginald McGinnis, 22–68. New York: Routledge, 2009.

Kiefer, Jeanne. "Anatomy of a Janeite: Results from *The Jane Austen Survey 2008.*" *Persuasions On-line* 29, no. 1 (Winter 2008). http://www.jasna.org/persuasions/on- line/vol30no02/index.html.

Lancaster, Kurt. *Interacting with* Babylon 5. Austin: University of Texas Press, 2001.

Lang, Andrew. *Letters to Dead Authors.* New York: Charles Scribner's Sons, 1888. Google Books, https://books.google.com/books?id=vbs-AAAAYAAJ.

———. *Old Friends: Essays in Epistolary Parody.* London: Longmans, Green & Co., 1890. Google Books, https://books.google.com/books?id=Jjs1AQAAIAAJ.

Langston, Camille A. "Sarah Josepha Hale's Rhetoric of 'Mental Improvement' and 'Women's Sphere' in *Godey's Lady's Book.*" In *Popular Nineteenth-Century American Women Writers and the Literary Marketplace,* edited by Earl Yarington and Mary De Jong, 118–36. Newcastle, UK: Cambridge Scholars, 2007.

Leavis, F. R. *The Great Tradition.* London: Chatto & Windus, 1948.

Le Faye, Deirdre. "'Three or Four Families': Suggestions for New Directions in Biographical Research" *Persuasions On-Line* 30, no. 2 (Spring 2010). http://www.jasna.org/persuasions/on- line/vo130no2/index.html.

Levine, Lawrence. *Highbrow/Lowbrow: The Emergence of Cultural Hierarchy in America.* Cambridge: Harvard University Press, 1988.

Lewis, Lisa, ed. *The Adoring Audience: Fan Culture and Popular Media.* London: Routledge, 1992.

Lockwood, Allison. *Passionate Pilgrims: the American Traveler in Great Britain, 1800–1914.* Rutherford, NJ: Fairleigh Dickinson University Press, 1981.

Looser, Devoney. *The Making of Jane Austen.* Baltimore: Johns Hopkins University Press, 2017.

Lynch, Deidre Shauna. "Cult of Jane Austen." In Todd, *Jane Austen in Context,* 111–20.

———. "Sequels." In Todd, *Jane Austen in Context,* 160–68.

———. *Janeites: Austen's Disciples and Devotees.* Princeton: Princeton University Press, 2000.

Macdonald, Gina, and Andrew Macdonald. *Jane Austen on Screen.* Cambridge: Cambridge University Press, 2003.

Malcolm, Gabrielle. *Fan Phenomena: Jane Austen.* Bristol, UK: Intellect Books, 2015.

Martin, Paul. *Popular Collecting and the Everyday Self: The Reinvention of Museums?* London: Leicester University Press, 1999.

Martineau, Harriet. *Harriet Martineau's Autobiography, with Memorials by Maria Weston Chapman.* London: Smith, Elder, & Co., 1877.

———. "Literary Lionism." *London and Westminster Review* 32 (April 1839): 139–50. http://books.google.com/books?id=rngeAQAAMAAJ.

Mayer, Robert. *Walter Scott and Fame: Authors and Readers in the Romantic Age.* Oxford: Oxford University Press, 2017.

Mirmohamadi, Kylie. *The Digital Afterlives of Jane Austen: Janeites at the Keyboard.* Basingstoke: Palgrave Macmillan, 2014.

Monaghan, David, Ariane Hudelet, and John Wiltshire, eds. *The Cinematic Jane Austen: Essays on the Filmic Sensibility of the Novels.* Jefferson, NC: McFarland, 2009.

Muensterberger, Werner. *Collecting: An Unruly Passion.* Princeton: Princeton University Press, 1994.

Mulvey, Laura. "Visual Pleasure and Narrative Cinema." *Visual and Other Pleasures,* 14–26. Bloomington: Indiana University Press, 1989.

Nelson, Elizabeth White. *Market Sentiments: Middle-Class Market Culture in Nineteenth-Century America.* Washington, DC: Smithsonian Institution, 2004.

Noonan, Mark J. *Reading The Century Illustrated Monthly Magazine: American Literature and Culture, 1870–1893.* Kent, OH: Kent State University Press, 2010.

Ott, Katherine. "Between Person and Profession: The Scrapbooks of Nineteenth-Century Medical Practitioners." In Tucker et al., *Scrapbook in American Life,* 29–41.

Palmer, Beverly Wilson, ed. *A Woman's Wit and Whimsy: The 1833 Diary of Anna Cabot Lowell Quincy.* Boston: Northeastern University Press, 2003.

Pande, Rukmini. *Squee from the Margins: Fandom and Race.* Iowa City: University of Iowa Press, 2018.

Pearson, Roberta. "Bachies, Bardies, Trekkies, and Sherlockians." In Gray et al., *Fandom: Identities and Communities in a Mediated World,* 98–109.

———. "'It's Always 1895': Sherlock Holmes in Cyberspace." In *Trash Aesthetics: Popular Culture and Its Audience,* edited by Deborah Cartmell, I. Q. Hunter, Heidi Kaye, and Imelda Whelehan, 143–61. London: Pluto Press, 1997.

Penley, Constance. "Brownian Motion: Women, Tactics, and Technology." In *Technoculture,* edited by Constance Penley and Andrew Ross, 135–61. Minneapolis: University of Minnesota Press, 1991.

Piggott, Patrick. *The Innocent Diversion: Music in the Life and Writings of Jane Austen.* London: Clover Hill, 1979.

Porter, Jennifer E. "To Boldly Go: *Star Trek* Convention Attendance as Pilgrimage." In *Star Trek and Sacred Ground: Explorations of Star Trek, Religion, and American Culture,* edited by Jennifer Porter and Darcee McLaren, 245–70. Albany, NY: SUNY Press, 1999.

Price, Kenneth M., and Susan Belasco Smith, eds. *Periodical Literature in Nineteenth-Century America.* Charlottesville: University of Virginia Press, 1995.

Pucci, Suzanne R., and James Thompson, eds. *Jane Austen and Co.: Remaking the Past in Contemporary Culture.* Albany, NY: SUNY Press, 2003.

Pugh, Sheenagh. *The Democratic Genre: Fan Fiction in a Literary Context.* Bridgend, UK: Seren, 2005.

Radway, Janice. *Reading the Romance: Women, Patriarchy, and Popular Culture.* Chapel Hill: University of North Carolina Press, 1984.

Reader, Ian, and Tony Walter, eds. *Pilgrimage in Popular Culture.* London: Macmillan, 1993.

Roach, Joseph. *Cities of The Dead: Circum-Atlantic Performance.* New York: Columbia University Press, 1996.

Robertson, Michael. *Worshiping Walt: The Whitman Disciples.* Princeton: Princeton University Press, 2008.

Rosenblatt, Betsy, and Roberta Pearson, eds. "Sherlock Holmes Fandom, Sherlockiana, and the Great Game." Special issue, *Transformative Works and Cultures* 23 (March 2017).

Rosenzweig, Roy, and David Thelen. *The Presence of the Past: Popular Uses of History in American Life.* New York: Columbia University Press, 1998.

Russo, Stephanie. "Austen Approved: Pemberley Digital and the Transmedia Commodification of Jane Austen." *Women's Writing* 25, no. 4 (November 2018): 512–524, DOI: 10.1080/09699082.2018.1510884.

Saler, Michael. "'Clap if You Believe in Sherlock Holmes': Mass Culture and the Re-Enchantment of Modernity, c. 1890–1940." *Historical Journal* 46, no. 3 (September 2003): 599–622.

Schechner, Richard. *Between Theatre and Anthropology.* Philadelphia: University of Pennsylvania Press, 1985.

Schickel, Richard. *Intimate Strangers: The Culture of Celebrity.* Garden City, NY: Doubleday, 1985.

Shealy, Daniel. "Louisa May Alcott's Juvenilia: Blueprints for the Future." *Children's Literature Association Quarterly* 17, no. 4 (Winter 1992): 15–18. https://muse.jhu.edu/article/249320.

Shreffler, Philip A. *Sherlock Holmes by Gas-lamp: Highlights from the First Four Decades of the Baker Street Journal.* New York: Fordham University Press, 1989.

Simonova, Natasha. *Early Modern Authorship and Prose Continuations: Adaptation and Ownership from Sidney to Richardson.* Basingstoke, UK: Palgrave Macmillan, 2015.

Southam, Brian. "Jane Austen and Winchester Cathedral." *Persuasions* 24 (2002): 226–40.

Stewart, Susan. *On Longing: Narratives of the Miniature, the Gigantic, the Souvenir, the Collection.* Durham, NC: Duke University Press, 1993.

Sun, Shuo. "The Reception of Jane Austen in China." PhD thesis, University of Nottingham, 2016. http://eprints.nottingham.ac.uk/38499/.

Tanselle, George Thomas. *Book-Jackets: Their History, Forms, and Use.* Charlottesville: Bibliographical Society of the University of Virginia, 2011.

Todd, Janet, ed. *Jane Austen in Context.* Cambridge: Cambridge University Press, 2005.

Thompson, James. "How to Do Things with Austen." In Pucci and Thompson, *Jane Austen and Co.*, 13–32.

Throsby, Corin. "Flirting with Fame: Byron's Anonymous Female Fans." *Byron Journal* 32, no. 2 (2004): 115–23. doi: 10.3828/BJ.2004.4.

Trilling, Lionel. "*Emma* and the Legend of Jane Austen" (1957). In *Jane Austen's Emma: A Casebook*, edited by Fiona Stafford, 83–100. Oxford: Oxford University Press, 2007.

Tucker, George Holbert. *A Goodly Heritage*. Manchester, UK: Carcanet New Press, 1983.

———. *Jane Austen the Woman: Some Biographical Insights*. New York: St. Martin's, 1994.

———. *More Tidewater Landfalls: Days beyond Recall Recollected*. Virginia Beach: Donning Co., 1975.

———. *Tidewater Landfalls*. Norfolk, VA: Landmark Communications, 1969.

Tucker, Susan, Katherine Ott, and Patricia P. Buckler, eds. *The Scrapbook in American Life*. Philadelphia: Temple University Press, 2006.

Tuckerman, Henry T. *A Month in England*. London: Richard Bentley, 1854. Google Books, https://books.google.com/books?id=FHcBAAAAQAAJ.

Turner, Victor. *From Ritual to Theater: The Human Seriousness of Play*. New York: PAJ Publications, 1982.

———. "Pilgrimage as Social Processes." In *Dramas, Fields, and Metaphors: Symbolic Action in Human Society*, edited by Victor Turner, 166–230. Ithaca, NY: Cornell University Press.

———. "Variations on a Theme of Liminality." In *Secular Ritual*, edited by Sally F. Moore and Barbara G. Myerhoff, 36–52. Amsterdam: Van Gorcum, 1977.

Turner, Victor, and Edith Turner. *Image and Pilgrimage in Christian Culture, Anthropological Perspectives*. New York: Columbia University Press, 1978.

Wagner, Tamara S. "Mrs. Hubback's *The Younger Sister:* The Victorian Austen and the Phenomenon of the Austen Sequel." *Victorian Web*, November 20, 2002. http://www.victorianweb.org/previctorian/austen/tsw7.html.

Walkley, Arthur Bingham. *Pastiche and Prejudice*. London: William Heinemann, 1921.

———. *Still More Prejudice*. 1925. Reprint, Freeport, NY: Books for Libraries Press, 1970.

Watson, Nicola J. *The Literary Tourist: Readers and Places in Romantic and Victorian Britain*. Basingstoke, UK: Palgrave Macmillan, 2006.

Wells, Juliette. *Everybody's Jane: Austen in the Popular Imagination*. London: Continuum, 2011.

———. *Reading Austen in America*. London: Bloomsbury Academic, 2017.

Yaffe, Deborah. *Among the Janeites: A Journey through the World of Jane Austen Fandom*. New York: Houghton Mifflin Harcourt, 2013.

Young, Jock. "The Subterranean World of Play." In *The Subcultures Reader*, edited by Ken Gelder, 148–56. London: Routledge, 2005.

ARCHIVAL SOURCES

Alberta and Henry Burke. Jane Austen Collection. Special Collections and Archives, Goucher College Library.

David Gilson Scrapbook. Special Collections and Archives, Goucher College Library.

George Holbert Tucker. Collection of Jane Austen Research Materials, 1975–87. Special Collections, Earl G. Swem Library, College of William & Mary.

Winn Family Jane Austen Collection. Special Collections and Archives, Goucher College Library.

NOVELS, SEQUELS, SPIN-OFFS

Alcott, Louisa May. *Little Women*. Modern Library. New York: Random House, 2000.

Austen, Jane. *Pride and Prejudice*. Oxford World's Classics. Edited by James Kinsley and Frank W. Bradbrook. Oxford: Oxford University Press, 1989.

Beck, Lily Adams. "The Darcys of Rosings." *"The Ladies!": A Shining Constellation of Wit and Beauty*. Boston: Atlantic Monthly Press, 1922. Google Books, https://books.google.com/books?id=O-woAQAAIAAJ.

Bonavia-Hunt, D. A. *Pemberley Shades*. New York: E. P. Dutton & Co., 1949.

Brinton, Sybil. *Old Friends and New Fancies: An Imaginary Sequel to the Novels of Jane Austen* (1913). Lakewood, CO: Revive, 1998.

Coolidge, Susan. *What Katy Did Next*. Boston: Roberts Brothers, 1886. Google Books, https://books.google.com/books?id=AMoXAAAAYAAJ.

Hale, Shannon. *Austenland*. New York: Bloomsbury, 2007.

FILMOGRAPHY

Austenland. Directed by Jarusha Hess, 2013; Sony Pictures Home Entertainment, 2014. DVD.

The Lizzie Bennet Diaries. YouTube web series, created by Bernie Su and Hank Greene, 2012. https://www.youtube.com/user/LizzieBennet.

Lost in Austen. Directed by Dan Zeff, 2008. London: ITV, 2009. DVD.

The Many Lovers of Jane Austen. YouTube, written by Amanda Vickery; BBC, 2011. https://www.youtube.com/watch?v=quPnwYadwBI.

Pride and Prejudice. Directed by Simon Langton, 1995. New York: A&E Television, 2001. DVD.

Pride & Prejudice. Directed by Joe Wright, 2005. Universal City, CA: Universal Home Entertainment, 2006. DVD.

Index